Modeling Metropolitan Economies
for Forecasting and Policy Analysis

MODELING
METROPOLITAN
ECONOMIES
FOR
FORECASTING
AND
POLICY ANALYSIS

MATTHEW P. DRENNAN

NEW YORK UNIVERSITY PRESS
New York and London
1985

Library of Congress Cataloging in Publication Data

Drennan, Matthew P., 1937–
   Modeling metropolitan economies for forecasting and
policy analysis

   Bibliography: p.
   Includes index.
   1. Urban economies.   2. Employment forecasting—United
States—Econometric models.   3. New York (N.Y.)—Economic
conditions—Econometric models.   4. Baltimore (Md.)—
Economic conditions—Econometric models.   5. Urban policy—
United States.   I. Title.
HT321.D74   1985   330.9173′2   85-13784
ISBN 0-8147-1781-0 (alk. paper)

*Clothbound editions of New York University Press
books are Smyth-sewn and printed on durable
and permanent acid-free paper.*

To my wife
Katherine Van Wezel Stone
and my children
Matthew and *Maureen*

CONTENTS

Contents

TABLES AND FIGURES

Tables

Figures

Appendix Tables

FOREWORD

It is with a great amount of personal pleasure and institutional pride that I write this Foreword to Professor Matthew Drennan's important contribution to regional economic forecasting. My pleasure stems from the fact that his pioneering effort is now being published after considerable delay in book form which will make his model, analysis, and policy prescriptions available to the broad scholarly and decision making community.

My institutional pride stems from the fact that the Conservation of Human Resources Project at Columbia University which I have directed since its establishment in the late 1940s provided the home and secured the financing for Professor Drennan's work. The U.S. Department of Labor was the funding agency.

The linkages between Drennan's work and the ongoing research of the Conservation Project go further. As Drennan makes clear in an early chapter, he adopted Richard Knight's method (VAPE) to estimate income for each regional industry. Knight's 1973 book, *Employment Expansion and Metropolitan Trade,* (Praeger), was an earlier contribution of the Conservation Project to metropolitan studies.

Drennan notes in his generous acknowledgment that I encouraged and supported his work despite an underlying skepticism about all economic forecasting. I want to make clear in the paragraphs that follow why I am comfortable with

Drennan's approach in the face of my pervasive skepticism about most econometric exercises.

To begin with, there is a considerable body of data available both for New York City and for the Standard Consolidated Area (SCA) covering a considerable span of years. Hence Drennan is not subject to the challenge faced by the regional imitators of Leontief, that is, engaging in mathematical symbol manipulation without data to test the effectiveness of his model.

Secondly Drennan has had the good fortune to develop, test, and use his model during the past two decades during which the national, regional and local economies, while subject to spurts and declines—and in the case of New York City buffetted by a serious financial crisis in 1975 with a long aftermath—nevertheless escaped major crises. One might argue that the loss by the City in the post World War II period of over 500,000 jobs in manufacturing represents a major "discontinuity." But the erosion was spread out over a quarter of a century and was accompanied by a significant if not equal expansion of employment in services, both public services and latterly business services.

While Professor Drennan demonstrates great acuity and skill in organizing his data and in specifying his model, he never permits himself to be captured by his own statistical results. He repeatedly makes use of the powerful propositions developed by macro- and microeconomists over many decades to illuminate, from different vantages, the reasonableness of his forecasting results.

Nowhere is this movement back and forth between model and economic analysis better demonstrated—and with high yield—than in Part Two, "Policy Analysis With the Model." Since it is unlikely that many mayors, county officials or governors will read Professor Drennan's book I am taking the liberty of identifying below some of his more important policy

insights and recommendations—those which commend themselves to me:

- Depopulation of selected urban areas is not to be equated
  with economic collapse.
- The key to effective urban economic development is to
  strengthen the competitive advantages of the city at a
  cost that governments—federal, state, and local—can
  afford to underwrite.
- Income redistribution is not a task for local government.
- The principal responsibility of the federal government
  is to help assure that the economy operates close to full
  employment under conditions of reasonable price
  stability.
- For those who like the President remain enamored with
  enterprise zones I especially commend Drennan's brief
  but incisive analysis (10.3). The President and his advis-
  ers might also profit from reading Drennan's brief positive
  comments on the UDAG program.
- Drennan also has some sensible guidance for local governments. Their principal responsibilities should be to do
  what they can to maintain fiscal integrity and to seek out
  policies that have the effect of keeping their relative costs
  from becoming uncompetitive. One important way to
  accomplish the last is for a city to become more efficient
  in the delivery of basic services from police to education.
- If cities avoid the imposition and continuance of taxes
  that have a depressing effect on investment and employment, they may not guarantee their long-term prosperity
  but they will be headed in the right direction.

The above are my selections from a much larger and richer
pool of important findings and recommendations. I may not as
yet be willing to discard my skepticism about modeling and
forecasting but I am more than pleased to recognize that Professor Drennan's effort is forcing me to reconsider. Let me

say my wish is that all other forecasters were as sound and as sensible as Professor Drennan.

Eli Ginzberg, Director
Conservation of Human Resources
Columbia University

ACKNOWLEDGMENTS

Support for this study was provided by the Employment and Training Administration, U.S. Department of Labor, under the authority of Title III, Part B of the Comprehensive Employment and Training Act of 1973. Points of view and opinions stated in this book do not necessarily represent the official position or policy of the Department of Labor.

Most of the assembling, checking and revising of the substantial data base for this study was performed expertly by Chris Hakusa. He also ran (and re-ran) all of the private sector equations, wrote, tested, and re-wrote all of the computer programs for forecasting with the model and for performing ex-post tests of the model, and finally assisted in the writing of Chapters 5 and 13. Few researchers are so extraordinarily lucky as to have the assistance of someone as gifted and as easy to work with as Chris Hakusa.

Georgia Nanopoulos-Stergiou provided me with an education in the intricacies of the City of New York's tax system. The revenue data base, and background for the fiscal sector were provided by her plus some of the draft of Chapter 7.

Eileen Friend and Georgia produced the summarized matrices from the vast Occupational Employment Survey data. Mauricio Gluck produced the quarterly data base. All the above are or were students in the Graduate School of Public Administration, New York University. Other students in my course, Empirical Studies in Urban Economics, contributed suggestions, ideas and criticisms.

Careful typing was carried out by Doreen Sczupiel and Michael Portantiere. Vicky Schumacher, with good cheer and breathtaking accuracy, typed the final version of the manuscript with able assistance from Janet Terry.

I am indebted to Dick Netzer, former Dean of the Graduate School of Public Administration for providing an environment so highly conducive to pursuing research. Likewise to his successor, Dean Alan Altshuler, who has strengthened that environment. Finally, I thank the one person who made this all possible, despite his misgivings about anybody's economic forecasts, Dr. Eli Ginzberg, Director of the Conservation of Human Resources and Hepburn Professor Emeritus of Economics, Columbia University.

1

Introduction

1.1 Purpose of the study

In 1977, the United States Department of Labor awarded a grant to the Conservation of Human Resources, Columbia University, to develop econometric models for two metropolitan areas: New York and Baltimore. The Labor Department had recognized that to improve the effectiveness of local job training programs required plausible short-term forecasts of employment, by industry and occupation, for metropolitan areas. Thus they decided to provide support for developing metropolitan area forecasting models. Given the policy goal of improving the expenditures of training funds, three major requirements of a metropolitan forecasting model followed.

1. The model should provide employment forecasts in as much industry detail as possible.
2. The model should provide forecasts of employment by detailed occupational categories.
3. The model methodology and data sources should be replicable for other metropolitan areas, large and small.

This study presents the results of the three-year work at Conservation of Human Resources on developing econometric models for New York and Baltimore. At the end of the first 18 months of this project, the Department of Labor decided that the remaining work be devoted to pursuing policy analysis and more qualitative analysis of the New York region based upon the model rather than improving and refining the model for Baltimore. However, to show that the model methodology is applicable to other metropolitan areas, a chapter is included here explaining the Baltimore model. It will be shown in following sections that the three major requirements have been met.

Clearly the interest in employment and general economic forecasts for metropolitan areas and cities is not limited to those involved in job training. In the public sector, state and local agencies charged with economic development responsibilities are continually faced with the question of the short-term and long-term prospects for the local economy. City and regional planning agencies must explicitly or implicitly frame their plans within the context of a future economic scenario for the area. And beleaguered budget agencies of large cities must look beyond the current fiscal year to future revenue prospects. But the tax revenue prospects, as they well know, are linked to the economic prospects for the area.

In the private sector, large businesses with a market in the metropolitan area have a far from casual interest in economic forecasts of the area. That is particularly the case for public utilities, but also true for banks, newspapers, and large real estate firms. Similarly, the financial institutions that deal with municipal bonds (including the bond rating agencies) see the same link that city budget agencies do, namely, that one cannot intelligently appraise revenue prospects without considering local economic prospects.

1.2 Why econometric models?

In the older cities of the Northeastern and North-Central states there is a new gospel: economic growth. As with most religions which click, this one is an import and it is from the

Sun Belt. But realistic policy makers and their advisors in local, state, and federal government recognize that belief is not sufficient for salvation. Good works are also required. So the nagging question is What must we do to make our older urban economies grow, or at least to stop declining?

There are no pat answers. Certainly there are no universal answers good for all places and all times. Previous work at Conservation in the urban area has indicated that beginning to formulate a tentative answer for a given place at a given time requires addressing some other questions beforehand: What is the structure of the local economy? How has it changed over time? What sectors are thriving, languishing, or holding their own? What handicaps and opportunities are presented by the thrust of technology and inexorable market forces? What are the positive and negative impacts of state and federal taxes and expenditures upon the local economy? How do changes in the local economy impact local government tax revenues? What are the positive and negative impacts of local government taxes and expenditures and policies upon the local economy? With plausible, but admittedly imperfect and incomplete, answers to these questions, it is *then* possible to ask what can be done to promote economic growth.

But how are plausible answers to the questions above obtained? One method which can encompass so many broad and interlinked questions is an econometric model of the local economy. With all of their imperfections and oversimplifications of a dynamic economy perpetually in flux, such models do link all of the diverse parts of the economy into a comprehensible whole. They do not produce ready-made answers but rather provide a framework which makes it possible to determine the key linkages within the economy, to sort out some major forces acting upon the economy, and to put quantitative flesh upon the bones of urban growth theories.

There are two functions which an econometric model of an economy can serve: analysis and forecasting. Much of the interest in the large-scale national models is focused upon their

forecasting role. But their greater value is in analysis, particularly policy analysis. For purposes of public policy, answers
to "What would happen if . . . ?" questions are more important than forecasting next year's GNP. For example, the model
constructed by Data Resources, Inc. has been used to estimate
the impact of an OPEC boost in world oil prices upon the rate
of inflation in the United States. It does not matter if the answer
is not exactly right. What matters is that the model provides a
measure of the magnitude of the effect.

Some of the kinds of policy questions which can be explored with a local area econometric model include the
following.

1. What would be the impact of an anticipated national
   recession on the local economy?
2. What would a full-employment growth path for the national economy imply for the local economy?
3. How would changes in local taxes affect employment in
   the different sectors of the local economy?
4. What is the sensitivity of local tax revenues to changes
   in the local economy?

It is important to recognize that there is much that econometric models cannot do. The real world is characterized by
discontinuities, such as changes in technology or abrupt
changes in terms of trade, which can never be anticipated with
an econometric forecast, and which can only be imperfectly
analyzed, after the fact, using an econometric model. Masters
of local area econometric models with good judgment, imagi-
nation, and an awesome stock of knowledge about the local
area can be valuable resources for both the local public and
private sector. Slaves of such models, usually lacking all of
the qualities listed above, can be, at worst (when they are
taken seriously) a public menace, and at best (when they are
not) a public nuisance.

1.3 Plan of study

This study is in two parts: Part I, "The Model" (chapters 2 through 8) and Part II, "Policy Analysis with the Model" (Chapters 9 through 13). Part I is necessarily narrower in scope than Part II, dealing with the presentation and explanation of the models and data and trends for specific places. Those whose eyes glaze over at the sight of an equation or an explanation of methodology can skip all of Chapters 2, 5, 7, and the latter parts of the other chapters in Part I where equations are presented. Part II does not deal with a specific place but with broad policy issues germane to urban economic development in all urban areas. The model applications and simulations presented in Part II, of course, do pertain to a specific place but the ramifications of the exercises are drawn out for all urban places.

In Chapter 2, the logic of the model is presented in a general manner. That is, it is not specific to New York or Baltimore and does not present estimated equations. Rather, a methodology is presented which can be applied to any metropolitan area. Chapter 3 explains the New York-Northeastern New Jersey Standard Consolidated Area (hereafter SCA) regional model and the New York City model, including all the variables used, the time-series data for those variables and the estimated regression equations. The Baltimore metropolitan area model is presented in Chapter 4. The development of annual industry-occupation employment forecasting matrices for the New York-New Jersey SCA and for New York City is explained in Chapter 5. A quarterly version of both the SCA and NYC model is presented in Chapter 6. Chapter 7 presents the fiscal sector which has been developed for New York City including the estimated regression equations for forecasting city tax revenues by source. Part I concludes with economic forecasts to 1990 for the New York-New Jersey SCA and New

York City using the SCA and NYC models, and those results are presented and analyzed in Chapter 8.

Part II begins (Chapter 9) with an overview of urban economic development. Chapter 10 deals with the federal role, and Chapter 11 with the local government role in urban economic development. The impact of local taxes on the local economy is analyzed in Chapter 12. The final chapter (13) considers the occupational structure of the local work force and job training in the development context.

PART 1

THE MODEL

2

The Structure of the Model

2.1 Export base theory

Urban areas are concentrations of economic activity. To exist a city must be the site for the production of goods or services that are demanded by markets in other parts of the nation and world. To be chosen as a site for the production of a particular good or service, the city must provide some special attraction—what economists term a "competitive advantage"—for that type of economic activity. Because of its competitive advantages, then, a city becomes a center for the production of goods and services that are sold externally. This exchange of goods or services produced in a city for income from outside sources is referred to as "export" activity. It is the foundation of a city's economic life.

These related concepts of competitive advantage and income derived from exports are at the heart of export base theory. The logic of the theory is compelling. The economic activities that are the source of export income are referred to as basic or export activities. Specialization in economic activities for which a competitive advantage exists is the source of that export income. The existence and growth of export activities lead to the development of economic activities which are supportive in character. The supportive activities are referred to as "local," since their production is consumed by local residents and firms rather than sold outside the urban area. If the supportive activities were swept away by some act of God, they would spring up again. But if a city's competitive advantage disappeared, export activities would shift to another location, and the urban area would eventually wither away.

According to this approach to urban economics, known as export base theory, export activities determine the economic health of a city. Export sector production is determined by external demand. This demand is related to the income and employment levels of local residents through a "multiplier" effect. Income derived from export activities recirculates through the local economy and thus multiplies the number of jobs in the community. Through this multiplier effect, one job in the export sector may be supporting two, three, or four jobs in a city's local sector, depending upon the residents' propensity to consume and the availability of locally produced goods and services.

The classic statement of export base theory given above is flawed in one important way, namely, the assumption that local economic activities (as opposed to export activities) passively respond to the level of area income determined by the export activities. Because the exports of one area are the imports of some other area, many types of local activities may be engaged in competition with external firms for the local market. That is not true of liquor stores and barbers, but it is certainly the case for financial institutions, business, legal, and education services plus manufacturing, construction, and parts of wholesale trade. If external firms gain the upper hand in the competition for the local market, the affected local industry will shrink regardless of the performance of the area's export industries and the level of total demand in the area. Of course, it works the other way too, and when local firms gain ascendancy in the local market over external competitors, locally produced services and goods are substituted for imports.

Export base theory is no useless abstraction. Rather, it is central to understanding the changing economic fortunes of cities. Urban areas in the United States are not self-sufficient entities. They are parts of a national and a world market, linked to one another through the interactive forces of trade and specialization. Like firms, cities compete for shares of national and, increasingly, world demand. Shifts in the composition of that demand benefit some areas and depress others depending upon the particular mix of export activities in a given city and depending upon the performance of local firms competing with imports. However, changes in a particular city's competitive advantage, due perhaps to technological change or the long-term effects of public policy, may also affect the economic growth of an urban area. The long-run fortunes of all firms in the city are inexorably linked to the success, or lack of it, of the city's export base in national and international competition for markets.

2.2 Brief review of regional econometric models

The underlying theory of regional econometric models requires little explanation, for it is simply a wedding of national macro models to regional export base theory. Regional econometric models can be described as the offspring of the national econometric models. One advantage of this relationship is that there is a wealth of theoretical and empirical work at the national level to draw upon. The Klein-Goldberger model, now over 30 years old, was the first large-scale econometric model of the United States' economy. There are many such models in use now, far more elaborate than the original model, which was comprised of less than 30 equations. Present national models seldom have fewer than 100 equations, and some have been estimated with quarterly rather than annual data. Among the most widely known models are those constructed by Data Resources Inc. (Otto Eckstein, et al.), Wharton Economic Associates (Lawrence Klein, et al.), and Chase Econometrics.

The major obstacle in the path of developing large-scale regional econometric models is the availability of data. There are two aspects to the problem of acquiring data. First, time-series data for regions do not go back in time as far as national data and are rarely available on a quarterly basis. That limits the number of observations and consequently the degrees of freedom. Second, data series for key variables are often simply unavailable for regions. Variables that should be present in some equations, on a priori grounds, are thus often left out, leading to errors of specification. Compounding the problems, even when data series for key variables are available, they are left out of equations because of the limited degrees of freedom noted above.

If the region of interest is small, that is, a metropolitan area rather than a state or group of states, those data problems become worse. Consequently, most large-scale regional ecomometric models have been estimated for states or groups of states. Models for metropolitan areas have been developed for Philadelphia (Glickman), Boston (Rothenberg, et al.), Buffalo (Crow, et al.), Los Angeles (Hall and Licari), Southern California (Moody and Puffer), Detroit (Mattila), and Santa Clara, California (Goldman). Also, models for San Francisco-Oakland, Phoenix, Tucson, and the Springfield, Massachusetts metropolitan area have been developed by Carol Taylor. An excellent review of the state and smaller area models which have been published is presented by Glickman *(Econometric Analysis of Regional Systems)* and will not be repeated here. The key features of the small area (as opposed to states or larger regions) models reviewed by Glickman are compared with the models presented in this study in Table 2.1.

Table 2.1
Comparison of Small-area Econometric Models

	Buffalo	Southern California	Los Angeles	Phila-delphia IV	NY-NJ SCA and NYC	Baltimore
Number of observations	8–17	9	12	25	21	19
Number of equations	35	18	29	228	289	34
Number of stochastic equations	23	13	19	105	159	25
Number of bivariate specifications	15	10	12	19	36	10
Number of stochastic equations with lags	4	1	0	37	34	1
Number of exogenous variables	14	3	4	49	32	4
Number of equations with $\bar{R}^2 > 0.90$	14	9	16	69	52	15
Number of equations with $\bar{R}^2 < 0.70$	1	2	0	0	23	4
Estimation techniques	OLS	OLS	OLS	OLS	OLS	OLS

SOURCE: N. Glickman, *Econometric Analysis of Regional Systems,* New York: Academic Press, 1977, and this study.

Of the small area models developed prior to this study, the most ambitious is the Philadelphia model, particularly the latest version (Philadelphia IV). That model has 228 equations of which 105 are stochastic (the others are identities). There are 37 equations with lagged variables, thus introducing dynamic as opposed to static relationships. The model has been estimated with 25 years of data, which is well above the range of observations for other small areas (nine to fifteen). The most innovative aspect of the Philadelphia IV model is the introduction of spatial disaggregation. The block of disaggregated spatial equations are linked to the macro model. The Philadelphia model yields estimates of variables for the entire area, the city of Philadelphia separately, and the suburban area as a residual.

The flexibility, the low cost, the theoretical correctness, and the possibility for as much industry detail as available data permits leads to the judgment that an econometric model is the best form for a usable model of a metropolitan area aimed at projecting industry employment and then occupational employment. Although there are data problems (noted above), they are no more serious than the data problems encountered in estimating small area input-output or economic base models.

This section is best summarized by a quote from Glickman, who developed Philadelphia IV and who was a student of Lawrence Klein.

> In sum, regional econometric models are rather simple, being constructed on annual data with static and largely recursive frameworks. They are structurally linked to national economies, often through the mechanism of a companion national econometric model. Nearly all (except Philadelphia IV and Boston) look at the regional economy as a point in space, thus ignoring important intraregional phenomena and policy issues. Yet, these models are relatively inexpensive to build when compared to alternative forecasting tools such as input-output. Since econometric models yield far more information than economic base models, they would appear to be a good compromise between these other tools.[1]

2.3 The ideal model structure and estimation problems

The ideal model structure requires both a great deal of industry disaggregation and a simultaneous system. In economic systems, causality is not unidirectional and so neither should it be in models which attempt to replicate interactions in the real world. Good simultaneous models have supply-side constraints built into them.

Linkages and feedbacks in the ideal model structure for a small area would be as follows.

1. Output in each export industry is a function of national exogenous variables and local endogenous price and wage variables.
2. Total export output determines total area income.
3. Output in each local industry is a function of total area income (2) and local endogenous price and wage variables.
4. Productivity in each industry is a function of national exogenous variables.
5. Output in each industry (1 and 3) divided by productivity (4) in the corresponding industry yields employment in each industry.
6. Population of the area is a function of lagged total income (2), lagged area unemployment, and endogenous wage variables.
7. Population determines area labor force.
8. Labor force and employment in all industries (5) determine area unemployment.
9. Area unemployment and changes in area total income determine local wages and prices.
10. Local wages and prices, along with national exogenous variables, determine output in each export industry (1).

Thus, linkage (10) returns us to (1) and we have a simultaneous system with supply side constraints (population, labor force, and unemployment influence local prices and wages).

Problems occur in estimating the ideal model. First, if there are a large number of industries, there are many equations and many exogenous variables. Strictly speaking, with large numbers of endogenous variables (that is, dependent within the system) on the right-hand side of equations, the equations should be estimated with two-stage least squares. That requires, first, regressing each endogenous variable (which appears on the right-hand side of equations) on all the exogenous variables excluded from the equation in which it appears. If there are say, 17 or more such exogenous variables and the number of observations is only 20, then two-stage, least-squares estimation cannot be used because there are not enough degrees of freedom (that is, $20 - 17 = 3$).

The second problem relates to regional data. The appropriate wage and price data for large numbers of area industries are not available. Also, because of changes in definition, consistent area data on unemployment and the labor force over a sufficiently long period of time is not available. Finally, the simultaneous linkages breakdown in practice if the estimated population equation or equations are not acceptable.

The choice then is either to abandon the extensive disaggregation by industry and perhaps to estimate a simultaneous system with far fewer equations (hoping the population equations work), or to abandon a simultaneous system. The choice in this study has been to abandon the simultaneous system because aggregation does too much violence to reality, as is brought out in Chapter 3 in the analysis of the export industries. In terms of the structure of the ideal model presented above, the linkages 1 through 5 have been developed in the models presented here.

2.4 Measures of regional output

In empirical studies which flow from the export base theory of urban economic development and growth, two major problems are confronted. The first is the identification of the export sector and its magnitude. The second is the choice of a measure of output in both the export and local sector.

Considering the first problem, the best way to identify the export sector is by a large-scale survey of firms in the area to determine where their output is shipped (that is, how much is sold within the region and how much outside). Aside from the difficulties of cost, time, response rates, and reliability of such information, the critical flaw is that it is only valid for the survey year. A regional econometric model requires time se-ries data on the export and local sectors. The only method available for developing such time series is the use of location quotients. Location quotients for a region can be calculated for each industry (i) and for each year (t) as follows.

$$LQ_{it} = \frac{RO_{it}/\Sigma RO_{it}}{NO_{it}/\Sigma NO_{it}}$$

where
  LQ_{it} = location quotient for region's industry i in year t
  RO_{it} = region's output in industry i in year t
  ΣRO_{it} = region's output in all industries in year t
  NO_{it} = national output in industry i in year t
  ΣNO_{it} = national output in all industries in year t

The location quotient compares a specific industry's rel-ative share of total regional output to that same industry's relative share of total national output. If a region's industry, such as retail trade, was 7 percent of total regional output and at the national level retail trade was also 7 percent of national output, then the location quotient for retail trade in the region would be 1.0 (that is, 7%/7%). If the steel industry in the Pittsburgh area was 10 percent of regional output and nation-wide the steel industry was 6 percent of the United States total output, then the location quotient for steel in the Pittsburgh area would be 1.67 (that is, 10%/6%).

Any regional industry for which the location quotient exceeds 1.0 is assumed to be an export industry, that is, producing more than what would be required locally, assuming local requirements are relatively (in percent terms) the same as national requirements. Any regional industry for which the location quotient is equal to or less than 1.0 is assumed to be a local industry, producing the same as or less than what is required locally.

The next step is to split the output of each export industry (that is, an industry with a location quotient greater than 1.0) into that part which is assumed to be for export and that part which is assumed to be for local requirements. The export component is calculated as follows.

$$X_{it} = RO_{it} - \left(\frac{NO_{it}}{\Sigma NO_{it}}\right)\Sigma RO_{it}$$

where
X_{it} = export component of region's industry i output in year t

The local component (L) is then

$$L_{it} = RO_{it} - X_{it}$$

The total export of the region is then

$$\Sigma X_{it}$$

Thus location quotients provide a means, albeit crude, for identifying the export sector (that is, estimating which industries are export oriented) and estimating its magnitude.

The second problem, noted above, is the choice of an appropriate measure of output. Physical output is not good because there are usually no measures of this available for trade and services. Dollar measures of output for a region, such as value added, are available annually only for manufacturing industries and then only for the larger metropolitan areas. Consequently, the measure usually settled for is employment because employment data by industry is widely available for metropolitan areas. The major shortcoming of using employment data is that, across industries, there is an implicit assumption that all jobs are equal (that is, each makes the same contribution to output), which is far from true. Over time, the shortcoming of using employment data is that it fails to take into account growth in productivity. An industry with no change in total employment over ten years can have a marked increase in output due to growth in productivity.

To avoid shortcomings of using regional employment data as a proxy for output, an income measure for each regional industry has been computed in this study. The method was first devised by Richard Knight.[2] In the U.S. National Income Accounts, detailed industry data on national income originating (value added less depreciation) are published annually.[3] Corresponding industry employment data are published by the Bureau of Labor Statistics.[4] From that data, value added per employee (hereafter VAPE) in each industry for each year can be calculated. Then making the assumption that national VAPE in a given industry and year is the same as the unobserved *regional* VAPE in that industry and year, it is possible to compute regional income for that industry and year by multiplying VAPE by regional employment in that industry. The calculation is set forth below.

$$\text{VAPE}_{it} = \frac{NI_{it}/IPD_t}{NE_{it}}$$

$$RI_{it} = RE_{it}\,(\text{VAPE}_{it})$$

where

VAPE_{it} = value added per employee, in constant dollars, for the United States in industry i and year t

NI_{it} = United States national income in industry i and year t

$\checkmark$ IPD_{it} = implicit price deflator for United States GNP, 1972 = 100 in year t

NE_{it} = United States employment in industry i and year t

RI_{it} = estimated regional income, in constant dollars, in industry i and year t

RE_{it} = regional employment in industry i and year t

The estimated regional income (RI) is a measure of productive activity or value added in the industry within the region. The sum of RI over all industries is comparable to national income (that is, net national product valued at factor prices), not personal income. To the extent that the region's true but unobserved value added per employee (VAPE) in any industry differs from the national VAPE in that industry, then the estimates of industry regional income are off. Such differences between the true and the estimated VAPE must certainly exist because of the following.

1. Differences in the industry mix within any two-digit industry exist.
2. Differences in hours worked exist.

Given the present state of regional published data, there is no avoiding that problem.

Nonetheless, the important point is that interindustry differences in VAPE are doubtless far greater than interregional differences in VAPE within the same industry. The dramatic differences in VAPE between industries are illustrated below.

Industry	VAPE in 1978 (1972 $)
Petroleum refining	$63,950
Security & commodity brokers	30,971
Leather manufacturing	7,668

SOURCE: U.S. Department of Commerce, Bureau of Economic Analysis, *Survey of Current Business,* July, 1979; U.S. Department of Labor, Bureau of Labor Statistics, *Employment and Earnings,* March, 1979.

Thus, the value of this method is that it explicitly recognizes differences in VAPE across industries. That is, it does not assume all jobs are equal. Some jobs generate more value added than others. The method also explicitly takes into account the fact of increasing productivity over time.

The method described above has been used to estimate annual time-series data on regional income (in constant dollars) for each industry. The extent of industry detail was limited by the regional employment data.

2.5 Identifying export industries and local industries

Using the estimated regional income by industry and national income by industry time-series data described above, location quotients were calculated. That was done for each industry and each year in every region. The purpose is to identify the export industries and to compute the magnitude of total export income over time. The calculation is represented below.

$$LQ_{it} = \frac{RI_{it}/\Sigma RI_{it}}{NI_{it}/\Sigma NI_{it}}$$

As noted above, RI is regional income in a specific industry (i) and a specific year (t). ΣRI is the total regional income (all industries) in that year. *NI* and ΣNI are the corresponding national income measures. Since the income of all industries was deflated by the same price index (the GNP implicit price deflator, 1972 = 100), there is no need to represent it in the calculation of the location quotient.

Time-series estimates of the constant dollar value of exports for each regional industry were calculated as follows.

$$XI_{it} = RI_{it} - \left(\frac{NI_{it}}{\Sigma NI_{it}}\right) \Sigma RI_{it}$$

Any regional industry for which *XI* is consistently (over time) positive and significantly above zero is thus identified as an export industry. All other regional industries are thus identified as local industries (that is, those industries for which *XI* is consistently negative or for which *XI* randomly fluctuates around zero). Of course for any industry i and year t in which $LQ > 1$, then necessarily $XI_{it} > 0$. Thus the calculation of XI_{it} is sufficient for determining which industries are export industries, and the calculation of LQ_{it} is not necessary. However, both are explained here because the location quotient concept is more familiar.

2.6 Specification of demand equations for export industries

In this study it was decided to rely on the location quotient to estimate which regional industries were export and which local. However, in the specification and estimation of export-industry demand equations, the *total* industry's income was used as the dependent variable and not the export component. The computation of the export component presumes a reliability of location quotients which is not well founded. Location quotients are adequate for identifying which industries a region appears to specialize in, that is, which are export oriented. But location quotients are too crude to split an industry's output accurately between that which is exported and sold locally.

Treating each export industry's regional income (value added) as a constant-dollar measure of industry output in the region, demand equations were estimated. The standard independent variables in demand equations are income and relative price. However, two considerations argued against using a relative price variable in most equations. First, since the purpose of the model is to make forecasts, it would be absurd to have the accuracy of the forecasts critically depend upon forecasts of relative prices for over 50 industries. Second, industry output in the region (at least among export industries) is in competition with output of the same industry in the rest of the world. Consequently, a national relative price variable would not be as appropriate as a regional price variable (that is, the industry price in the region relative to the industry price in the rest of the world).

On an *a priori* basis, there are a number of factors which determine the level of demand for the output of a particular export industry in a region. Those factors are:

1. total demand in the national economy
2. stage of the business cycle
3. relative prices
4. costs of production in the local area versus elsewhere
5. output of a major customer industry

Identifying the important factors is only the first step. The difficult next step is to find quantitative measures (variables) which truly represent those factors. The variables which have been chosen are very effective in explaining, over time, the regional income for most of the export industries. Not all of the variables appear in every equation of course. Listed below are the key variables, at least one of which has been used in almost every equation, corresponding to the five factors named above.

1. United States GNP in 1972 dollars
2. United States unemployment rate
3. price index of particular industry divided by price index for all industries
4. consumer price index of the region divided by the consumer price index of the United States
5. the particular industry's output

The regional multiplier is central to export base theory. The level of total regional income is determined by export income times the multiplier. That is,

$$\Sigma RI_{it} = k(\Sigma XI_{it})$$

where k is the multiplier, ΣXI is the sum of the export component of all export industries (that is, those for which XI is positive) and ΣRI is total regional income. The equation above should not be estimated by regression because the right-hand variable (ΣXI) is included in the left-hand variable (ΣRI). Thus, the statistical estimate of the multiplier (k) would be biased. However, an unbiased estimate of k can be derived by estimating the following equation.

$$\Sigma LI_{it} = a + b\,\Sigma XI_{it} + u_i$$

where LI is the region's total local income. By definition, then,

$$\Sigma LI_{it} + \Sigma XI_{it} = \Sigma RI_{it}$$

The estimate of the coefficient b is unbiased, and it can be shown (see page 49) that

$$b + 1 = k$$

As was pointed out above, equations for estimating the export component, *XI*, of each export industry have not been developed. Consequently, in order to use the model for forecasting, it was necessary to estimate ΣXI indirectly. The following equation was estimated in order to forecast ΣXI based on the individual export industries' forecasts of *RI*.

$$\Sigma XI_{it} = c + d\,\Sigma RIX_{it}$$

where ΣRIX_{it} is *total* income in all the export industries, not total regional income.

The structure of the forecasting model as explained up to this point is represented below

$$RI_{1t} = f[N_t]$$
$$RI_{2t} = g[N_t]$$
$$\cdot \qquad \cdot$$
$$\cdot \qquad \cdot$$
$$\cdot \qquad \cdot$$
$$RI_{mt} = h[N_t]$$

where *N* is a vector of independent variables, mostly national and widely forecasted. RI_1 is forecasted regional income in export industry number 1, RI_2 is forecasted regional income in export industry number 2, and so on.

$$\Sigma RIX_{it} = RI_{1t} + RI_{2t} + \cdots + RI_{mt}$$

Then, ΣXI_{it}, the export-component sum, is forecasted by substituting the value of ΣRIX_{it} in the following equation.

$$\Sigma XI_{it} = c + d \, \Sigma RIX_{it}$$

Total local income is then estimated.

$$\Sigma LI_{it} = a + b \, \Sigma XI_{it}$$

Finally, the forecast total regional income is

$$\Sigma RI_{it} = \Sigma LI_{it} + \Sigma XI_{it}$$

2.7 Specification of demand equations for local industries

Regional income (RI) in each local industry has been used as the dependent variable in every local industry equation. The main independent variables used are total regional income (ΣRI), the unemployment rate in the United States, and some relative price (across industries) and relative cost (region versus nation) variables. As explained before, there are a priori grounds for not including total regional income in some local industry equations because their share of the local market may be more affected by external competitors than by the size of total regional income. The United States unemployment rate was used instead of a regional unemployment rate because a consistent series over time was not available for the latter.

For forecasting purposes, an estimate of total regional income (ΣRI) is required to forecast income in each local industry. The method of deriving a forecast of ΣRI was explained in Section 2.6. That forecast of ΣRI, however, is viewed as an interim value, a necessary input for the local-industry income equations. Once forecasts of all the income of local industries is obtained, the final forecast of total regional income is

$$\Sigma RI_{it} = \Sigma RIL_{it} + \Sigma RIX_{it}$$

where

ΣRIL_{it} = sum of forecast regional income in all local industries

ΣRIX_{it} = sum of forecast regional income in all export industries

ΣRI_{it} = forecast total regional income for all industries

2.8 Specification of productivity equations

The estimates of regional income by industry developed in this study are calculated as the product of national value added per employee (constant dollars) in that industry, VAPE, and regional employment in that industry, *RE*, as shown below.

$$RI_{it} = RE_{it}(\text{VAPE}_{it})$$

In sections 2.6 and 2.7 the method for forecasting *RI* by industry was explained. In order to forecast regional employment by industry, it is necessary to forecast national VAPE by industry.

Ordinary least-squares equations have been estimated for projecting national VAPE by industry, in 1972 dollars. Because VAPE is a measure of productivity (although an imperfect one because it is value added per employee rather than value added per manhour) in most industries it has a strong secular trend. Thus, most of the VAPE equations have a single argument: a time trend or real aggregate national income per employee. A strong cyclical component in some industry's VAPE required the addition of the unemployment rate in the United States as a second independent variable. A considerable advantage of this regional forecasting model over prior efforts is that by forecasting industry VAPE separately, historically differential growth rates in productivity among industries are explicitly taken into account.

2.9 Derivation of employment

Given forecasts of regional income by industry (RI_{it}), and value added per employee by industry ($VAPE_{it}$), forecasts of regional employment by industry (RE_{it}) are derived algebraically; that is,

$$RE_{it} = \frac{RI_{it}}{VAPE_{it}}$$

Thus, forecasted employment trends depend not only upon the projected growth of output in a particular industry but also upon the projected trend in productivity (real VAPE) for that industry. Explicitly accounting for productivity growth in forecasting industry employment is an improvement over using forecasting models in which the effect of productivity growth is only present implicitly or is simply an average which is the same for all industries.

Notes

1. N. Glickman, "Son of 'The Specification of Regional Econometric Models,' " *Papers of the Regional Science Association,* No. 32 (1975), p. 162.

2. R. Knight, *Employment Expansion and Metropolitan Trade* (New York: Praeger, 1973).

3. U.S. Department of Commerce, Bureau of Economic Analysis, "National Income and Product Accounts," *Survey of Current Business,* July issues.

4. U.S. Department of Labor, Bureau of Labor Statistics, *Employment and Earnings, United States, 1909–78,* July, 1979.

3

The Regional Models of the New York-Northeastern New Jersey Standard Consolidated Area and New York City

3.1 The region, the time span, and the industries

The region defined for this model is the New York-Northeastern New Jersey Standard Consolidated Area (hereafter SCA). The SCA is comprised of New York City (five counties), Long Island (two counties), three other suburban counties in New York State, and eight urban and suburban counties in northeastern New Jersey. The list of counties included in the SCA is shown in Table 3.1. There are three parts to the model:

1. data and equations for the entire SCA
2. data and equations for New York City, a subpart of the SCA
3. data (but not equations) for the non-New York City part of the SCA

The model equations can be used to forecast SCA income and employment, and New York City (hereafter NYC) income and employment. Forecasts of the non-NYC part of the SCA can be derived by subtraction.

Table 3.1
New York-Northeastern New Jersey Standard Consolidated Area

New York Counties	New Jersey Counties
New York City	Bergen
Bronx	Essex
Brooklyn	Hudson
Manhattan	Middlesex
Queens	Morris
Staten Island	Passaic
Non-New York City	Somerset
Nassau	Union
Suffolk	
Westchester	
Rockland	
Putnam	

SOURCE: U.S. Department of Labor, Bureau of Labor Statistics, *Employment, Hours, and Earnings, States and Areas, 1939–82*, January, 1984.

All of the model time-series equations have been estimated with annual data between 1958 and 1978 (21 observations). The fiscal equations for estimating city government tax revenues by source have been estimated over a shorter period because the present revenue system has been in effect only since the mid-1960s (see Chapter 7).

The basic employment and income data are for 53 industries. There are of course three sets of that detailed industry data: one for the SCA, one for NYC, and one for the non-NYC part of the SCA. The industry definitions closely correspond to the two-digit Standard Industrial Classification (S.I.C.) code. The list of industry names and their S.I.C. codes are presented in Appendix Table 1.

The entire model consists of 289 equations of which 159 are stochastic and the others are identities. There are 16 exogenous national variables and 12 regional exogenous variables plus four lagged variables. Considering the regional parts, the SCA model has 114 equations of which 54 are stochastic. The NYC model has 122 equations of which 56 are stochastic.

The NYC part has more equations than the SCA part because of the inclusion of a fiscal submodel. The equations for the national value added per employee, 53 in all, can be applied both in the SCA and NYC models.

In opting for a very high degree of disaggregation (53 industries), the possibility of developing a simultaneous-equation model was foreclosed. In a fully simultaneous model, all of the endogenous variables are simultaneously determined. In an industry-by-industry model such as this, a simultaneous structural form would require endogenous variables for output, employment, wages, and prices in each industry plus aggregate endogenous variables for regional population, labor force, migration, and unemployment, all of which (with appropriate exogenous variables and lagged endogenous variables) would be jointly determined.

Such a structure imposes data requirements which simply cannot be met for small regions (that is, below the state level) unless one is willing to settle for disaggregation only within the manufacturing sector (for which regional data is more complete) and aggregation in nonmanufacturing. That is what Glickman did in developing the Philadelphia model, which is partly simultaneous.[1] The nonmanufacturing part of the Philadelphia model is split into only six sectors, whereas in this model there are 33 nonmanufacturing industries, each with its own output, value added per employee, and employment equation. For an economy such as Philadelphia (or more so Pittsburgh, Cleveland, and Detroit), which is largely driven by its manufacturing export base, Glickman's aggregation of nonmanufacturing and his specification of those equations as local activities is a tolerable tradeoff to gain a partially simultaneous system. For an economy such as the New York area (and more so New York City), which is largely driven by its nonmanufacturing activities, to gain a partially simultaneous system is to bury or obscure the substantive reality of central interest in order to achieve econometric elegance. That is an unacceptable tradeoff. Consequently, the model presented here is recursive, not simultaneous.

3.2 Historical economic trends

As noted above, the model equations have been estimated between 1958 and 1978. The historical sketch of broad trends presented here, however, goes beyond that period. In the sections on policy analysis and tests of the model, data for years after 1978 are also presented.

Over the 25 years from 1958 to 1983, real income in the SCA expanded at an annual rate of 2.0 percent.[2] Typical of metropolitan areas' economic growth, expansion in the city was markedly lower (1.0 percent per year), while expansion in the rest of the region was markedly higher (3.3 percent per year). Because real income growth in the city was slower than productivity growth, city employment declined by an average of −0.2 percent per year over those 25 years (See Table 3.2).

From 1958 to 1969, real income and employment increased in both parts of the SCA. The recessions of 1969 and 1970 and between 1973 and 1975 hit the region very hard, particularly NYC. Total real income in NYC in 1975 was 15.5 percent below the 1969 level and employment was down 514,000 from 1969. Real income increased, from 1975 to 1983 in both parts of the SCA as recovery got underway. By 1983, employment in the SCA had surpassed the prior peak of 6,701,000 in 1969 by 145,000 jobs. However, employment in NYC in 1983, at 3,344,000, was still below the 1969 peak of 3,797,000 but nonetheless was above the depressed 1975 level.

Employment changes by sector are shown in Table 3.3 for the region and the city. The SCA had employment gains in all sectors, between 1958 and 1969, albeit small ones in manufac-

Table 3.2
Total Income and Employment in the Region, 1958–1983

Year	Income (billion 1972 $)		
	SCA	NYC	Rest of SCA
1958	$53.5	$33.6	$19.9
1969	77.0	43.9	33.1
1975	71.5	37.1	34.4
1983	87.9	43.1	44.8
Average Annual Percent Change			
1958–1983	2.0	1.0	3.6
1958–1969	3.4	2.5	4.7
1969–1975	− 1.2	− 2.8	0.6
1975–1983	2.6	1.9	3.4
Employment (thousands of jobs)			
Year	SCA	NYC	Rest of SCA
1958	5,528	3,479	2,049
1969	6,701	3,797	2,904
1975	6,304	3,283	3,021
1983	6,846	3,344	3,502
Average Annual Percent Change			
1958–1983	0.9	− 0.2	2.2
1958–1969	1.8	0.8	3.2
1969–1975	− 1.0	− 2.4	0.7
1975–1983	1.0	0.2	1.9

SOURCE: Income data calculated. Employment data from U.S. Department of Labor, Bureau of Labor Statistics, *Employment and Earnings, States and Areas, 1939–78,* 1980, and *Employment and Earnings,* March, 1984.

turing. The city lost 128,000 manufacturing jobs in that growth period when most other sectors of city employment expanded. In the period of decline, from 1969 to 1975, the SCA had a net loss of 397,000 jobs; the city's loss was 514,000 jobs. The largest losses in both the SCA and NYC were in manufacturing. Excepting government, no sector of NYC employment had a gain in jobs, from 1969 to 1975. From 1975 to 1983, most sectors of the SCA increased in employment. Government

Table 3.3
Changes in Employment by Sector, SCA and NYC, 1958–1983 (thousands)

	SCA			NYC		
Sector	1958– 1969	1969– 1975	1975– 1983	1958– 1969	1969– 1975	1975– 1983
Mining and construction	+14	−48	+19	−10	−25	+7
Manufacturing	+35	−451	−107	−128	−289	−105
Transportation and communication	+39	−56	—	+2	−55	−33
Wholesale and retail trade	+244	−37	+117	+15	−114	−26
Finance, insurance, and real estate	+129	−20	+119	+92	−46	+74
Services	+406	+76	+426	+206	−13	+197
Government	+306	+139	−33	+142	+25	−54
Total Change	+1173	−397	+541	+318	−514	+61

SOURCE: U.S. Department of Labor, Bureau of Labor Statistics, *Employment and Earnings, States and Areas, 1939–78,* 1980, and *Employment and Earnings,* March, 1984.

employment in the city fell sharply, reflecting the fiscal emergency layoffs. Employment in services and finance expanded strongly in NYC, from 1975 to 1983, and there were also gains in mining and construction. Manufacturing, transportation, and trade continued to decline but at slower rates.

Because the changes in employment by sector have not been proportional, the SCA, and especially the city, have had dramatic changes in the mix of employment (see Table 3.4). In 1958, 27.4 percent of city jobs were in manufacturing. By 1983 only 12.9 percent were in manufacturing. The sectors which showed relative increases were services, government, and finance insurance and real estate.

3.3 The export industries

Using the method described in Chapter 2, the export industries of the city and SCA have been identified. Table 3.5 presents the list of SCA export industries, their total income

Table 3.4
Employment Shares by Sector, SCA and NYC

Sector	Percentage of Total Employment			
	1958		1983	
	SCA	NYC	SCA	NYC
Mining and construction	4.2%	3.3%	3.2%	2.7%
Manufacturing	31.2	27.4	17.7	12.9
Transportation and communication	8.6	9.3	6.7	7.1
Wholesale and retail trade	20.4	21.1	21.2	18.2
Finance, insurance, and real estate	8.5	10.7	10.2	14.8
Services	15.2	16.5	25.5	28.9
Government	11.8	11.6	15.6	15.5
Total	100%	100%	100%	100%

SOURCE: See Table 3.3.

and the estimated export component in 1958 and 1983. Table 3.6 presents the same information for the city export industries.

Manufacturing accounted for one-third of the SCA export income in 1958 but was only one-fifth in 1983. Both the service sector and financial sector exceeded the export income of the manufacturing sector by 1983. In 1983, the financial sector had become the most important export sector of the region, accounting for 31 percent of SCA export income.

There have been dramatic shifts in importance of export industries. In 1958, apparel manufacturing, with exports of $1.2 billion, ranked first, while communication, with exports under $0.3 billion, ranked fifteenth out of 22 export industries. By 1983, the export component of communication, which more than quadrupled since 1958, was 33 percent larger than that of apparel. The only manufacturing industries which had gains in export income were chemicals (which includes production of pharmaceuticals and cosmetics) and printing and publishing.

Because the city is included in the SCA and in terms of income is one-half of the SCA, the pattern of changes in export industries presented in Table 3.6 is similar to that of the SCA.

Table 3.5
Export Industries of the SCA (millions 1972 $)[a]

SIC. Code	Sector and Industry	Abbreviated Name	1958		1983	
			Income	Export Component	Income	Export Component
	Manufacturing					
23	Apparel	APP	$1,984	$1,248	$1,378	$ 762
27	Printing and publishing	PRNT	1,631	677	2,271	1,101
28	Chemicals	CHEM	1,830	530	2,859	1,373
31	Leather	LETH	247	12	144	−6
38	Instruments	INST	853	444	1,022	257
39	Miscellaneous manufacturing	MMAN	884	530	663	338
	Transportation and communication					
44	Water transportation	WATT	787	552	534	324
45	Air transportation	AIRT	310	129	1,191	690
47	Transportation services	TSRV	203	124	507	296
48	Communication	COMM	1,394	227	3,180	1,017
	Trade					
50, 51	Wholesale trade	WHOL	4,489	1,026	8,480	3,001
	Finance, insurance, and real estate					
60	Banking	BANK	1,708	615	3,659	1,557
62	Securities	SEC	937	712	3,779	3,269
63	Insurance carriers	INSC	1,238	448	1,596	506
64	Insurance agents	INSA	401	112	977	458
65, 66 & 67	Real estate and combined financial, and holding, and investment companies	RECH	1,780	956	1,133	91
	Services					
73	Business services	BSRV	1,673	991	4,343	1,951
78	Motion pictures	FILM	178	40	291	133
80	Health services	MED	1,451	58	4,433	−245
81	Legal services	LEGL	702	331	1,920	935
82	Educational services	EDUC	311	[b]	1,211	551
84, 89	Miscellaneous services and museums	MSVM	791	237	2,002	586
	Total all export industries		$25,782	$9,999	$47,571	$18,944

[a] Parts may not add to totals due to rounding.
[b] Not an export industry in 1958.
SOURCE: Calculated for this study.

Table 3.6
Export Industries of NYC (millions 1972 $)

			1958		1983	
SIC Code	Sector and Industry	Abbre-viated Name	Income	Export Com-ponent	Income	Export Com-ponent
	Manufacturing					
23	Apparel	APP	$ 1,581	$1,116	$ 967	$ 665
27	Printing and publishing	PRNT	1,252	649	1,325	751
31	Leather	LETH	187	38	94	21
39	Miscellaneous manufacturing	MMAN	641	417	384	224
	Transportation and communication					
44	Water transportation	WATT	668	520	264	160
45	Air transportation	AIRT	286	171	951	705
47	Transportation services	TSRV	180	130	331	227
48	Communication	COMM	953	215	1,883	822
	Trade					
50, 51	Wholesale trade	WHOL	3,399	1,209	3,950	1,263
	Finance, insurance, and real estate					
60	Banking	BANK	1,345	658	2,726	1,935
62	Securities	SEC	901	760	3,410	3,160
63	Insurance carriers	INSC	928	431	887	352
64	Insurance agents	INSA	313	130	528	273
65, 66, & 67	Real estate and com-bined financial, and holding, and invest-ment companies	RECH	1,474	955	843	450
	Services					
73	Business services	BSRV	1,239	808	2,455	1,282
78	Motion pictures	FILM	148	61	222	144
80	Health services	MED	883	a	2,195	206
81	Legal services	LEGL	538	303	1,315	832
82	Educational services	EDUC	193	a	684	360
83, 86	Social services and nonprofit organizations	MEMB	382	30	845	332
84, 89	Miscellaneous services and museums	MSVM	600	250	1,151	456
	Total all export industries		$18,091	$8,851	$27,410	$14,620

[a] Parts may not add to totals due to rounding.
[b] Not an export industry in 1958.
SOURCE: Calculated for this study.

However, manufacturing is even less prominent among NYC export industries and the declines since 1958 have been more severe. The transformation of the city's economy in 25 years is in large part revealed by ranking the major export industries, then and now (see Table 3.7). Wholesale trade, apparel manufacturing, and real estate ranked respectively first, second, and third in 1958, and together accounted for 37 percent of the city's export income. By 1983, securities, banking, and business services held the three top places, in that order, together accounting for 45 percent of all export income. Industries included among the top ten in 1983 but not in 1958 are legal services, communications, air transportation, and miscellaneous services. And industries no longer among the top ten in 1983 are real estate, water transportation, insurance carriers, and miscellaneous manufacturing. In general, it can be said that the production and distribution of goods are on the wane in New York while activities related to providing services to business and other large institutions are on the rise. That finding, which might have been obscured in a less-disaggregated model, underscores the error of some naïve regional econometric models which assume that goods production is the export sector and everything else is the local sector.

The transformation of the region's and city's export base over 25 years is highlighted by employing a functional taxonomy of export industries different from the conventional categories (manufacturing, services, among others). Each of the export industries can be categorized into one of three groups: goods production and distribution, corporate services, and consumer services. The first is self-explanatory. The second is difficult to define. Primarily, corporate services include those export industries which *are* export industries by virtue of their serving a national and even international corporate market with financial services, business services, communication, and transportation. They also provide services locally

Table 3.7
Top Ten Export Industries of NYC, 1958 and 1983

	1958			1983	
Rank	Industry	Export Component (million 1972 $)	Rank	Industry	Export Component (million 1972 $)
1	Wholesale trade	$1,209	1	Securities	$ 3,160
2	Apparel	1,116	2	Banking	1,935
3	Real estate, combined financial, holding and investment companies	955	3	Business services	1,282
4	Business services	808	4	Wholesale trade	1,263
5	Securities	760	5	Legal services	832
6	Banking	658	6	Communication	822
7	Printing and publishing	649	7	Printing and publishing	751
8	Water transportation	520	8	Air transportation	705
9	Insurance carriers	431	9	Apparel	665
10	Miscellaneous manufacturing	417	10	Miscallaneous services and museums	456
	Total top ten	$7,523		Total top ten	$11,871
	As percent of city exports	85.0%		As percent of city exports	81.2%

SOURCE: Calculated from Table 3.6.

to consumers as well as local business, in the same way, of course, that any export industry also responds to local demand. But banking and securities, for example, are not export businesses (using the traditional mechanical procedure) because of an unusually large proportion of neighborhood branch banks and retail stockbrokers' offices in the New York region. They are truly export industries because of the significant volume of their business emanating from corporations and other large institutions around the nation and the world.

The third group, consumer services, includes two large export industries: private health and education.

In 1958, the goods production and distribution group of SCA export industries was the largest of the three groups, accounting for half the real income of all SCA export industries. But by 1983 the corporate-services group was far and away the largest, having grown 3.2 percent per year compared with growth of only 1.3 percent per year in the goods-production and distribution group (see Table 3.8).

Even in 1958, the corporate services group dominated the NYC export groups, representing over half the income of all city export industries. From 1958 to 1983, real income of the city's goods production and distribution group fell 0.4 percent per year on average while corporate services income expanded 2.6 percent per year and consumer services income (fueled by federal health-care dollars) grew 4.0 percent per year. Thus, by 1983, 75 percent of the city's income generated from its 22 export industries was accounted for by corporate services and consumer services.

3.4 Export industry equations

As explained in Chapter 2, ordinary least-squares, time-series regression equations have been estimated for each export industry of the SCA and for each export industry of NYC.

Table 3.8
Real Income of Export Industries by Major Groups, 1958 and 1983[a]

Area and year	Goods Pro-duction and Distribution[b]	Corporate Services[c]	Consumer Services[d]	Total Export Industries
	(million 1972 $)			
SCA				
1958	$12,705	$11,315	$1,762	$25,782
1983	17,351	24,578	5,644	47,571
Average annual percent change, 1958–1983	1.3	3.2	4.8	2.5
NYC				
1958	$ 7,728	$ 9,287	$1,076	$18,091
1983	6,984	17,548	2,879	27,410
Average annual percent change, 1958–1983	−0.4	2.6	4.0	1.7

[a] Parts may not add to total due to rounding.
[b] NYC includes apparel, printing and publishing, leather, miscellaneous manufacturing, water transportation, and wholesale trade. SCA includes all of those plus chemicals and instruments.
[c] NYC includes air transportation, transportation services, communication, banking, securities, insurance carriers, insurance agents, real estate, business services, motion pictures, legal services, social services and nonprofit organizations, and miscellaneous services and museums. SCA includes all of those except social services and non-profit organizations.
[d] NYC and SCA include health services (private) and educational services (private).
SOURCE: Computed from Tables 3.5 and 3.6.

The dependent variable is always the total income (not the export component) of the specific export industry, in millions of 1972 dollars. Because the industry income is a measure of value added, it is thus a measure of dollar output and the equations are demand equations. The export component was not used as the dependent variable because it is recognized that the calculation of export components presumes that location quotients truly indicate the extent of export activity in an industry. That is an unacceptable presumption. The chief value of location quotients in this model is to identify which industries are export oriented over time. To assume that year-to-year changes in any industry's calculated export component reflects real economic changes would be placing too much faith in a mechanical procedure.

Appendix Tables 2 and 3 present the estimated equations for the SCA export industries and the NYC export industries, respectively.

Of the 22 equations for SCA export industries, 11 have adjusted R^2 values above 0.90 and another nine have values above 0.70. Of the 21 city export industry equations, nine have adjusted R^2 values above 0.90 while seven have values above 0.80. Only one equation has an adjusted R^2 below 0.70 (insurance carriers: .699).

Although some adjusted R^2 values are not as high as one would like, the t statistics (which measure the statistical significance of individual partial regression coefficients) are generally excellent. Higher R^2 values (and poor t statistics) could have been obtained by accepting equations with serious multicolinearity. But in fact all estimated equations with serious multicolinearity were rejected. That rule has been applied throughout, so all estimated equations presented in this report are not multicolinear. It is generally believed that multicolinearity is not a serious handicap in equations used for forecasting. But it is a serious handicap for analysis because the separate effect of an independent variable can be obscured. Given the extensive disaggregation in this model (53 industries) and the tendency for errors to cancel when aggregating individual industry income forecasts to obtain a total SCA or NYC income, then it seems far better to trade off explanatory power of individual industry equations for statistical significance of partial regression coefficients. Also, higher R^2 values can usually be obtained by using the lagged value of the dependent variable as an explanatory variable. There are two problems about that. First, it tends to produce multicolinearity. Second, it tends to reduce the likelihood of the equation catching turning points in the economy.

At least one of three particular independent variables appears in every regional and city export equation, excepting the equation for business services in the SCA (SYBSRV). Those variables are the gross national product in constant dollars (UGNP), the national unemployment rate (UUNEMPR), and the ratio of the regional CPI to the national CPI (SCPIUS). On a priori grounds, demand for the output of an export industry would be positively related to aggregate demand in the national economy, as measured by the real GNP. In most of the equations in which UGNP appears, the sign on its partial regression coefficient is positive and highly significant. Cyclically sensitive export industries are by definition responsive to the stages of the business cycle. The national unemployment rate reflects those stages, rising in recessions and falling in expansions. In every equation in which the unemployment rate (UUNEMPR) appears, its sign is negative as expected and highly significant.

The third variable which appears in so many equations requires some explanation. On a priori grounds, the appropriate relative price variable to use in a regional export-industry demand equation would be the industry output price in the region relative to the industry output price in the nation. Lacking regional data on detailed industry prices, a proxy variable has been used which presumably reflects the rate of overall price increases in the region relative to the nation, that is, the regional consumer price index divided by the national consumer price index. To the extent that the consumer price index (CPI) is an aggregate manifestation of cost pressures across industries, then when the regional CPI rises faster than the national CPI, it suggests that regional export industries are at a competitive disadvantage viz-à-viz competitors outside the region. Hence, one would anticipate a negative sign on that relative price variable. The sign on SCPIUS is almost always negative and statistically significant.

One advantage of this model for forecasting is that two of the three key independent variables, real GNP and the unemployment rate, are widely forecast by national econometric models. The third key variable, the CPI ratio, does not require an explicit projection of each CPI to make a forecast. Rather, only an assumption is required about whether inflation in the region will be faster, slower, or the same as in the nation.

3.5 Aggregate income equations

Table 3.9 at the end of this section presents the set of aggregate equations (as opposed to individual industry equations) for determining export income, local income, and total income. The set of equations corresponds to the explanation in Chapter 2 of the forecasting of total income in the city and the SCA respectively. Using the city equations to illustrate a forecast, the steps are as follows.

1. The equations in Appendix Table 3 are used to forecast the income of each city export industry.
2. Equation CA1 (Table 3.9), an identity, calculates total income of all city export industries as a sum, CEXP21.
3. That sum, CEXP21, is put into equation CA2 which forecasts the aggregate *export component* (CEXP1) of the city export industries.
4. The prior year's aggregate export component (LCEXP1) is inserted into equation CA3 along with lagged city population (LCPOP) to forecast the current year's aggregate local income component, CLOCY1.
5. Total city income (CALLY) in the current year is determined with equation CA4 as the sum of current-year, aggregate export component income, CEXP1 (from

Table 3.9
NYC and SCA Aggregate Income Equations

Equation Number		Equations	Adjusted R^2	Durbin Watson	Standard Error
CA1	CEXP21	$= \Sigma$City Export Industries' Income			
CA2	CEXP1	$= +12{,}934 + .5883$CEXP21 $- 14{,}924$SCPIUS	.984	1.16	143.0
		(31.9) (8.8)			
CA3	CLOCY1	$= -13{,}602 + 1.390$LCEXP1 $+ 3.470$LCPOP	.926	1.99	478.1
		(14.1) (5.8)			
CA4	CALLY	$=$ CEXP1 $+$ CLOCY1			
CA5	CLOCY2	$= \Sigma$City Local Industries' Income			
CA6	CALLY*	$=$ CEXP21 $+$ CLOCY2			
CA7	CYERROR	$=$ CALLY $-$ CALLY*			
SA1	SEXP22	$=$ SCA Export Industries' Income			
SA2	SEXP1	$= 19{,}631 + .3793$SEXP22 $- 19{,}360$SCPIUS	.963	0.93	294.1
		(18.4) (4.7)			
SA3	SLOCY1	$= -67{,}814 + 2.009$SEXP1 $+ 6.294$L2SPOP	.981	1.60	796.6
		(9.7) (12.1)			
SA4	SALLY	$=$ SEXP1 $+$ SLOCY1			
SA5	SLOCY2	$= \Sigma$SCA Local Industries' Income			
SA6	SALLY*	$=$ SEXP22 $+$ SLOCY2			
SA7	SYERROR	$=$ SALLY $-$ SALLY*			
SA8	SPOP	$= 13{,}581 - 191.2$LUUNEMPR $+ .03947$L2SALLY	.752	1.11	199.4
		(2.9) (6.8)			

Guide to Table 3.9

Definitions of Variables

CEXP21	total income of all (21) NYC export industries, millions of 1972 $
SEXP22	total income of all (22) SCA export industries in millions of 1972 $
CEXP1	export income component of all NYC export industries in millions of 1972 $
SEXP1	export income component of all SCA export industries in millions of 1972 $
CLOCY1	local income component of all NYC industries in millions of 1972 $
LCEXP1	CEXP1 value in prior year
SLOCY1	local income component of all SCA industries in millions of 1972 $
CALLY	total income, all industries, in NYC in millions of 1972 $
SALLY	total income, all industries in SCA in millions of 1972 $
CLOCY2	total income of all (32) NYC local industries in millions of 1972 $
SLOCY2	total income of all (31) SCA local industries in millions of 1972 $
LCPOP	population of NYC in prior year in thousands
L2SPOP	population of SCA, lagged two years in thousands
LUUNEMPR	United States unemployment rate in prior year
L2SALLY	value of SALLY lagged two years
L2CALLY	value of CALLY lagged two years
SCPIUS	CPI for region divided by consumer price index for United States

equation CA2), and curent-year aggregate local component income, CLOCY1 (from equation CA3).

6. The estimate of total city income, CALLY, from equ-
   tion CA4, is the main explanatory variable in many of
   the individual local industry income equations, which
   are presented in the next section.

7. Once the individual local industry incomes are forecast,
   equation CA5 is used to calculate the sum of local industries' total income (CLOCY2).

8. A second estimate of total city income (CALLY) is derived with equation CA6. The difference between the
   two total income estimates is computed in equation
   CA7.

It is important to make clear how the two total city-income
estimates are calculated. The first, from equation CA4, is the
sum of aggregate export component income (CEXP1 from
equation CA2) and aggregate local component income
(CLOCY1 from equation CA3). The second estimate of total
city income (from equation CA6) is the sum of total income of
all export industries (CEXP2 from equation CA1) and total
income of all local industries (CLOCY2 from equation CA5).
An important part of the testing of this model has been to
determine, over the time for which the equations were estimated, which estimate of total city income is closer to the
actual. The same holds true for the SCA. The final section of
this chapter (3.8) presents the results of that testing.

There is a population equation for the SCA (SA8) but not
for the city because an acceptable equation could not be estimated. The SCA population equation is appealing on a priori
grounds, with population inversely related to the prior year's
unemployment rate and positively related to total income,
lagged two years, but it is not sufficiently accurate to be of
much use. It is a promising beginning but requires further
work.

Population forecasts are required to forecast more than two years ahead for the SCA and more than one year ahead for the city. That is because equation SA3, used to forecast the aggregate local income component, SLOCY1, includes as an independent variable the region's population, lagged two years (L2SPOP). Similarly, equation CA3, for forecasting the city aggregate local income component (CLOCY1), includes as an independent variable the city's population, lagged one year (LCPOP). Alternative equations estimated for SLOCY1 and CLOCY1 without population as an independent variable all have standard errors three to five times larger. Given that year-to-year variations in SLOCY1 and CLOCY1 are much larger in percentage than year-to-year variations in population, it seems appropriate to use the equations with population as an explanatory variable and to project population outside the model.

Empirical estimates of the export income marginal multiplier for the city and the region can be derived from the following alternative forms of equations CA3 and SA3 respectively.

$$\text{Alternative CA3} \quad \text{CLOCY1} = 13{,}133 + 1.405 \text{ LCEXP1}$$
$$(8.5)$$
$$R^2 = .79 \qquad \text{SEE} = 803$$

$$\text{Alternative SA3} \quad \text{SLOCY1} = 4911 + 3.981 \text{ LSEXP1}$$
$$(12.4)$$
$$R^2 = .89 \qquad \text{SEE} = 2082$$

According to export base theory, changes in total income are some multiple of changes in export income; that is,

$$\text{CALLY} = a + k \text{ CEXP1} \qquad (1)$$

or

$$CALLY = k\,CEXP1 \tag{2}$$

The coefficient k is the marginal multiplier. If either equation (1) or (2) is estimated, the estimate of k will be biased because the right-hand variable, CEXP1, is included in the left-hand variable, CALLY, and is a substantial part of it; that is,

$$CALLY = CEXP1 + CLOCY1 \tag{3}$$

However, bias can be avoided as follows. Rearranging equation (3) and substituting for CALLY from equation (1) yields

$$CEXP1 + CLOCY1 = a + k\,CEXP1 \tag{4}$$
$$CLOCY1 = a + k\,CEXP1 - CEXP1 \tag{5}$$
$$CLOCY1 = a + (k - 1)\,CEXP1 \tag{6}$$

If equation 6 is estimated by regression, the estimated regression coefficient on CEXP1, call it "b," is an estimate of $(k - 1)$. Hence, an estimate of k can be derived as

$$k = b + 1 \quad \text{because} \quad b = (k - 1)$$

So from alternative equation CA3, the estimate of the city-income marginal multiplier is

$$k = 1.405 + 1 = 2.405$$

And from alternative equation SA3 the estimate of the region income marginal multiplier is

$$k = 3.981 + 1 = 4.981$$

Thus the estimated city income marginal multiplier, 2.4, is about half the SCA multiplier of 5.0. Because the region is much larger than the city and has more of a self-sufficient economy, it would be expected that the SCA multiplier be much larger. In a study of many metropolitan areas, it was found that the income multiplier tends to be larger for larger metropolitan areas.[3]

3.6 Local industry equations

The full set of local industry income equations for the SCA and for NYC are presented in Appendix Tables 4 and 5. As with the export industry equations, the dependent variable is always the total income of the specific local industry, in millions of 1972 dollars.

In 21 of the 31 SCA local industry equations, total SCA income (SALLY) appears as an independent variable. Of the 32 city local industry equations, the total city income variable (CALLY) appears in 18. The absence of a total income variable from some of the local industry equations points up the limited usefulness of the method based on the location quotient for identifying which industries are local and which export. To take extreme cases, the mining industry falls into the set of local industries for the SCA and the city using location quotients. Certainly all of the mining industry employees in the city sit at desks of central administrative offices, and almost all of the SCA mining industry employees do likewise. It is patently absurd to assert that the level of economic activity of the mining industry in the city or SCA is a function of total city or SCA income, as is the case for liquor stores and other truly local activities. The other extreme case is local transit which, based on the location quotient, falls in the export category for the SCA and the city. It is difficult to conceive of the sense in which the region "exports" mass-transit rides. Consequently, the local transit industry was included with local industries. But location quotients are far from useless. In dealing with the unusual New York-Northeastern New Jersey region, their use effectively avoided the antiquated error of assuming all goods production is export oriented and everything else (banking, securities, business services, communication, among other businesses) is local.

Of the 31 SCA local industry equations, 2 are identities by default; that is, no acceptable regression equations were estimated. For the same reason, there are 6 identities among the 32 city equations. For the most part, the dependent variable in each of those equations, industry income in constant dollars, showed little variation over the period of estimation.

Of the 29 regression equations estimated for SCA local industries, nine have adjusted R^2 values above 0.90 and 13 have adjusted R^2 values between 0.80 and 0.90. Among the 26 city regression equations, nine have R^2 values above 0.90 and nine have R^2 values between 0.80 and 0.90.

Local industries are often, of course, cyclically sensitive, just as export industries are. Consequently, the unemployment rate (UUNEMPR) in the United States appears as an explanatory variable in most of the local industry equations. On a priori grounds, it would be appropriate to use the local unemployment rate rather than the national rate. However, over the estimating period, between 1958 and 1978, the local unemployment rate has been redefined, and a consistent historical series is not available. Thus the unemployment rate in the United States is much more reliable statistically than any small-area rate.

Some of the explanatory variables in local-industry equations are not forecast in national models or within this model. They include city and SCA population. Fortunately the population variables only appear in three SCA equations and three city equations. The region's housing starts (SNEWHST) only appears in one equation. Consequently, forecasts of those variables outside the model would have little impact on the aggregated forecast of total income of local industries.

3.7 Value added per employee equations

As explained in Chapter 2, forecasts of income by industry are translated into forecasts of industry employment by dividing income by value added per employee (VAPE). That requires forecasts of VAPE by industry.

Ordinary least-squares, time-series equations have been estimated for the national value added per employee (1972 $) in each of 53 industries. The estimated equations are presented in Appendix Table 6.

Four of the VAPE equations are identities by default. That is, the historical pattern of industry VAPE appeared to be random fluctuations around the mean. It is particularly troubling that for some of the SCA and city major export industries good VAPE equations have not been estimated (such as, for banking, securities, insurance carriers, business services, and legal services).

Of the 49 regression equations for industry VAPE, almost all have as the key explanatory variable either a time trend (YEARRANK) or a measure of aggregate value added per employee in all industries (UYPE or UGNPE). Because VAPE appears to be cyclically sensitive in a number of industries, the national unemployment rate is used as an explanatory variable.

The qualtiy of the 49 VAPE regression equations is not as high as the industry income equations. Only nine of the 49 have R^2 values above 0.90, 13 have R^2 values between 0.80 and 0.90, while 5 have R^2 values below 0.70. However, the variability of industry value added per employee over time tends to be much less than the variability of industry income.

3.8 Testing the model by simulating the past

The foregoing sections of this chapter have described the numerous estimated regression equations of the regional and city model, all of which are presented in Appendix tables. Evaluating a large number of ordinary least-squares regression equations, however, is not the same thing as evaluating the quality of the model. As Glickman has pointed out, there is a "forest-trees" problem. Having focused on the trees, it is now necessary to see the forest. Glickman has stressed that there are two basic issues for every econometric model:

1. How closely do the model predictions "fit" the actual data over the period for which the model equations have been estimated?
2. How closely do the model predictions of future values "fit" the actual data?

This section deals with the first issue (the second issue is considered in the next section).

> The first step in the evaluation of regional econometric models is to view their performance in replicating economic activity during the sample period through ex post tests . . . using the known values of the exogenous variables and lagged endogenous variables during the sample period, one may calculate a set of predicted endogenous variables (Y) and compare them with the actual values.[4]

The SCA and NYC models have been so used to replicate the period between 1960 and 1978. Because some variables are lagged two years, it was not possible to extend the simulation back to 1958, the first year of the period for which the equations were estimated.

Actual and predicted values of total income and total employment for the region and the city are shown in Table

3.10. There are two predicted values for total SCA income (SALLY and SALLY*) and two for total city income (CALLY and CALLY*) because of the two alternative methods for estimating those totals within the model (see Section 3.5 and Table 3.9).

One measure of the accuracy of such predictions is the root mean square error (RMSE) which is calculated as follows.

$$\text{RMSE} = \sqrt{\frac{\Sigma(\text{Actual} - \text{Predicted})^2}{n}}$$

The RMSE is of course in the same units as the variable, in this case millions of 1972 dollars. Based on comparing the RMSE for the two methods, it appears that SALLY is a more accurate predictor than SALLY* and similarly CALLY is more accurate than CALLY*, as shown below.

	Predicted Values			
	SALLY	*SALLY**	*CALLY*	*CALLY**
RMSE	$ 901	$ 1,229	$ 840	$ 946
Actual mean	$71,317	$71,317	$39,973	$39,973
RMSE/mean	1.26%	1.72%	2.10%	2.37%

Also, the SCA predicted values are more accurate than the city predicted values. That is not surprising given that the SCA is the whole of a geographically cohesive economic region while the city is a part. The city boundaries are less economically meaningful than the SCA boundaries.

The RMSE as a percent of the actual mean of SCA income is under 2 percent, while for the mean of NYC income it is somewhat above 2 percent. That indicates a reasonably good "fit" between actual and predicted values. Indeed, given the magnitude of some of the actual year-to-year changes (shown below), it is impressively good.

Table 3.10
SCA and NYC Actual and Predicted Income Totals, 1960–1978
(million 1972 $)

Year	Actual SALLY	Predicted SALLY	Predicted SALLY*	Actual minus Predicted SALLY	Actual minus Predicted SALLY*
			SCA		
1960	57541.	57634.	58697.	−93.	−1156.
1961	59012.	58441.	57800.	571.	1212.
1962	61194.	61671.	61880.	−477.	−686.
1963	62443.	62566.	62231.	−123.	212.
1964	65337.	64996.	64723.	341.	614.
1965	68007.	68069.	68242.	−62.	−235.
1966	71001.	71003.	71798.	−2.	−797.
1967	72677.	73601.	73811.	−924.	−1134.
1968	75938.	75715.	76152.	223.	−214.
1969	77017.	75692.	76738.	1325.	279.
1970	75509.	73616.	73629.	1893.	1880.
1971	75318.	74430.	73753.	888.	1565.
1972	77146.	76633.	76539.	513.	607.
1973	79215.	77979.	78337.	1236.	878.
1974	73655.	75523.	75297.	−1868.	−1642
1975	71516.	72365.	69305.	−849.	2211.
1976	74778.	74824.	74237.	−46.	541.
1977	77683.	77546.	78065.	137.	−382.
1978	80272.	81565.	83058.	−1293.	−2786.
			NYC		
1960	35601.	36610.	36536.	−1009.	−935.
1961	36413.	36815.	35240.	−402.	1173.
1962	37214.	36854.	37559.	360.	−345.
1963	37457.	38040.	37506.	−583	−49.
1964	39069.	38456.	38472.	613.	597.
1965	39940.	39809.	39833.	131.	107.
1966	41208.	40974.	41577.	234.	−369.
1967	42073.	42263.	42372.	−190.	−299.
1968	43788.	43061.	43158.	727.	630.
1969	43924.	43228.	43381.	696.	543.
1970	42599.	42306.	41389.	293.	1210.
1971	41945.	40780.	40862.	1165.	1083.
1972	42166.	40769.	41820.	1397.	346.
1973	42277.	41236.	42238.	1041.	39.
1974	38782.	40189.	39928.	−1407.	−1146.
1975	37137.	37612.	35275.	−475.	1862.
1976	38370.	36822.	37688.	1548.	682.
1977	39397.	39070.	39815.	327.	−418.
1978	40315.	41354.	42587.	−1039.	−2272.

SOURCE: Computed for this study.

| | Year to-Year Percentage Change | |
	SALLY	CALLY
1967–1968	+4.5%	+4.1%
1973–1974	−7.0	−8.3

Another measure of the reliability of a model is the extent to which the predicted values show the same direction of change as the actual values. On that basis also the model is impressively good.

| | Predicted Values | | | |
	SALLY	SALLY*	CALLY	CALLY*
Number of year-to-year changes, 1960–1978	18	18	18	18
Predicted changes in:				
same direction as actual	16	16	16	15
opposite direction	2	2	2	3

The predictions of employment for the SCA and the city (Table 3.11) are somewhat less accurate than the better income predictions (and again those for the SCA are better than those for the city). The reason is that the employment predictions are derived from the individual industry income predictions, the sum of which is SALLY* (or CALLY* as the case may be), and those are the least accurate income predictions.

| | Predicted Values | |
| | Total SCA Employment | Total NYC Employment |
	(thousands)	
RSME	105	86
Actual mean	6,282	3,521
RSME/mean	1.67%	2.44%
Predicted changes in		
same direction as actual	13	14
opposite direction	5	4

Table 3.11
SCA and NYC Actual and Predicted Employment Totals, 1960–1978 (thousands)

	NYC Employment			SCA Employment		
Year	Actual	Predicted	Actual Minus Predicted	Actual	Predicted	Actual Minus Predicted
1960	3,538	3,601	− 63	5,712	5,680	+ 32
1961	3,526	3,442	+ 84	5,722	5,634	+ 88
1962	3,559	3,495	+ 64	5,838	5,853	− 15
1963	3,533	3,519	+ 14	5,869	5,834	+ 35
1964	3,560	3,527	+ 33	5,944	5,932	+ 12
1965	3,577	3,565	+ 12	6,077	6,105	− 28
1966	3,615	3,601	+ 14	6,231	6,264	− 33
1967	3,662	3,690	− 28	6,364	6,462	− 98
1968	3,722	3,705	+ 17	6,512	6,563	− 51
1969	3,797	3,732	+ 65	6,701	6,586	+ 115
1970	3,745	3,631	+ 114	6,686	6,497	+ 189
1971	3,609	3,521	+ 88	6,536	6,411	+ 125
1972	3,566	3,439	+ 127	6,563	6,502	+ 61
1973	3,540	3,407	+ 133	6,624	6,465	+ 159
1974	3,447	3,444	+ 3	6,543	6,483	+ 60
1975	3,283	3,070	+ 213	6,304	6,030	+ 274
1976	3,199	3,083	+ 116	6,262	6,254	+ 8
1977	3,187	3,201	− 14	6,338	6,397	− 59
1978	3,234	3,303	− 69	6,521	6,608	− 87

SOURCE: Actual employment from U.S. Department of Labor, Bureau of Labor Statistics, *Employment and Earnings, States and Areas, 1939–78,* 1980. Predicted employment computed for this study.

How well does the model compare with other regional econometric models? Glickman has constructed a comparison table for the few regional models which have made available ex post measures of their accuracy.[5] As he points out, it is unfortunate that so few ex post tests have been published. The common measure used in Glickman's table is the mean absolute percent error (MAPE) calculated as follows.

$$\text{MAPE} = \frac{\Sigma(|\text{Actual} - \text{Predicted}|)/(\text{Actual Value})}{n} \cdot 100$$

Table 3.12
Comparison of MAPE Statistics for Regional Econometric Models

Regional Model	Gross Regional Output or Income (percent)		Total Employment (percent)	
	MAPE	*RANK*	*MAPE*	*RANK*
SCA	0.95	2	1.45	5
NYC	1.35	4	1.70	7
Philadelphia I	4.32	8	1.56	6
Philadelphia IV	0.98	3	0.66	2
Northeast Corridor	2.05	6	1.40	4
Buffalo	1.87	5	3.39	8
Los Angeles	2.08	7	0.88	3
Mississippi	0.94	1	0.41	1

SOURCE: N. Glickman, *Econometric Analysis of Regional Systems,* New York: Academic Press Inc., 1977, p. 69. SCA and NYC data from this study.

The MAPE statistics for SCA and NYC total income and employment are compared with MAPE statistics for corresponding aggregate variables in the other models in Table 3.12. Based on the MAPE for gross regional output or income, the SCA model ranks second best and the NYC model ranks fourth, out of the eight models included. But based on the MAPE for total employment, the SCA and NYC models are below average, ranking fifth and seventh respectively. However, the comparison is not quite fair for the models of this study because their estimation period includes the unusually volatile years from 1973 to 1978. The latest version of Glickman's model, Philadelphia IV, is one of the best shown but its period of estimation, from 1948 to 1971, does not include the worst of the postwar recessions, between 1973 and 1975, and the subsequent recovery. An examination of the error terms for the SCA and NYC models in Tables 3.10 and 3.11 clearly shows that the errors became larger on average in the 1970s.

Table 3.13
Total Employment, Actual and Forecast, SCA and NYC, 1979–1981[a]

Year	SCA Total Employment (thousands)			NYC Total Employment (thousands)		
	Actual	Forecast	Error	Actual	Forecast	Error
1979	6,642	6,622	+20	3,279	3,379	−100
1980	6,705	6,640	+64	3,302	3,357	−55
1981	6,791	6,502	+276	3,358	3,302	+56

[a] Forecast employment computed for this study.
SOURCE: Actual employment from Bureau of Labor Statistics, U.S. Department of Labor.

3.9 Testing the model by predicting the future

As noted in Section 3.8, the second basic issue for an econometric model is to determine how closely the model predictions of future values "fit" the actual data. The "future" in this case is the three-year period, from 1979 to 1981, following the period for which the model equations were estimated (1958 through 1978). All of the values for exogenous variables used in this test are actual because of course the years between 1979 to 1981 of the "future" are now past. The reason this type of testing is different from that used in Section 3.8 is that the model equations have been estimated with data ending in 1978. By "forecasting" 1979 through 1981, the model is being used to predict for years beyond the estimation period.

Table 3.13 compares actual with forecasted employment from 1979 to 1981 in the SCA and NYC. The errors (actual minus predicted) for the SCA in 1979 and 1980 are impressively small: +20,000 or one-third of 1 percent in 1979 and +64,000 or about 1 percent in 1980. The 1981 error of +276,000 (4 percent) is disappointingly large. Also, the fact that the errors are all positive and increasing suggests that the SCA model has a downward bias (that is, the forecasts are too low).

Table 3.14
Employment by Sector, Actual and Forecast, SCA and NYC, 1979–1981 [a]

Year		Mining and Construction	Manufacturing	Transportation, Communication, and Public Utilities	Wholesale and Retail	Finance, Insurance, and Real Estate	Services	Government
				SCA Employment (thousands)				
1979	A	195.5	1,377.7	465.4	1,406.2	605.4	1,500.6	1,091.1
	F	181.0	1,381.6	455.2	1,424.6	650.3	1,435.4	1,093.8
	E	+14.5	−3.9	+10.2	−18.4	−44.9	+65.2	−2.7
1980	A	202.1	1,340.4	468.9	1,401.1	630.9	1,579.5	1,080.7
	F	172.0	1,342.3	466.1	1,444.5	664.5	1,455.9	1,094.8
	E	+30.1	−1.9	+2.8	−43.4	−33.6	+123.6	−14.1
1981	A	206.6	1,321.1	468.6	1,404.1	661.8	1,649.8	1,066.1
	F	162.7	1,283.4	459.8	1,447.3	602.2	1,459.2	1,087.1
	E	+43.9	+37.7	+8.8	−43.2	+59.6	+190.6	−21.0
				NYC Employment (thousands)				
1979	A	72.0	518.6	258.7	621.1	429.7	858.6	520.2
	F	71.9	556.8	280.7	607.8	476.1	855.7	530.3
	E	+0.1	−38.2	−22.0	+13.3	−46.4	+2.9	−10.1
1980	A	78.1	495.7	257.0	612.8	448.2	893.7	516.3
	F	65.0	538.8	282.5	586.8	490.3	860.2	532.8
	E	+13.1	−43.1	−25.5	+26.0	−42.1	+33.5	−16.5
1981	A	84.1	485.2	255.8	611.6	473.0	933.3	514.4
	F	63.3	532.7	277.8	575.2	452.2	871.6	529.5
	E	+20.8	−47.5	−22.0	+36.4	+20.8	+61.7	−15.1

[a] A = actual, F = forecast, E = error.
SOURCE: Actual employment from Bureau of Labor Statistics, U.S. Department of Labor.

The NYC errors do not suggest a downward bias. Also, they do not become larger over time. The smallest error, $-55,000$ in 1980, is 1.7 percent. The largest, $-100,000$ in 1979, is 3.0 percent.

The total employment forecasts are, of course, sums of forecasted employment in each industry. The breakdown by sector is presented in Table 3.14 for both the SCA and NYC. The comparison of actual and forecasted SCA employment brings out that a substantial part of the aggregate error and the downward bias can be attributed to two sectors: services and construction. The errors in those sectors for the SCA are positive and increasing. Also in relative terms, for any year the errors in those two sectors tend to be the largest.

For New York City, the services sector errors are also positive and increasing, although the relative (and absolute) sizes of the errors are considerably smaller. Offsetting that apparent downward bias in the services sector in NYC is an apparent upward bias in the NYC manufacturing sector (that is, the errors are all negative and large).

Notes

1. N. Glickman, *Econometric Analysis of Regional Systems* (New York: Academic Press, 1977).

2. Real income for the SCA and NYC refers to the measure explained in Chapter 2 and calculated for this study. It is comparable to real national income (domestic), which is the sum of value added for all domestic industries.

3. R. Knight, *Employment Expansion and Metropolitan Trade* (New York: Praeger, 1973).

4. Glickman, op. cit., pp.65–69.

5. Glickman, op. cit., p. 69.

4

The Regional Model
of the
Baltimore Metropolitan Area

4.1 The region, the time span, and the industries

The region defined for this model is the Baltimore Standard Metropolitan Statistical Area (hereafter Baltimore SMSA or simply SMSA). It consists of the county of Baltimore and four suburban counties: Anne Arundel, Carroll, Harford, and Howard.

The original object was to develop parallel city and SMSA models, as in the case of New York. But investigation revealed that detailed city employment data was only available back to 1970. Consequently, it has been possible to develop a model for the entire Baltimore SMSA only, and not for the city of Baltimore. The model thus includes data and equations for the SMSA only.

All of the model time-series equations have been estimated with annual data from 1958 to 1976 (19 observations). The basic employment and income data are for 28 industries. The industry definitions correspond to the Standard Industrial Classification code. The list of 28 industries and their SIC codes are presented in Appendix Table 7.

Because Baltimore is a smaller area than the New York-Northeastern New Jersey SCA (and smaller than New York City), the available employment data for industries is given in less detail. Prior to 1978, there is no industry breakdown within the finance, insurance, and real-estate sector and none within the services sector.

The Baltimore model consists of 86 equations. Of those, 53 are the same national value added per employee (VAPE) equations developed for the SCA and NYC models required to derive forecasts of industry employment from forecasts of industry income. Since the VAPE equations are not area specific, they can be utilized for any region. Given the greater industry aggregation for Baltimore noted above, weighted combinations of appropriate VAPE forecasts are required.

Of the 33 equations specific to the Baltimore SMSA, 25 are stochastic and eight are identities. There are 11 export industry equations, all of which are stochastic. There are five equations for determining aggregate regional income (two are stochastic, three are identities) and 17 local industry equations, of which 12 are stochastic.

4.2　Historical economic trends

Table 4.1 presents total income (in 1972 dollars) and total employment of the Baltimore SMSA for selected years between 1958 and 1983. In the 11 years from 1958 to 1969, real income rose at an average annual rate of 3.6 percent. From 1969 to 1975, a period which includes the recession of 1969 and 1970 and the severe recession of 1973 to 1975, growth of real income slowed to 1.1 percent per year. In the most recent period, from 1975 to 1983 income growth accelerated to 3.0 percent annually.

Total employment increased by 185,000 jobs from 1958 to

Table 4.1
Total Income and Employment, Baltimore SMSA, 1958–1983

			Employment (thousands)						
Year	Total Income (million 1972 $)	Total Employment	Mining and Construction	Manu-facturing	Transportation and Communication	Wholesale and Retail	Finance, Insurance, and Real Estate	Services	Government
1958	$ 5,724	613.2	38.2	198.4	55.1	122.9	32.4	76.7	89.5
1969	8,490	797.9	43.0	206.4	55.6	170.8	42.1	129.3	150.7
1975	9,045	839.9	42.5	161.0	54.0	192.2	48.5	154.5	187.2
1983	11,431	938.5	45.2	139.8	57.7	220.5	59.5	212.8	203.0
			Average Annual Percent Change						
1958–1969	3.6%	2.4%	1.1%	0.4%	0.1%	3.0%	2.4%	4.9%	4.9%
1969–1975	1.1	0.9	−0.2	−4.1	−0.5	2.0	2.4	3.0	3.7
1975–1983	3.0	1.4	0.8	−1.8	0.8	1.7	2.6	4.1	1.0

SOURCE: Income data calculated. Employment data from U.S. Department of Labor, Bureau of Labor Statistics, *Employment and Earnings, States and Areas, 1909–78*, 1980, and *Employment and Earnings*, March, 1984.

Table 4.2
Changes in Employment by Sector in Baltimore SMSA

Sector	Employment Change (thousands)	
	1958–69	1969–83
Mining and construction	+4.8	+2.2
Manufacturing	+8.0	−66.6
Transportation and communication	+0.5	+2.1
Wholesale and retail	+47.9	+49.7
Finance, insurance, and real estate	+9.7	+17.4
Services	+52.6	+83.5
Government	+61.2	+52.3
Total	+184.7	+140.6

SOURCE: Calculated from Table 4.1.

1969. About one-third of that gain was accounted for by growth in government employment. Employment continued to expand, from 1969 to 1975, but at a much slower rate—0.9 percent per year. The job gain in the period since 1975 has been about 100,000, despite continuing losses in manufacturing employment.

From 1969 to 1975, the Baltimore area sustained a 22 percent reduction in manufacturing employment, or 45,000 jobs. In the more recent period, between 1975 and 1983, manufacturing employment has continued to decline (down 21,000 more jobs) but not as sharply.

Table 4.2 shows changes in employment by sector. All sectors showed gains in employment from 1958 to 1969. From 1969 to 1983 the total gain was 44,000 less than that of the earlier period because of a large decline in manufacturing.

Table 4.3 shows how the mix of employment has changed since 1958. Manufacturing jobs accounted for 32.4 percent of all employment in 1958, but by 1983 that sector's share was down to 14.9 percent. The biggest gains in share are in the services sector and government. The changes in employment shares for the Baltimore SMSA are similar to those for the

Table 4.3
Employment Shares by Sector in Baltimore SMSA

Sector	Percent of Total Employment	
	1958	1983
Mining and construction	6.2	4.8
Manufacturing	32.4	14.9
Transportation and communication	9.0	6.1
Wholesale and retail	20.0	23.5
Finance, insurance, and real estate	5.3	6.3
Services	12.5	22.7
Government	14.6	21.6
Total	100.0	100.0

SOURCE: Calculated from Table 4.1.

New York-Northeastern New Jersesy SCA (see Table 3.4). That reflects a general pattern throughout the nation (and particularly in large metropolitan areas), over the past 25 years, of relative declines in manufacturing jobs and relative gains in service and government jobs.

4.3 Export industry equations

Using the method described in Chapter 2, the export industries of the Baltimore SMSA have been identified. Table 4.4 lists the export industries, their total income, and the estimated export component in 1958 and 1976.

Although the location quotients indicate the listed set of industries as export oriented, only two stand out in terms of an export component which is a significant part of their total income (that is, in excess of 15 percent). They are primary metals and transportation other than railroad. Those two had combined exports, of $353 million in 1976, 51 percent of total SMSA exports. Primary metals, the area's most important export industry, had a decline in real income from 1958 to

Table 4.4
Export Industries in Baltimore SMSA (million of 1972 $)

SIC Codes	Industry Name	Abbre- viated Industry Name	1958		1976	
			Income	Export Com- ponent	Income	Export Com- ponent
15–17	Construction	CNST	391.0	55.1	571.7	55.8
	Manufacturing					
27	Printing	PRNT	99.6	a	150.6	6.5
28	Chemicals	CHEM	152.0	13.0	210.6	4.2
33	Primary metals	PMET	501.0	331.5	493.4	290.8
	Transportation and communication					
40	Railroads	RR	119.5	a	97.0	12.6
41–47	All other transportation	TRAN	254.7	80.3	363.9	62.5
48, 49	Communication, electricity, and gas	CMEG	252.9	a	467.4	34.1
	Trade					
50, 51	Wholesale trade	WHOL	332.3	a	735.9	41.2
52–59	Retail trade	RETL	665.8	a	1,051.0	63.3
60–67	Finance, insurance, and real estate	FIRE	419.6	31.8	610.1	57.9
70–86, 89, 7–9	Services	SERV	618.6	a	1,485.5	68.9
	Total all export industries		3,807.0	511.7	6,237.1	697.8

[a] Not an export industry in 1958.
SOURCE: Calculated for this study.

1976. Transportation other than railroads showed a gain in real income of 65 percent. However, past trends do not necessarily reveal present and future prospects. If more detailed employment data for Baltimore were available within the services and financial sectors, they would likely reveal a number of emerging growth industries. Aside from its other shortcomings, the location quotient approach to sorting out export industries from local industries, even when done over a long time span as in this study, can conceal more than it reveals when the industry data is too highly aggregated. Qualitative data on

Baltimore dealt with in the policy analysis section (Part II) reveals a much more upbeat picture of the region's economy.

Appendix Table 8 presents the estimated export industry equations for the Baltimore SMSA. Seven of the 11 equations have adjusted R^2 values above 0.90. The only poor equation among the set is for the primary metals industry. As with the SCA and NYC export industry income equations, the United States GNP, the national unemployment rate, and the regional CPI divided by the United States CPI, are the most important explanatory variables. One export industry which has been in a long-run decline, railroad transportation, has, as a significant negative explanatory variable in its income equation, the income of the other transportation industries (also an export industry). That captures the substitution effect of other modes of transport for rail. Three of the 11 export equations have only a single explanatory variable (the United States GNP) and two of those three are broad aggregations of industries, namely, the financial and services sectors. Not surprisingly, both of those equations exhibit severe autocorrelation with Durbin-Watson statistics well under one.

4.4 Aggregate income and population equations

The set of aggregate equations for determining income of all export industries, all local industries, total income, and population are shown in Table 4.5 The procedure is not quite the same as that outlined in Chapter 2 and as estimated for the SCA and NYC in Chapter 3 because it was not possible to estimate a good equation linking the aggregative export component to the aggregate income of export industries.

The steps in making a forecast are as follows.

1. The equations in Appendix Table 8 are used to forecast the income of each export industry in the SMSA.

Table 4.5
Baltimore SMSA Aggregate Income Equations, 1958–1976 ($n = 19$)

Equation Number	Dependent Variable	Constant	Independent Variables, Coefficients, and t Statistics (in parentheses)	Adjusted R^2	Durbin-Watson	Standard Error
BA 1	BEXP2	=	ΣSMSA export industries income			
BA 2	BLOCY2	= −6.610	+ 0.5001 BEXP2 (28.7)	.976	1.2	$63.1 million
BA 3	BALLY	= BEXP2	+ BLOCY2			
BA 4	BLOCY2*	=	ΣSMSA local industries income			
BA 5	BPOP	= 1,332	+ 0.09065 L2BALLY (13.9)	.923	0.4	32.1 thousand

2. Equation BA1, an identity, calculates total income of all export industries as a sum, BEXP2.
3. Equation BA2 estimates total income of all local industries (BLOCY2) as a function of total income of all export industries (BEXP2).
4. Total SMSA income (BALLY) is determined with equation BA3, an identity, as the sum of total income of all export industries (BEXP2, from equation BA1) and total income of all local industries (BLOCY2, from equation BA2).
5. The estimate of total income, BALLY, from equation BA3, is the main explanatory variable in the individual local industry income equations, which are presented next.
6. Once each individual local industry income is forecasted, equation BA4 is used to derive a second estimate of total income in all local industries as a sum, BLOCY2*.

The last equation (BA5) forecasts the Baltimore SMSA population as a function of total income lagged two years (L2BALLY). It is not sufficiently accurate to be of much use in making short-term population forecasts.

4.5 Local industry equations

The equations for estimating constant-dollar income in each local industry in Baltimore are presented in Appendix Table 9. For five of the 17 local industries, no acceptable regression equations have been estimated; thus, they are shown as identities, equal to their prior year's income. Some of the equations are quite good. But as with the SCA and NYC local industry equations, total area income, BALLY, does not appear in every equation because it was not statistically significant or had the wrong sign when included. Six of the 12 stochastic equations have adjusted R^2 values above 0.90 while five have R^2 values less than 0.80.

4.6 Applying the model methodology to other metropolitan areas

As explained in Chapter 2, in order to convert a forecast of industry income into a forecast of industry employment, value added per employee (VAPE) must also be forecast. Income is divided by VAPE to estimate employment. For the Baltimore industries which exactly correspond to the SCA and NYC industries, no additional VAPE equations need be estimated, since the same equations can be used. (Recall that VAPE by industry is a national variable and hence does not differ among areas in this model.) However, for the more aggregated Baltimore industries (such as, services), a weighted combination of forecasted VAPE in component industries must be computed.

The chief purpose of this chapter is to demonstrate that the model methodology is applicable to other metropolitan areas. Having assembled the data base on the national income of the United States by 53 industries, corresponding national employment by industry, and having computed the time series on real national income per employee by industry (VAPE), it is a simple matter to generate time-series data on regional income for any region. What is required is the particular region's employment data by industry over time. For areas with less industry detail on employment than New York (such as, Baltimore), the national income and national employment data can be so aggregated that VAPE can be calculated for any grouping of industries required.

5

Estimating and Forecasting Employment by Industry and Occupation for the SCA and NYC

5.1 The industry-occupation matrices

Approximately 20 percent of all the households in the U.S. completed the "long form" in the 1970 census. On that long form, households were asked to provide detailed information about their members' jobs, including number of people in the household employed, county of employment, industry of employment, and occupation.

Under a grant from the U.S. Department of Labor, the New York and New Jersey State Labor Departments worked with the New York-New Jersey portion of that detailed employment data and estimated, from the 20 percent sample, total employment, and converted the data to a place-of-work base, so that the data for any given area would reflect the number of people that *work* (rather than *reside*) in that area.

Based on that census data and their adjustments to it, the state labor departments developed a huge industry-occupation matrix for 1970 for each of several geographic regions in the New York-New Jersey area, including New York City and the

18-county New York-New Jersey SCA. Those industry-occupation matrices are based upon over 200 occupations and
over 300 industries. Each cell in one of those 1970 area matrices
indicates the number of employees in the specified occupation
and the specified industry. Using the 1970 matrix and other
data, a similar matrix was produced for 1974, and a 1985 matrix
was projected by the state labor departments, largely on the
basis of the differences between 1970 and 1974. Those New
York and New Jersey state labor departments' matrices, with
more than 300 industries and 200 occupations, contain roughly
75,000 cells each. To make their data relevant to this study,
the huge matrix was collapsed to a more manageable size.

The object of combining the 300 or more industries was
to have the industry breakdown correspond to the 53 separate
industries in the SCA. and NYC models. With two exceptions,
that objective was achieved. Insurance carriers (SIC 63) and
insurance agents (SIC 64) had to be combined into a single
industry for the industry-occupation matrix. The state and
local government industry of the model (SIC 92 & 93) had to
be split into six subgroups based upon the type of public employment. The six are

1. education
2. health services
3. public utilities
4. local transit
5. construction
6. all other state and local

Consequently there are 57 industry categories in the industry-
occupation matrices computed for this study.

The 200 or more occupations were collapsed to a more
manageable 47, while retaining virtually all of the important
distinctions. As each subgroup of obviously related occupa-

tions was considered, the type and amount of training required for each occupation was the most important criterion used in the aggregating procedure. Doctors and dentists were combined, for example, because of the similar amount and type of training involved, while registered nurses were kept separate due to the lesser amount of training involved.

The actual values involved were also examined, and some combinations were made when an occupation had very few members. Judges, for example, were combined with lawyers because there are very few judges, also because of the oft-taken lateral step between the two professions.

There are eight broad categories of occupations: professionals; managers, officials, proprietors; sales workers; clerical; crafts and kindred workers; operatives; services; and other labor. Each of these categories then has a number of subdivisions. A full list of the 47 occupations is presented in Appendix Table 10.

Thus, the aggregating procedure yielded a 57-industry by 47-occupation matrix for the years 1970, 1974, and 1985, for the SCA and for NYC. For the purposes of using this data in conjunction with the industry employment data, and in order to create similar matrices for other years, each matrix of actual employment values was converted into a matrix of percents. Within each *industry*, each occupation's employment value was divided by that industry's total employment value, thereby yielding a percent occupational breakdown for each industry. The calculating procedure is explained below.

Let N be a matrix of order 47 (occupation rows) $\times$ 57 (industry columns) for the region for 1970. Let n_{ij} be an element of N such that n_{ij} = the number of employees in occupation i (i = 1 to 47) and industry j (j = 1 to 57) in the SCA in 1970. Let $N_j = \Sigma n_{ij}$, that is, the total number of employees in industry j in the SCA in 1970. Compute $P_{ij} = (n_{ij}/N_j) \times 100$, that is, the percent of employees of occupation i in industry j. Then Σp_{ij} = 100 percent, for industry j.

Calculating P_{ij} for all industries and occupations yields a new matrix P of order 47 × 57 such that every column (industry) of P sums to 100 percent, and every element P_{ij} indicates the percent of employees of industry j which are in occupational category i.

Through arithmetic interpolation similar matrices of percents were created for all the years in between 1970 and 1974, and between 1974 and 1985. So, for example, if in 1970 the percent of all education employees who were high school teachers was 22 percent, and by 1974 it fell to 18 percent, the 1973 matrix would contain a value of 19 percent for this cell.

By applying those matrices of percents to the industry employment values for New York City and for the New York-New Jersey SCA for the years 1970 through 1978 actual, and 1979 through 1985 projected, the occupational breakdown for each industry for those years was obtained. The procedure is explained below.

Let P be the computed matrix of percents of order 47 (occupations) by 57 (industries) for the region in 1976. The first column of P, then, is the percent occupational breakdown within industry 1 in the region in 1976. Column one sums to 100%, as does every other column of P. Let $E(76)_1$, be total employment in industry 1 in the region in 1976. Multiplying every element in column one by $E(76)_1$ yields an estimate of the number of employees in industry 1 in each of 47 occupational categories. That is,

$$E(76)_1 \times P_{1,1} = OE(76)_{1,1}$$

$$E(76)_1 \times P_{2,1} = OE(76)_{2,1}$$

$$\begin{matrix} \cdot & \cdot & \cdot \\ \cdot & \cdot & \cdot \\ \cdot & \cdot & \cdot \end{matrix}$$

$$E(76)_1 \times P_{47,1} = OE(76)_{47,1}$$

where the P's are the percents of employees in industry 1 in each of 47 occupational categories. That is, they are the elements of column 1 of P. Then the products

$OE(76)_{1,1}$ = Number of employees of industry 1 in occupational category 1 in the region in 1976

$OE(76)_{2,1}$ = Number of employees of industry 1 in occupational category 2 in the region in 1976

$OE(76)_{47,1}$ = Number of employees of industry 1 in occupational category 47 in the region in 1976

By definition,

$$\Sigma P_{i1} = 100\%$$

or 1.0, in decimal form. So it follows that,

$$\Sigma OE(76)_{i1} = E(76)_1$$

that is, summing the number of employees in each of 47 occupational categories in industry 1 in the region in 1976 equals total employment in industry 1 in 1976.

Repeating the process for each of the 57 industries yields an industry-occupation employment matrix for the region for 1976. Every element in the matrix indicates the numbers of employees in a given industry (column) in a given occupation (row).

The 1978 matrix for the SCA is presented in its entirety in Appendix Table 11 (An explanation of the industry abbreviations can be found in Appendix Table 1; for the occupation abbreviations, see Appendix Table 10).

5.2 Forecasting annual employment by industry and occupation

As noted in Section 5.1, the State Labor Departments prepared industry-occupation matrices for 1970, 1974, and 1985 for both the SCA and the city. Having aggregated those matrices into 57 industries and 47 occupations, the percent matrices were calculated. By arithmetic interpolation, percent matrices were computed for all other years (1971 to 1973 and 1975 to 1984). The models described in Chapter 3 can be used to forecast annual employment by industry for 1979 and later (the models were estimated for 1958 to 1978). A forecasting program has been prepared which takes the forecasts of employment by industry, for the city or region, for any future year through 1985 and performs the multiplications with the percent matrix for that year and thus computes a forecasted industry-occupation matrix. It must be stressed that, although the State Labor Department prepared its own employment forecast in order to construct their 1985 industry-occupation matrix, this model does not assume that that forecast of levels is best or appropriate. All that is assumed is that the 1985 percent distribution of occupations within each industry implicit in the Labor Department forecast is correct. Also note that the relative occupational distribution does not remain fixed over time within any industry.

6

The Quarterly Versions of the SCA and the NYC Models

6.1 Cyclical or short-term versus intermediate or long-term forecasting

The models presented in Chapter 3 have been estimated with annual data and of course can be used to make annual forecasts of income and employment by industry. Annual data obscures much of the cyclical or short-term changes in economic time series which are of great interest. Consequently, at the national level, quarterly econometric models (estimated with quarterly time-series data) are used to make short-term forecasts, and annual econometric models are used to make intermediate or long-term forecasts (see, for example, the models of Data Resources Inc. and Wharton Econometric Forecasting Associates).

In order to make short-term forecasts of the regional and city economies, quarterly models have been estimated. The quarterly models are not export base models. Rather, the income in each of seven sectors is regressed upon corresponding national income variables, among others. Almost all of the explanatory variables are national. The calculation of regional or city income in each sector, as in the annual models, uses the national income or value added per employee (VAPE). That is,

$$\text{VAPE}_{it} = \frac{NY_{it}}{NE_{it}}$$

$$CY_{it} = CE_{it}(\text{VAPE}_{it})$$

$$\text{CALLY}_t = \Sigma CY_{it}$$

where

NY_{it} = national income, in 1972 \$, of sector i (i = 1 to 7) in quarter t

NE_{it} = national employment in sector i in quarter t

VAPE_{it} = value added per employee, in 1972 \$, in sector i and quarter t

CY_{it} = city income, in 1972 \$, of sector i in quarter t

CE_{it} = city employment of sector i in quarter t

CALLY_t = total city income, in 1972 \$, the sum of city income in seven sectors, in quarter t

The chief reason that the quarterly models are much more aggregated (seven sectors rather than 53 industries) is that the quarterly national income data required for computing VAPE is only published by broad sectors. The far more detailed national income by industry, used in computing VAPE for the annual models, is only published annually.

The seven sectors of the quarterly models are mining and construction; manufacturing; transportation, communication and public utilities; wholesale and retail trade; finance, insurance and real estate; services; and government. The SCA model and the NYC model have both been estimated over the period from the first quarter of 1958 through the fourth quarter of 1978 (84 quarters). In addition to quarterly real income by sector, total real income by quarter has been computed for the region and the city. It is the sum of income in the seven sectors.

The computed income data for the city reveals a good deal about the recession and expansion pattern of the city's economy over the past 25 years. That history is described and analyzed before presenting the estimated model equations.

6.2 Cyclical history of the New York City economy

National recessions have never left New York unscathed. In order to appraise the possible effects of a future recession upon the city's economy and the city government's tax revenues, it is helpful to know what has happened in past recessions. It is even more helpful to know why it happened.

Figure 6.1 plots the performance of the city's economy and the United States economy over the past six recessions. In Figure 6.1, the aggregate dollar measures of economic activity (national income in constant dollars and New York City total income in constant dollars, CALLY) have been converted to index numbers. Both city and national income have been set equal to 100 for the period a few quarters before the nationally defined business cycle peak. Thus the figure compares relative performance of the city and U.S. economies. Table 6.1 presents the data used in the construction of Figure 6.1.

One almost consistent pattern about the city's performance in the six past recessions is that city income (which is the same as net city output, or city value added) has turned down prior to the national peak in all but the most recent recession (1981 to 1982). In the recession of 1957 and 1958 and that of 1969 and 1970, city income had peaked two quarters before the national peak. It peaked one quarter before the national peak in the mild recession in 1960 and 1961. In the fourth recession, included in the data span used here, the recession between 1973 and 1975, city income reached its high three quarters prior to the national peak. In the 1980 recession, city

Figure 6.1
United States and NYC in Six Recessions

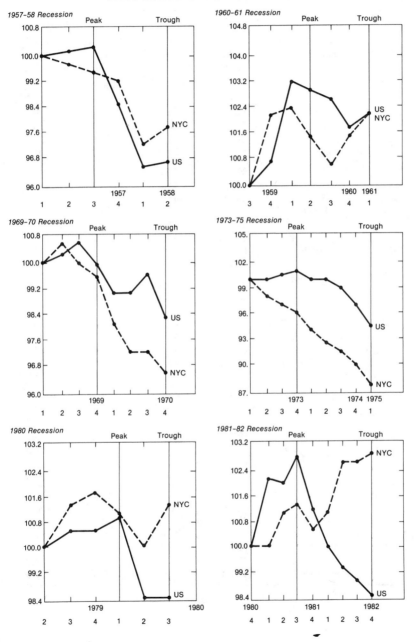

Table 6.1
National Income and NYC Income in Six Recessions

		National Income	NYC Income	National Income	NYC Income
				Index Numbers	
Year	Quarter	(billions 1972 $)		(Beginning Quarter = 100)	
1957	1	$ 567.0	$39.2	100.0	100.0
	2	567.3	39.1	100.1	99.7
	PEAK 3	567.9	39.0	100.2	99.5
	4	558.7	38.9	98.5	99.2
1958	1	547.9	38.1	96.6	97.2
	TROUGH 2	548.1	38.3	96.7	97.7
1959	3	593.8	40.9	100.0	100.0
	4	597.9	41.8	100.7	102.2
1960	1	612.9	41.9	103.2	102.4
	PEAK 2	611.7	41.5	103.0	101.5
	3	609.6	41.1	102.7	100.5
	4	604.5	41.5	101.8	101.5
1961	TROUGH 1	606.7	41.8	102.2	102.2
1969	1	897.5	50.7	100.0	100.0
	2	900.3	51.0	100.3	100.6
	3	903.0	50.7	100.6	100.0
	PEAK 4	897.2	50.5	100.0	99.6
1970	1	889.5	49.8	99.1	98.2
	2	889.7	49.3	99.1	97.2
	3	894.3	49.3	99.6	97.2
	TROUGH 4	881.8	49.0	98.3	96.6
1973	1	1,020.5	49.1	100.0	100.0
	2	1,019.3	48.2	99.9	98.2
	3	1,023.9	47.7	100.3	97.1
	PEAK 4	1,033.0	47.1	101.2	95.9
1974	1	1,022.1	46.1	100.2	93.9
	2	1,018.3	45.4	99.8	92.5
	3	1,007.8	44.9	98.8	91.4
	4	991.3	44.2	97.1	90.0
1975	TROUGH 1	961.9	43.0	94.3	87.6
1979	2	1,190.9	46.6	100.0	100.0
	3	1,198.2	47.2	100.6	101.3
	4	1,196.3	47.4	100.5	101.7
1980	PEAK 1	1,201.2	47.1	100.9	101.1
	2	1,171.4	46.6	98.4	100.0
	TROUGH 3	1,171.4	47.2	98.4	101.3

Table 6.1 (Continued)

				Index Numbers	
Year	Quarter	National Income	NYC Income	National Income	NYC Income
		(billions 1972 $)		(Beginning Quarter = 100)	
1980	4	1,182.3	47.6	100.0	100.0
1981	1	1,206.9	47.6	102.1	100.0
	2	1,205.7	48.1	102.0	101.1
	PEAK 3	1,215.0	48.2	102.8	101.3
	4	1,196.2	47.9	101.2	100.6
1982	1	1,182.0	48.1	100.0	101.1
	2	1,175.0	48.9	99.4	102.7
	3	1,169.0	48.9	98.9	102.7
	TROUGH 4	1,163.1	49.0	98.4	102.9
1984	1	1,279.8	50.6	100.0	100.0

SOURCE: National Income from "The National Income and Product Accounts of the United States," Table 1.8, Supplement to the *Survey of Current Business,* September, 1981, and various July issues of the *Survey of Current Business,* U.S. Department of Commerce. NYC Income calculated in this study.

income peaked one quarter before the national peak. Are downturns in the city's economy harbingers of national recession? Is city income what business cycle watchers call a leading indicator? Not knowing the reason why the local economy has turned down early in five of the last six recessions, it would be hazardous to presume that it will turn down before the U.S. economy in future recessions.

In the two earliest recessions (1957 to 1958 and 1960 to 1961), not only did city income decline before the national peak, but it also rose before the trough or bottom of the recession. Early decline and early recovery are the chief characteristics of leading indicators. But in the next two recessions (1969 to 1970 and 1973 to 1975), there is no pattern of early recovery by the city economy. In fact just the opposite occured (not shown on Figure 6.1). City income continued down long after the national economy reached its lowest point. In the most recent two recessions (1980 and 1981 and 1982) the pattern of moderate decline and early recovery resumed.

Another feature which splits the middle two recessions from both the earlier two and the later two is the performance of the city relative to the nation. Figure 6.1 shows that city income did not decline as much, in percentages, as national income in the first two and the last two recessions. However, in the middle two recessions (1969 and 1970 and 1973 to 1975), the city suffered larger percent declines than the nation. There are a number of reasons for that adverse change in pattern which are addressed below.

Figure 6.1 brings out the severity of the recession of 1973 to 1975 compared with the earlier three. Indeed it seems strange to call this recession by the same name as the others. From the peak to the bottom, national income in constant dollars fell 6.9 percent. From the peak in city income, three quarters before the national peak, the drop to the bottom eight quarters later was 12.4%. Over the period for which city income data is available (1957 to 1983), there has never been a steeper two-year decline. Indeed, tracing back the U.S. data on real national income, no two-year period prior to the recession of 1973 to 1975 showed a steeper decline since the 19 percent drop, in 1945 to 1947 brought on by rapid demobilization at the end of World War II.

Understanding the reasons for the magnitude of the decline in city income between 1973 and 1975, and also the reasons why that recession and the prior one broke with the pattern of both the two earlier and two most recent recessions (that is, early recovery and less decline than the United States economy) requires looking outside the context of individual national recessions with their peak and trough boundaries. The requirement of looking beyond the conventional recession context for an explanation of the New York economy's performance in the 1970s is evident upon examination of Table 6.2.

Table 6.2
Contraction and Expansion in Recessions and Recoveries in the United States and NYC

| | Average Annual Percent Change | |
	Real National Income	Real City Income
Recessions—Peak to Trough		
1957–3 to 1958–2	−4.6	−2.4
1960–2 to 1961–1	−1.1	+1.0
1969–4 to 1970–4	−1.7	−3.0
1973–4 to 1975–1	−5.6	−7.0
1980–1 to 1980–3	−4.9	+0.4
1981–3 to 1982–4	−3.4	+1.3
Recoveries—Trough to Peak		
1958–2 to 1960–2	+5.6	+4.1
1961–1 to 1969–4	+4.6	+2.2
1970–4 to 1973–4	+5.4	−1.3
1975–1 to 1980–1	+4.5	+1.3
1980–3 to 1981–3	+3.7	+2.1
1982–4 to 1984–1[a]	+8.0	+2.6

[a] Not a peak, but the latest quarter available for national income.
SOURCE: Calculated from the data of Table 6.1.

Table 6.2 presents average annual rates of contraction and expansion in the six recessions and recoveries for the United States and New York City. It clearly shows that the city fared better than the nation in the first two recessions and the last two recessions. Indeed, city real income actually rose from the peak to the trough of three of those four recessions. And it also clearly shows that the city fared worse than the nation in the middle two recessions.

In the recoveries, the income of the city consistently expanded at a slower rate than that of the United States. But of central interest is the fact that during the national recovery between 1970 and 1973, when real national income grew at an annual rate of 5.4 percent, real city income declined at a rate of −1.3 percent per year. The divergence in growth between the city and the nation in that period of expansion is wider than it had been during any other recovery and even wider than in any recession. So, real income in the city declined in the recession of 1969 and 1970, continued to decline in the following national recovery between 1970 and 1973, and then declined precipitously during the recession of 1973 to 1975. If one ignores the national time boundaries of peaks and troughs, the entire stretch from 1969 to 1975 is more comprehensible if it is considered as a local depression.

In the second quarter of 1969, real city income reached an all-time high of $51.0 billion (1972 dollars). Twenty-six quarters later, or six and one-half years, real city income was $42.9 billion, 16 percent lower, and at the level of 1961. During that entire six-and-one-half year period, there were only three consecutive quarters of increase in real city income. That long downhill history is plotted in Figure 6.2.

There are a number of reasons why New York suffered a massive economic decline. There are short-run and long-run factors, internal and external factors, which contributed to the decline. The two most important factors, which are both short-run and external, are the national recessions of 1969 and 1970 and 1973 to 1975. New York is not now and never was immune to the ups and downs of the U.S. economy.

Some of the long-run factors were evident before the city economy peaked in 1969. The most pervasive of those was the rising cost of doing business in New York relative to other places. Some of those costs are measurable, such as wages, taxes, and energy. Some are not easily measured, such as congestion, crime, and red tape. The congestion costs increased for both goods and people, partly because of the deteriorating transport infrastructure (such as highways, streets, subways, rail-freight systems, commuter trains, and water freight systems). The deterioration has not been fully arrested in the postdepression period, but with 453,000 fewer jobs in the city in 1983 than in 1969, and almost 800,000 fewer resi-

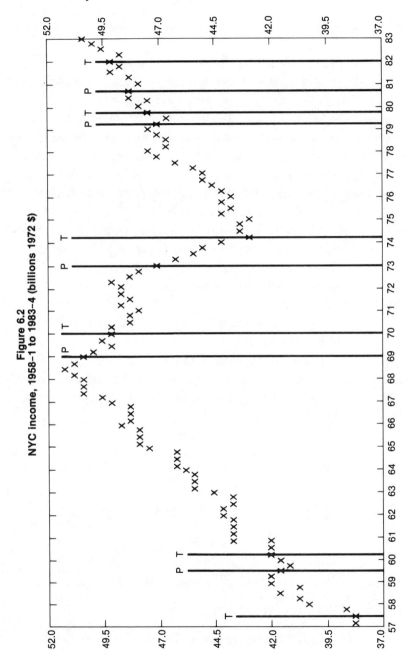

Figure 6.2

NYC income, 1958–1 to 1983–4 (billions 1972 $)

dents, the pressures on the transport infrastructure have been lessened.

A related but external long-run factor was the putting in place of the interstate highway system combined with the long-run decline in the real cost of intercity transport for both goods and people. (That long-run decline abruptly ended in late 1973 with the quadrupling of world crude-oil prices). The factor is related because the juxtaposition of rising relative costs of operating businesses in New York and the falling relative costs of moving goods (and people) into New York made it clear to many firms that they could serve the New York market without being in New York or its environs. In the garment industry in the days before the interstate-highway system was completed, it was said that eastern Pennsylvania was overnight from New York in terms of truck runs. Now, North Carolina is overnight from New York.

The advent of containerization of ocean cargo plus the substitution of intercontinental jet travel for passenger ships sent the New York City area of the Port of New York into a tailspin from which it has never recovered. The impact on the city's economy was not only on dock jobs but also on railroads, as shown below.

Year	NYC Employment	
	Water Transportation	Railroads[a]
	(thousands)	
1958	71.9	30.6
1969	49.3	13.1
1983	17.0	5.3
	Average annual percent decrease	
1958–1969	−3.4	−7.4
1969–1983	−7.3	−6.3

[a] Does not include local transit.
SOURCE: New York State Department of Labor.

From more than 100,000 jobs in 1958, jobs in water transportation and the railroads dropped to 62,000 in 1969 and then shrank to only 22,000 by 1983. The collapse of port activity had an impact upon trucking and wholesale trade as well, but it does not show up in employment declines until after 1969.

One factor in the decline between 1969 and 1975, which was not evident prior to 1969, is the mechanization of back-office functions in the securities industry. The bull market of the late 1960s brought with it tremendous increases in the volume of daily trading. As a result, employment in the securities industry in the city almost doubled in four years, rising from 56,000 in 1965 to 105,000 in 1969. But then the computerization of back-office functions, the accompanying demise of smaller brokerage firms, and the end of the bull market wiped out most of that employment gain in the six years after 1969. Securities-industry employment in 1978 in New York was 33 percent below the 1969 peak but daily volume was 153 percent higher. That kind of technological shock and the resulting job loss is not directly connected to recession or expansion and is not predictable.

Another factor dating from about 1969 and not directly connected to the national recession is the decline in employment in corporate headquarters in New York, as corporate head offices or parts of them were moved out of the city. From a total of 184,000 headquarter jobs (that is, city employment at central administrative offices of manufacturing and mining firms and offices of insurance companies) in 1969, there was a drop of almost 50,000 by 1976. That dispersion was not unique to New York. All of the largest United States cities lost headquarters in the 1960s and 1970s. But the long-run factors noted above—rising relative costs of doing business in New York, including congestion costs, and the deteriorating infrastructure—may have hastened the departures.

One external shock which contributed to the New York depression was the quadrupling of world crude-oil prices in

1973 and 1974 and further increases later. Although domestic crude oil prices were kept below world prices by government controls through most of the 1970s, New York and all of the Northeastern States were hurt more than the rest of the nation for three reasons. First, the Northeast uses proportionately more oil and less natural gas than the rest of the nation for heating, generating electricity, and industrial uses. And, although all energy prices rose sharply, oil prices increased the most. Second, the Northeastern States import much of their heating oil, and the world market prices of such oil products had increased more than domestic prices. Third, because of the strict state environmental laws, the Northeastern States require low-sulfur oil, which is sold at a premium over standard grades.

The last factor in explaining the New York depression is complex because it is both an effect and a cause. Because of the steep economic decline which began in mid-1969, the city's population decreased in the 1970s. The loss from 1970 to 1980 was about 800,000. That was not simply a shift to the suburbs which left the region the same size or even bigger, for the entire New York-Northeastern New Jersey metropolitan complex (which includes New York City) registered a population loss of 974,000. There are only about ten cities in the United States with populations larger than 800,000, which was the population loss in New York in ten years. Consequently, the local industries which primarily serve local consumers contracted. Of course, the population-related contraction of local industries did not occur until some time after the long economic decline was underway. In 1973, the total income (1972 $) of city industries which are classified as local in the annual model (that is, industries without an export component) was $18.0 billion. The total income of industries classified as export that year was $24.3 billion. From 1973 to 1975 the export industries' income plummeted $2.8 billion, but by 1978 they had recovered, reaching $25.0 billion. But the income of local industries in 1978 had not reached the 1973 level. It was $15.3 billion, or $2.7 billion below 1973. Indeed, even by 1983, the income of local industries totalled only $15.7 billion, well below the level of ten years earlier.

6.3 The sector output and productivity equations

The period over which output and productivity equations have been estimated extends from the first quarter of 1958 through the fourth quarter of 1978. The quarterly series on total city income (CALLY) and total SCA income (SALLY) do not correspond exactly with the annual series on total city and SCA income. That is, for any year, the averge of total income for four quarters is not equal to annual total income; it is, in fact, higher, as illustrated below.

	1978	
	CALLY	SALLY
	(millions of 1972 $)	
Average of four quarters	$45,545	$87,668
Annual	40,178	80,186
Difference	$ 5,367	$ 7,482
Percent difference	11.8	8.5

The source of the discrepancy is all in finance, insurance, and real estate. With the more detailed annual data on national income, it was possible to remove large amounts of imputed interest and imputed rent in the industries of banking, real estate, and credit agencies other than banks. Those imputed amounts (the imputed interest in negative) distorted the value added per employee (VAPE) in the affected industries and so they were removed from the industry national income data before computing VAPE. Relying on the quarterly national-income data by sector alone, it is not possible to remove the imputed interest and rent because that data is not published quarterly. But because the sector is an aggregation of several industries, the distortion evident in the annual industry data becomes minor in the quarterly data.

The estimated quarterly regression equations for the SCA and NYC are shown in Tables 6.3 and 6.4 respectively. The first SCA equation has total SCA income in 1972 dollars (SALLY) as a function of national income in 1972 dollars (UALLY), the ratio of the region's CPI to the national CPI (SCPIUS), the United States unemployment rate (UUNEMPR), and the region's population lagged for eight quarters (L8SPOP). The signs on the partial regression coefficients conform with a priori expectations. That is, the region's real income is directly related to real national income and lagged population, and inversely related to the CPI ratio and the unemployment rate. All four explanatory variables are highly significant. The population variable was included in the equation because it appears likely that the local income component of SALLY is sensitive to total population, but as explained in Section 6.2, the response appears to be lagged. Also, for forecasting purposes, it is much better to use lagged population because regional population forecasts are subject to large errors. With a short-term quarterly model, forecasts rarely are extended beyond eight quarters from the present. Consequently, forecasts of SALLY at most require estimates of population for the current period.

The second SCA quarterly equation has real per-capita regional income (SYPCAP) as a function of real per-capita national income (UYPCAP) and the national unemployment rate. The per-capita income equation and the total income equation together provide a means for indirectly estimating the region's population (SPOP), as shown in the identity

Table 6.3
SCA Quarterly Sector Income Equations ($n = 84$)[a]

Dependent Variable	Constant	Partial Regression Coefficients, Independent Variables, and t Statistics (in parentheses)				Adjusted R^2	Durbin-Watson	Standard Error
SALLY =	−399.1	+ 25.70 UALLY (13.2)	− 71.269 SCPIUS (4.2)	− 1217 UUNEMPR (8.4)	+ 8.774 L8SPOP (9.1)	.974	0.47	$1,156
SYPCAP =	+2,605	+ .7024 UYPCAP (61.6)	− 82.45 UUNEMPR (16.3)			.979	0.51	61.3
SYMF =	+41,094	+ 19.60 UYMF (9.0)	− 20,190 SCPIUS (5.8)	− 924.3 UUNEMPR (19.9)		.881	0.34	539
SYTC =	+4,192	+ 4.994 UALLY (32.5)	− 140.5 UUNEMPR (7.7)	− 12.65 DUMDEP (0.2)		.938	0.38	216
SYWR =	+8,202	+ 40.17 L2UYWR (23.7)	− 321.7 UUNEMPR (10.1)			.877	0.36	369
SYBF =	+10,371	+ 73.95 UYBF (25.8)	− 394.0 UUNEMPR (9.0)			.892	0.14	522
SYSV =	+5,025	+ 74.46 UYSV (51.6)	− 318.7 UUNEMPR (9.7)			.970	0.19	389
SYGV =	+1,741	+ 68.11 UYGV (52.9)	− 133.3 UUNEMPR (4.1)			.971	0.81	388
SYMC =	+2,067	+ .01994 SALLY (7.2)	− 112.6 UUNEMPR (10.6)			.582	0.34	211

$$SPOP = \frac{SALLY}{SYPCAP}$$

SALLY* = SYMF + SYTC + SYWR + SYBF + SYSV + SYGV + SYMC
SALLY* − SALLY = ERROR

[a] For a definition of the variables, see Guide to Tables 6.3 and 6.4.

Table 6.4
NYC Quarterly Sector Income Equations ($n = 84$)[a]

Dependent Variable	Constant	Partial Regression Coefficients, Independent Variables and t Statistics (in parentheses)				Adjusted R^2	Durbin-Watson	Standard Error
CALLY =	−29,663	− 32,389 SCPIUS (3.7)	+ 12.10 CPOP (12.0)	+ 24.13 UALLY (14.3)	− 874.8 UUNEMPR (8.4)	.932	0.62	$828
CYPCAP =	+5,008	− 544.6 SCPIUS (0.4)	+ 67.33 DUMDEP (1.2)	+ .5746 UYPCAP (14.1)	− 156.2 UUNEMPR (13.2)	.901	0.36	129
CYMF =	+24,108	− 6,452 SCPIUS (2.1)	− 477.3 DUMDEP (3.9)	− 17.04 L3UYMF (12.8)	− 714.7 UUNEMPR (24.0)	.951	0.69	290
CYTC =	+4,167	− 66.17 DUMDEP (1.5)	+ 1.691 UALLY (13.9)	− 154.6 UUNEMPR (10.7)		.775	0.35	171
CYWR =	+1,995	+ 6916 SCPIUS (5.2)	− 10.81 L2UYWR (8.7)	− 242.0 UUNEMPR (16.5)		.842	0.53	170
CYBF =	−1,289	+ .2841 CALLY (21.0)				.841	0.14	392
CYSV =	−4,288	+ 9634 SCPIUS (6.2)	+ 27.12 UYSV (22.0)	− 254.1 UUNEMPR (13.9)		.954	0.50	217
CYGV =	−16,805	+ 20,809 SCPIUS (7.9)	+ 15.76 UYGV (8.5)	− 170.1 UUNEMPR (6.8)		.914	0.94	297
CYMC =	−4,432	+ 7033 SCPIUS (7.8)	− 18.88 L3UYMC (9.5)	− 57.90 UUNEMPR (5.8)		.649	0.65	112

$$CPOP = \frac{CALLY}{CYPCAP}$$

CALLY* = CYMF + CYTC + CYWR + CYBF + CYSV + CYGV + CYMC
CALLY* − CALLY = ERROR

[a]For a definition of the variables, see Guide to Tables 6.3 and 6.4.

Guide to Tables 6.3 and 6.4

The prefix 'S' indicates an SCA variable and the prefix 'C' indicates a NYC variable. All variables are quarterly, unless otherwise indicated and the estimation period is from the first quarter of 1958 through the fourth quarter of 1978.

Dependent Variables

SALLY & CALLY	= total income, in millions of 1972 $, of SCA and NYC
SYPCAP & CYPCAP	= per capita income, in 1972 $, of the SCA & NYC
SYMF & CYMF	= manufacturing sector income in millions of 1972 $ of the SCA and NYC
SYTC & CYTC	= transportation, communication, and public utilities income in millions of 1972 $ of the SCA and NYC
SYWR & CYWR	= wholesale and retail trade income in millions of 1972 $ of the SCA and NYC
SYBF & CYBF	= finance, insurance, and real estate income in millions of 1972 $ of the SCA and NYC
SYSV & CYSV	= services sector income in millions of 1972 $ of the SCA and NYC
SYGV & CYGV	= government income in millions of 1972 $ of the SCA and NYC
SYMC & CYMC	= mining and construction income in millions of 1972 $ of the SCA and NYC
SPOP & CPOP	= population in thousands by year of the SCA and NYC

Independent Variables

UALLY	= total United States national income in billions of 1972 \$
SCPIUS	= ratio of the CPI for the region to consumer price index for the nation
UUNEMPR	= United States unemployment rate
L8SPOP	= population of the SCA, in thousands, lagged eight quarters
UYPCAP	= per capita United States national income, in 1972 \$
UYMF	= United States national income in the manufacturing sector in billions of 1972 \$
DUMDEP	= dummy variable for local area depression; DUMDEP = 1 for second quarter of 1969 through first quarter of 1975, and DUMDEP = 0 for all other quarters.
L2UYWR	= United States national income in the wholesale and retail trade sector in billions of 1972 \$, lagged two quarters
UYBF	= United States national income in the finance, insurance, and real estate sector in billions of 1972 \$
UYSV	= United States national income in the services sector in billions of 1972 \$
UYGV	= United States national income in the government sector in billions of 1972 \$
L3UYMF	= United States national income in the manufacturing sector in billions of 1972 \$, lagged three quarters
L3UYMC	= United States national income in the mining and construction sector, in billions of 1972 \$, lagged three quarters

$$\text{SPOP} = \frac{\text{SALLY}}{\text{SYPCAP}}$$

Total regional income can be estimated with the first equation and also as the sum of estimated income in the seven sectors (see identity for SALLY* in Table 6.3). The difference between the two is ERROR. Alternatively, because the mining- and construction sector income (SYMC) equation is so poor, with an adjusted R^2 of .582, ERROR can be set equal to zero in making a forecast (that is, SALLY = SALLY*), and the identity for SALLY* can be used to solve for SYMC rather than the stochastic equation for SYMC.

The quarterly city income equations are similar to the SCA equations, but they are of lesser quality because the explanatory power (as measured by the adjusted R^2) tends to be lower, and some variables have the wrong signs, notably the ratio of the consumer price index for the region to the consumer price index for the United States (SCPIUS). It is positive (incorrect) in four sector equations, negative in one, and negative in the stochastic equation for total city income (CALLY). The implication of that curious result for forecasting (noting the magnitude of the partial regression coefficients on the SCPIUS variable) is that a rise in SCPIUS, *ceteris paribus,* will have a net increase effect upon the sum of sector income (CALLY*) but will decrease total city income (CALLY) as estimated with the first equation. Thus if SCPIUS is presumed to change in the same direction for several quarters, *ceteris paribus,* the divergence between CALLY* and CALLY (that is, ERROR) increases. However, given the size of changes in SCPIUS (the largest absolute quarter-to-quarter change in that variable since 1958 was .005), the net effect is small. A quarterly rise in SCPIUS of .005 raises the sum of sector income (CALLY*) $144 million and reduces the total city income (CALLY) $162 million. The latter change is only 20 percent of the standard error of the equation for CALLY.

In the stochastic equation for total city income (CALLY), the current value for city population, which is endogenous, appears on the right-hand side. But in forecasting, projections of city population are not required because, with a separate equation for per-capita city income (with all exogenous variables on the right), the equation for CALLY and the city population identity can be solved simultaneously for CALLY and CPOP. Strictly speaking, the validity of that procedure requires a two-stage least squares estimation of the total city income equation, that is, the actual values of CPOP should not be used in estimating the equation for CALLY but rather the estimated values of CPOP from an equation in which the independent variables are all of those in the system of equations which do not appear in the CALLY equation. But that refinement remains to be done.

As with the SCA equations, total city income can be forecasted as the sum of the sectors (CALLY*) and forecasted in the manner explained above. The difference (ERROR) can be set equal to zero and then the identity for CALLY* can be used to solve for CYMC rather than use the stochastic equation for forecasting that sector's income because it is a poor equation. For testing purposes, it is better to not set ERROR = 0 but rather see what happens to the size of ERROR in forecasting one through eight quarters forward.

Although both the city and SCA equations are very good in terms of explanatory power and statistical significance, the Durbin-Watson statistic for every single equation is terrible, indicating autocorrelated residuals. Equations with such pronounced autocorrelation are not reliable for making forecasts. Employing the method described below, the autocorrelation has been removed from the equations, and the resulting adjusted equations can then be used to forecast the dependent variables.[1]

For each quarterly stochastic equation shown in Tables 6.3 and 6.4, it has been assumed that the relationship among the disturbance terms (the residuals) is of the form

$$u_t = bu_{t-1} + e_t$$

Using the residuals of the individual equations as observations (u_t and u_{t-1}), the "b" coefficients have been estimated for each equation. For this example, the steps will be illustrated for one equation only. With the estimated "b" for the total city income (CALLY) equation residuals, variables which appear in the original CALLY equation are adjusted as follows.

$$CALLY'_t = CALLY_t - bCALLY_{t-1}$$
$$SCPIUS'_t = SCPIUS_t - bSCPIUS_{t-1}$$
$$CPOP'_t = CPOP_t - bCPOP_{t-1}$$
$$UALLY'_t = UALLY_t - bUALLY_{t-1}$$
$$UUNEMPR'_t = UUNEMPR_t - bUUNEMPR_{t-1}$$

Then regressing $CALLY'_t$ (as computed above) on the set of adjusted variables, the equation below is estimated

$$CALLY'_t = A + a_1 SCPIUS'_t + a_2 CPOP'_t$$
$$+ a_3 UALLY'_t + a_4 UUNEMPR'_t$$

The estimated partial regression coefficients, a_1 through a_4 are then used to replace the original coefficients in the CALLY equation shown on Table 6.4. The constant term of that original equation is replaced by

$$a_0 = \frac{A}{1 - b}$$

So the CALLY equation corrected for autocorrelation then would be

$$CALLY_t = a_0 + a_1 \, SCPIUS_t + a_2 \, CPOP_t$$
$$+ \, a_3 \, UALLY_t + a_4 \, UUNEMPR_t$$

Repeating the procedure for every stochastic equation in Tables 6.3 and 6.4, the resulting equations corrected for auto-correlation have been computed and are presented in Tables 6.5 and 6.6. The corrected equations are, of course, the ones to be used in making forecasts.

In order to use the quarterly models to forecast employment by sector, equations for forecasting quarterly value added per employee are required. As with the annual models, employment forecasts are derived as

$$CE_{it} = \frac{CY_{it}}{UVAE_{it}}$$

where
CE_{it} = estimated city employment in sector i and quarter t
CY_{it} = estimated city income in sector i and quarter t
$UVAE_{it}$ = estimated United States value added per employee in sector i and quarter t

The estimated equations for the quarterly value added per employee for each of seven sectors are presented in Table 6.7. The independent variables are the same in all seven equations. United States national income per employee in all sectors in 1972 $ (UYPE), and the United States unemployment rate

Table 6.5
SCA Quarterly Equations Corrected for Autocorrelation[a]

SALLY   = +11,834 + 31.18 UALLY   − 13.506 SCPIUS − 1.125 UUNEMPR + 3.935 L8SPOP

SYPCAP = +2,617 + .6629 UYPCAP   − 54.65 UUNEMPR

SYMF   = +44,728 + 18.78 UYMF   − 24.799 SCPIUS − 691.4 UUNEMPR

SYTC   = +4,072 + 4.506 UALLY   − 48.61 UUNEMPR + 103.0 DUMDEP

SYWR   = +9,043 + 25.72 L2UYWR   − 132.0 UUNEMPR

SYBF   = +7,895 + 77.98 UYBF   − 35.15 UUNEMPR

SYSV   = +5,200 + 59.69 UYSV   − 35.48 UUNEMPR

SYGV   = +1,623 + 67.00 UYGV   − 89.62 UUNEMPR

SYMC   = +2,063 + .0168 SALLY   − 65.53 UUNEMPR

[a] For a definition of the variables, see Guide to Tables 6.3 and 6.4.

Table 6.6
NYC Quarterly Equations Corrected for Autocorrelation[a]

CALLY	=	− 12,449 − 10,899 SCPIUS	+ 7.858 CPOP	+ 16.82 UALLY	− 911.5 UUNEMPR
CYPCAP	=	+ 6,060 − 1,637 SCPIUS	+ 42.91 DUMDEP	+ .5010 UYPCAP	− 88.44 UUNEMPR
CYMF	=	+ 29,633 − 12,933 SCPIUS	− 275.3 DUMDEP	− 15.40 L3UYMF	− 605.9 UUNEMPR
CYTC	=	+ 4,039 + 16.30 DUMDEP	+ 1.299 UALLY	+ 74.09 UUNEMPR	
CYWR	=	+ 4,486 + 4,062 SCPIUS	− 10.84 L2UYWR	− 167.7 UUNEMPR	
CYBF	=	+ 4,975 + .1555 CALLY			
CYSV	=	− 2,457 + 7,296 SCPIUS	+ 26.37 UYSV	− 141.7 UUNEMPR	
CYGV	=	− 14,639 + 18,347 SCPIUS	+ 16.78 UYGV	− 134.8 UUNEMPR	
CYMC	=	− 2,657 + 5,067 SCPIUS	− 15.87 L3UYMC	− 46.71 UUNEMPR	

[a] For a definition of the variables, see Guide to Tables 6.3 and 6.4.

Table 6.7
Quarterly United States Value Added per Employee Equations, by Sector, 1958-1 to 1978-4 (n = 84)

Sector	Dependent Variable	Independent Variables, Partial Regression Coefficients, and t Statistics (in parentheses)	Adjusted R^2	Durbin-Watson	Standard Error (1972 $)
Mining and construction	UVAEMC =	$-12{,}103 + 1.991$ UYPE $+ 253.5$ UUNEMPR (17.1) (3.9)	.782	1.44	$782
Manufacturing	UVAEMF =	$-7{,}280 + 1.593$ UYPE $+ 163.1$ UUNEMPR (35.9) (6.6)	.940	0.65	298
Transportation, communication, and public utilities	UVAETC =	$-16{,}096 + 2.496$ UYPE $+ 332.0$ UUNEMPR (37.8) (9.1)	.946	0.71	443
Wholesale and retail trade	UVAEWR =	$+4{,}865 + .3628$ UYPE $- 60.08$ UUNEMPR (14.3) (4.3)	.734	1.45	171
Finance, insurance, and real estate	UVAEBF =	$+19{,}446 + .9063$ UYPE $- 392.0$ UUNEMPR (8.3) (6.4)	.583	0.31	738
Services	UVAESV =	$+3{,}128 + .5760$ UYPE $- 78.36$ UUNEMPR (28.8) (7.1)	.917	1.00	134
Government	UVAEGV =	$-674 + .9329$ UYPE $- .1531$ UUNEMPR (15.4) (0)	.740	0.72	407

Dependent Variables:
All dependent variables are value added per employee for the United Sttes (indicated by the prefix UVAE), in 1972 $, for the sector named.

Independent Variables:
UYPE   = United States national income per employee, in 1972 $
UUNEMPR = United States unemployment rate

(UUNEMPR). In the first three equations, the unemployment rate variable has a positive sign but is highly significant. That may reflect the cyclical pattern of productivity (as crudely measured by real value added per employee) in some sectors. Namely, it shows the greatest gains at the bottom and early recovery period of a recession (when the unemployment rate is high) and shows sluggish growth or declines near the peak and during the contraction.

6.4 Testing the quarterly model by predicting the future

The quarterly models described in this chapter have been estimated with data through the fourth quarter of 1978. The city quarterly model has been used to "forecast" the four quarters of 1979, and those forecasted values are compared with the actual values in order to appraise the predictive accuracy of the model.

Actual and forecasted income by sector (Table 6.8) suggests an upward bias in the forecasts for three sectors. That is, the residuals are consistently negative (manufacturing, transportation, and wholesale and retail trade), and show a downward bias in the other four sectors (the residuals are consistently positive). The forecast of total city income simultaneously with city population is probably as good a forecast as one could expect, with the smallest residual virtually zero (first quarter) and the largest residual only 1.4 percent of actual city income (second quarter). The preferred forecast of city income as the sum of the sectors' forecasted income is almost as good with the smallest residual 0.2 percent of actual city income (fourth quarter), and the largest residual 0.6 percent of actual income (second quarter). The forecasts of income in Table 6.8 have been made with the equations corrected for autocorrelation (Table 6.6).

Table 6.8
NYC Income, Actual and Forecast, for Four Quarters of 1979
(millions of 1972 $)

		1979			
		1	2	3	4
Total city income (single	Actual	$45,634	$45,079	$45,385	$45,664
equation)	Forecast	45,637	45,710	45,865	46,022
	Residual	−3	−631	−480	−358
City population (thousands)	Actual	N.A.	N.A.	N.A.	N.A.
	Forecast	6,929	6,954	6,962	6,974
	Residual	N.A.	N.A.	N.A.	N.A.
Manufacturing	Actual	7,903	7,687	7,567	7,523
	Forecast	8,452	8,472	8,442	8,352
	Residual	−549	−785	−875	−829
Transportation, communica-	Actual	4,976	4,787	4,875	4,862
tion, and public utilities	Forecast	5,148	5,132	5,134	5,135
	Residual	−172	−345	−259	−273
Wholesale and retail trade	Actual	5,387	5,401	5,470	5,447
	Forecast	5,652	5,595	5,600	5,557
	Residual	−265	−194	−130	−110
Finance, insurance, and real	Actual	12,365	12,267	12,503	12,627
estate	Forecast	12,073	12,084	12,108	12,133
	Residual	+292	+183	+395	+494
Services	Actual	8,336	8,334	8,472	8,610
	Forecast	8,332	8,265	8,283	8,332
	Residual	+4	+69	+189	+278
Government	Actual	5,680	5,607	5,497	5,585
	Forecast	5,574	5,425	5,283	5,292
	Residual	+106	+182	+214	+293
Mining and construction	Actual	986	997	1,001	1,011
	Forecast	890	821	760	778
	Residual	+96	+176	+241	+233
Total city income (sum of	Actual	$45,634	$45,079	$45,385	$45,664
sectors)	Forecast	46,121	45,799	45,610	45,579
	Residual	−487	−720	−225	+85

Table 6.9
United States Value Added per Employee, Actual and Forecast, for
Four Quarters of 1979 (1972 $)

		1979			
Sector		*1*	*2*	*3*	*4*
Manufacturing	Actual	$15,039	$14,741	$14,521	$14,503
	Forecast	14,873	14,243	14,260	14,133
	Residual	+166	+498	+261	+370
Transportation, communica-	Actual	19,219	18,553	18,722	18,706
tion, and public utilities	Forecast	19,051	18,068	18,098	17,904
	Residual	+168	+485	+624	+802
Wholesale and retail trade	Actual	8,660	8,702	8,812	8,812
	Forecast	9,356	9,206	9,207	9,171
	Residual	−696	−504	−395	−359
Finance, insurance, and real	Actual	29,095	28,707	29,158	29,277
estate	Forecast	29,286	28,894	28,889	28,783
	Residual	−191	−187	+269	+494
Services	Actual	9,907	9,769	9,819	9,911
	Forecast	10,355	10,118	10,120	10,064
	Residual	−448	−349	−301	−153
Government	Actual	10,882	10,744	10,637	10,696
	Forecast	11,656	11,279	11,286	11,204
	Residual	−774	−535	−649	−508
Mining and construction	Actual	$14,066	$14,317	$14,430	$14,418
	Forecast	15,868	15,083	15,107	14,951
	Residual	−1,802	−766	−677	−533

Actual and forecasted value added per employee, by sector and quarter, are shown in Table 6.9. The forecast values have been derived using the equations in Table 6.7. Forecasts of employment by sector and quarter (Table 6.10) are derived as

$$\left(\begin{array}{c} \text{Forecast Sector} \\ \text{Employment} \end{array} \right) = \frac{\text{Forecast Sector Income}}{\begin{array}{c}\text{Forecast Sector Value} \\ \text{Added per Employee}\end{array}}$$

The forecasts of total employment as the sum of sector em-

Table 6.10
**NYC Employment, Actual and Forecast, for Four Quarters of 1979
(thousands)**

Sector		1979			
		1	2	3	4
Manufacturing	Actual	526	522	521	519
	Forecast	568	595	592	591
	Residual	− 42	− 73	− 71	− 72
Transportation, communication,	Actual	259	258	260	260
and public utilities	Forecast	270	284	284	287
	Residual	− 11	− 26	− 24	− 27
Wholesale and retail trade	Actual	622	621	621	618
	Forecast	604	608	608	606
	Residual	+ 18	+ 13	+ 13	+ 12
Finance, insurance, and real	Actual	425	427	419	431
estate	Forecast	412	418	419	422
	Residual	+ 13	+ 9	+ 10	+ 9
Services	Actual	841	853	863	869
	Forecast	805	817	819	828
	Residual	+ 36	+ 36	+ 44	+ 41
Government	Actual	522	522	517	522
	Forecast	478	481	468	472
	Residual	+ 44	+ 41	+ 49	+ 50
Mining and construction	Actual	70	70	69	70
	Forecast	56	54	50	52
	Residual	+ 14	+ 16	+ 19	+ 18
Total employment	Actual	3,265	3,272	3,280	3,289
	Forecast	3,194	3,257	3,240	3,257
	Residual	+ 71	+ 15	+ 40	+ 32

SOURCE: Actual employment from U.S. Department of Labor, Bureau of Labor Statistics.

ployment are almost as good as the total income forecasts. The largest percent error is 2.2 percent (first quarter) and the smallest percent error is 0.5 percent (second quarter). The errors in the other two quarters are very close to 1 percent. Forecasts of employment for individual sectors are not nearly as accurate as the forecasts of total employment, which is to be expected because errors tend to be offsetting.

The tentative conclusion, then, based on the test for 1979, is that the quarterly city model is a workable model. That is, it yields plausible and reasonably accurate forecasts.

Note

1. See Harry Kelejian and Wallace E. Oates, *Introduction to Econometrics,* New York: Harper and Row, 1974, pp. 195–207.

7

Fiscal Sector of the New York City Model

7.1 The New York City revenue system

New York City's fiscal crisis in 1975 has stimulated interest in forecasting the city government's revenues. From the City's Office of Management and Budget to the Financial Control Board to the U.S. Treasury Department, there is a keen concern over the outlook for city revenues from taxes and other sources. The reason, of course, is that expected revenues are a key part, perhaps the central part, of the New York City Financial Plan aimed at meeting all financial obligations and continuing on a fiscally sound basis.

A fiscal sector of New York City model has been developed in order to forecast individual city tax revenues. The fiscal sector is, of couse, linked to city economic variables, so that different forecasts of economic conditions lead to different forecasts of city tax revenues. Because the larger region, the SCA, embraces parts of two states and myriad local governments, all with different tax systems, no attempt was made to develop a fiscal sector for the SCA model.

About two-thirds of the New York City government's

Table 7.1
New York City Revenue for Fiscal Years 1968, 1978, and 1983

Revenue Source (million $)	1968	1978	1983	Average Annual % Change, 1968–1983
Property tax	$1,599	$3,230	$3,787	5.9%
Sales tax	410	931	1,515	9.1
Personal income tax	170	700	1,331	14.7
General corporation tax	200	467	767	9.4
Commercial rent tax	79	194	334	10.1
Utility tax	41	109	202	11.2
Stock transfer tax	254	290	171	−2.6
Unincorporated business tax	30	89	145	11.1
Financial corporation tax	26	136	107	9.9
Other taxes, fees, charges, and miscellaneous	366	929	1,560	10.2
Total own-source revenues	$3,175	$7,075	$9,919	7.9%
State and federal transfers	2,763	5,784	5,814	5.1
Total revenues	$5,938	$12,859	$15,733	6.7%
Consumer price index (1967 = 100)	104.3	196.1	288.6	7.0%

SOURCE: The City of New York, *Comprehensive Annual Report of the Comptroller,* fiscal years 1968, 1981, and 1983. Consumer price index for N.Y.-Northeastern New Jersey area from U.S. Department of Labor, Bureau of Labor Statistics.

operating revenue in the most recent fiscal year (1983) is from local taxes, fees, and charges. The rest is from state and federal transfers. Table 7.1 presents historical data on the city's revenues, both the total and the major sources. The tax revenues shown in Table 7.1 and used throughout this chapter are tax revenues received by the city in a given fiscal year. They are not the same as tax *liabilities incurred* in a given fiscal year. It might be better to use liabilities rather than revenues in analyzing links between economic activity and city taxes, but it has not been possible because historical data on city tax liabilities are not available.

The first revenue shown in Table 7.1 is that received in 1968, when the current revenue system became fully effective. Between 1968 and 1983, the average annual rate of inflation, as measured by the consumer price index, was 7.0 percent. With the exception of the property tax (the major single tax) and the stock transfer tax (which is being phased out), all the own-source revenues shown increased at a higher rate than inflation. But much of the growth in excess of inflation can doubtless be attributed to tax-rate increases rather than to an expanding tax base. From 1968 to 1976 alone there were 13 rate increases on ten taxes, many increases in fees and user charges, plus some new revenue sources.

Eight of the nine major taxes listed in Table 7.1 are described below.

General Sales Tax

The present city sales tax rate is 4 percent. The New York state sales tax rate is also 4 percent. There is an additional one-quarter of 1 percent levied regionwide earmarked for the Metropolitan Transportation Authority. The biggest increase in sales tax revenues (38 percent) occured in fiscal year (hereafter FY) 1975, when the rate was boosted from 3 to 4 percent. The state sales tax rate has been 4 percent since its introduction in 1965. As a share of the city's own-source revenues, the sales tax revenues amounted to 15 percent in FY 1983.

Personal Income Tax

The personal income tax is imposed on the city taxable income of resident individuals, estates, and trusts. Taxable income is city-adjusted gross income less city deductions and city personal exemptions. Nonresidents with earnings in the city are also taxed, but at a much lower rate.

The tax first became effective January 1st, 1966. The rate

structure was mildly progressive with a minimum rate of 0.4 percent and a maximum rate of 2.0 percent on taxable income in excess of $30,000. During fiscal year 1972, there was an 80 percent increase in the rate schedule on residents which became effective for calendar year 1971. The maximum rate was then 3.5 percent on taxable income over $30,000. A further increase in rates became effective for calendar year 1976 and the maximum rate was boosted to 4.3 percent on taxable income over $25,000.

For nonresidents, the city personal income tax is imposed on wages, salaries, and net earnings from self-employment earned within the city. Income earned elsewhere is, of course, not taxed. The tax first became effective in 1966 with a rate of 0.25 percent on wages and salaries, and 0.375 percent on net earnings from self-employment. In 1971 the nonresident rates were increased to 0.45 percent on wages and salaries and 0.65 percent on net earnings from self-employment.

Revenues from the personal income tax grew 14.7 percent per year on average from FY 1968 to FY 1983 (see Table 7.1). The largest increases occurred in FY 1972 and FY 1977 when rate increases became effective. As a percent of total own-source revenues, the personal income tax share has risen from 5.4 percent in FY 1968 to 13.4 percent in FY 1983.

Unincorporated-business Tax

The unincorporated-business tax first became effective in 1966. Since its inception, the tax rate has been 4 percent of the unincorporated business taxable income earned in New York City. This tax is levied on any individual or unincorporated entity, including a partnership, fiduciary, or corporation in liquidation, engaged in any trade, business, profession, or occupation, wholly or partly carried on within the city. In 1971, professions (doctors, lawyers, and accountants) previously exempted became subject to the tax.

Revenues from the unincorporated business tax expanded at an average annual rate of 11.1 percent from FY 1968 to FY 1983. They represent a very small share (only 1.5 percent) of total own-source revenues.

General Corporation Tax

The general corporation tax is basically a tax upon the net income of corporations. The NewYork City general corporation tax was put into effect in 1966 when there was a major overhaul of the city's taxing authority and Charter revision. Prior to that time, the city had imposed a tax on gross receipts of businesses.

Originally, the general corporation tax was imposed on all domestic and foreign corporations doing business in the city. This was revised in 1972 so that a corporation which employed capital, owned or leased property, or maintained an office in the city also became subject to the tax.

The tax is imposed on every domestic or foreign corporation for the privilege of doing business, or employing capital, or owning or leasing property, or maintaining an office in the City of New York. Corporatioins deriving income from activities within and outside the city allocate their entire net income and capital according to formulae established for each. That part of net income (or capital) allocated to activities within the city is subject to the tax.

The tax rate on allocated net income was originally set at 5.5 percent in 1966. It was increased to 6.7 percent in 1971 and then to 10.05 percent in 1975. In 1977 the rate was reduced to 9.5 percent and then cut to 9.0 percent in 1978.

Revenues from the general corporation tax have not

grown as rapidly as revenues from the personal income and unincorporated business taxes. As a share of total own-source revenues, the general corporation tax was 7.7 percent in FY 1983.

Financial Corporation Tax

The financial corporation tax was first imposed on banks and financial corporations in 1966 as a franchise tax for the privilege of doing business in the city. Like many changes in 1966, this tax replaced a previous tax based on gross receipts, the financial-business tax.

Currently, federal taxable income, with various additions and subtractions, forms the base. All of net income is subject to the tax unless it is derived from business within and outside of the city, in which case net income must be apportioned either by separate accounts or by a formula perscribed by the city's Finance Department.

There are essentially two broad types of financial corporation taxpayers: commercial banks and savings institutions. Since 1973, allocation of income using separate accounts and utilizing the federal definition of taxable income seems to have reduced city net income for many banks. Foreign income and expenses of large city commercial banks (which are international banks) appear to have played a major role in this reduction.

As shown in Table 7.1, revenues from the financial corporation tax totaled only $107 million in FY 1983, thus accounting for only 1.1 percent of the city's total own-source revenues.

Utility Tax

The utility tax is imposed by the city on the gross income of all utilities, common carriers, and vendors of utility services. The revenue is almost all derived from telephone and electricity usage, not from transportation. Since 1966 the tax rate has been 2.35 percent on the gross income of utilities. Revenues from the utility tax were 2.0 percent of total own-source revenues in FY 1983.

Commercial Rent Tax

The commercial rent or occupancy tax is a tax upon leases of commercial space. The tax rate is applied to the annual lease payment, which is based upon the number of square feet of space rented and the price per square foot. The maximum rate of 7.5 percent is applied to space leased at a price above $7.00 per square foot. In FY 1983 revenues were 3.4 percent of total own-source revenues.

Property Tax

The property tax is New York City's largest single revenue source, accounting for 38 percent of own-source revenues in FY 1983. In comparison with earlier years, however, that tax has become a smaller component of total revenue as the city has diversified its tax structure and as revenues from the property tax have risen much slower than other revenues.

The property tax is calculated at a rate per dollar of assessed value of the city's taxable real estate. The portion of real-estate taxes that can be raised for operating purposes is

limited by the New York State Constitution to 2.5 percent of
the average full value of taxable real estate for the most recent
five years minus adjustments for certain short-term debt pay-
ments. The city is also authorized to levy a real estate tax
outside the 2.5 percent limit to cover the principal and interest
on all long-term indebtedness of the city.

Historical data on the property tax base, rates, and revenues are presented in Table 7.2. The full value or market value
of taxable property was $130 billion in Fy 1983 and has in-
creased at an average annual rate of 8.5 percent from FY 1978
to FY 1983. The assessed value is much lower, $43.8 billion in
FY 1983, and has grown at a slower rate—only 2.6 percent per
year. Consequently, the computed equalization ratio (column
3), that is, ratio of assessed value to market value, has dropped
from 72.4 percent in FY 1968, to 44.8 percent in FY 1978, and
to 33.7 percent in FY 1983.

The city, as many other jurisdictions in New York State,
has historically assessed real property at less than market
value. The State Board of Equalization and Assessment calculates the ratio of assessed value to full value and in the
process issues a "special equalization ratio" to reflect estimated market values in the fiscal year for which the tax will
be levied. Since there is a time lag between issuance of the
special ratios and final determination of the equalization rate,
changes can be made in the ratios originally set in prior years.
Their data include sales information and sample appraisals.
The equalization ratio shown is a computed average.

As shown in Table 7.2, the property tax collections in any
fiscal year are less than the tax levy. The problem of tax arrears
is most serious with the city's large stock of walk-up apartment
buildings. After nonpayment for three years (one year in the
case of abandoned buildings), the city institutes foreclosure
proceedings.

Table 7.2
The New York City Property Tax: Base, Rates, and Revenues for Fiscal Years 1968, 1978, and 1983 (millions of $)

Fiscal Year	(1) Full Value of Real Estate	(2) Assessed Value of Real Estate	(3) Equalization Ratio[a]	(4) Property Tax Rate[b]	(5) Property Tax Levy[c]	(6) Property Tax Collections[d]	(7) Collection Ratio[e]
1968	$44,903	$32,486	72.4%	$5.11	$1,660	$1,599	96.3%
1978	86,246	38,612	44.8	8.75	3,379	3,230	95.6
1983	129,951	43,825	33.7	9.12	3,996	3,787	94.8
				Average Annual Percent Increase or Decrease			
1968–1978	6.7%	1.7%			7.4%	7.3%	
1978–1983	8.5	2.6			3.4	3.2	

[a] Column 3 = Column 2/Column 1.
[b] Dollars per $100 of assessed value.
[c] Column 5 = (Column 4) × (Column 2).
[d] Same as property tax revenues shown in Table 7.1.
[e] Column 7 = Column 6/Column 5.
SOURCE: The City of New York, *Comprehensive Annual Report of the Comptroller,* fiscal years 1981 and 1983.

7.2 Tax revenue equations

The city's own-source revenue system either taxes or imposes charges on virtually every aspect of the local economy. Consequently, revenue equations have been specified which link tax revenues to measures of the local economy. Because the current city system of taxes has been in effect only since 1967, the number of annual observations on revenue items is limited. Further, because of large rate changes, as with the personal income tax, a consistent series is only available for ten years. Finally, judgments about structural changes in the city's economy led to a decision to eliminate years prior to 1975 in estimating some tax revenue equations. That imposes statistical limitations on revenue equations because the number of observations (years) is small. It limits the number of explanatory variables which can be used and still obtain significant results.

The estimated revenue equations are presented in Table 7.3. All seven of the equations have been estimated in log form. As noted above, the estimation period varies. The first equation regresses the log of property tax revenues (LTXPROP) on the log of deflated market value of property lagged two years, LDMVAL $(T-2)$, and on the log of the GNP implicit price deflator, $1972 = 100$ (LUDALL). The second equation is for the personal income tax revenues, deflated (LDTXPI). The explanatory variables are the log of total city income in 1972 dollars (LCALLY) and a measure of tax rate change (RATE).

The remaining five equations each have two explanatory variables: the log of the GNP implicit price deflator (LUDALL) and either the log of total city income in 1972 dollars (LCALLY) or the log of private city income in 1972 dollars (LCYPVT). Private city income is equal to total city income less government and the nonprofit industries. The city income

Table 7.3
NYC Tax-revenue Equations

Period	n	Dependent Variable		Constant	Independent Variables, Partial Regression Coefficients, and t Statistics (in parentheses)		Adjusted R^2	Durbin-Watson
1970–1984	15	LTXPROP	=	−2.8487 (1.8)	+ 0.5771LDMVAL $(T-2)$ (4.6)	+ 0.8993LUDALL (16.5)	0.96	1.24
1975–1984	10	LTXSALE	=	−1.6650 (0.2)	+ 0.2245LCALLY $(T-1)$ (0.3)	+ 1.2263LUDALL (6.3)	0.98	0.62
1972–1984	13	LDTXPI	=	−18.873 (4.1)	+ 2.347LCALLY (5.4)	+ 0.156RATE (3.1)	0.84	1.38
1975–1984	10	LTXGB	=	−36.895 (3.0)	+ 3.9428LCYPVT (2.9)	+ 0.4469LUDALL (1.1)	0.93	1.81
1968–1984	17	LTXUTIL	=	+2.4663 (0.9)	− 0.5439LCYPVT (2.1)	+ 1.5626LUDALL (31.3)	0.98	1.13
1975–1984	10	LTXUB	=	−48.306 (4.8)	+ 4.7314LCYPVT (4.2)	+ 0.7360LUDALL (2.3)	0.97	2.03
1968–1984	17	LTXFIN	=	+37.571 (2.5)	− 3.9387LCALLY (2.8)	+ 1.8072LUDALL (8.0)	0.81	2.07

variable(s) in these equations is, of course, the same variable derived in the city economic model explained in Chapter 3. Thus, the results from a forecast of the city economy can be used to generate a corresponding forecast of city tax revenues.

Of the seven equations shown, five have adjusted R^2 values above $+0.90$ and all have acceptable Durbin-Watson statistics, except for the sales tax equation. In the next and final chapter of Part I, these equations plus the full economic model of Chapter 3 are used to generate a forecast through 1990.

8

A Forecast of
the Region's and
the City's Economies

8.1 Three scenarios for the future

The annual versions of the SCA and NYC model have been used to generate long-term forecasts for 1987 and 1990. Forecasts of some key independent variables required as inputs for the models are shown in Table 8.1. The national forecast indicates moderate growth. Real GNP is projected to grow 3.6 percent per year from 1983 to 1990. From the high of 9.4 percent in 1983, the unemployment rate is expected to improve, falling to 6.4 percent by 1990, which is still well above a targeted full-employment rate of 5.0 percent. The crude measure of productivity, real national income per emplyee, is projected to expand 0.9 percent per year over the projection period. The national rate of inflation, as measured by the CPI, is projected to average 5.2 percent per year, 1983 to 1990.

A key variable in the regional and city models is the ratio of the regional CPI to the national CPI (SCPIUS). Three scenarios are assumed which result in three different projections for the SCA and the city economies. The "middle" case assumes inflation in the region at the same rate as nationally, 5.2

Table 8.1
National Economic Scenario and Regional Inflation Assumptions

	Actual 1983	Forecast 1987	Forecast 1990	Forecast Average Annual Percent Change, 1983–1990
GNP (billion 1972 $)	$1,535	$1,737	$1,070	3.6
Nonagricultural employment (millions)	90.0	101.7	107.9	2.6
Unemployment rate (percent)	9.4	6.7	6.4	
National income per employee (thousand 1972 $)	$13.5	$14.0	$14.4	0.9
Consumer price index, U.S. (1967 = 100)	298.3	363.3	424.1	5.2
Consumer price index, NY-NJ area (1967 = 100)				
High		342.6	392.3	4.5
Middle	288.6	351.7	410.5	5.2
Low		360.0	427.9	5.8
Ratio of CPI region/CPI U.S.				
High		0.943	0.925	
Middle	0.968	0.968	0.968	
Low		0.991	1.009	

SOURCE: 1983 actual data from Bureau of Economic Analysis, U.S. Department of Commerce, and Bureau of Labor Statistics, U.S. Department of Labor. Forecasts based upon a distillation of national forecasts as of April, 1984.

percent per year between 1983 and 1990. The "high," or favorable, case assumes a slower rate of inflation in the region, 4.5 percent per year average to 1990. The "low," or unfavorable, case assumes a higher rate of inflation in the region than in the nation, 5.8 percent per year, between 1983 and 1990.

8.2 SCA and NYC forecasts of income and employment by industry

Summary projections of real income (or output) and employment for the SCA and NYC are presented in Table 8.2. Three forecast scenarios are shown corresponding to three

Table 8.2
**Projections of Total Income and Employment, SCA and NYC,
1983 to 1990**

Year	SCA		New York City	
	Income *(billion 1972 $)*	Employment *(thousands)*	Income *(billion 1972 $)*	Employment *(thousands)*
1983	$87.9	6,846	$43.1	3,344
Projected				
— High	98.6	7,336	47.9	3,535
1987 — Middle	97.4	7,235	47.8	3,523
— Low	96.1	7,133	47.7	3,510
— High	104.9	7,636	50.0	3,607
1990 — Middle	101.8	7,408	49.7	3,582
— Low	98.9	7,170	49.5	3,553
Projected average annual percent change				
— High	2.6%	1.6%	2.1%	1.1%
1983–1990 — Middle	2.1%	1.1%	2.0%	1.0%
— Low	1.7%	0.7%	2.0%	0.9%

SOURCE: Computed for this study.

assumptions about inflation in the region compared with the United States inflation.

High Regional inflation rate less than national inflation rate (that is, improving competitive position viz-à-viz the United States).

Middle Regional inflation rate equal to national inflation rate (that is, neutral competitive position viz-à-viz the United States).

Low Regional inflation rate greater than national inflation rate (that is, deteriorating competitive position viz-à-viz the United States).

Real income in the region (SCA) and the city (NYC) are projected to grow at 2.1 percent and 2.0 percent respectively, per year (middle case). If regional inflation is lower than national inflation (high case), growth is projected at 2.6 percent (SCA) and 2.1 percent (NYC) per year. If regional inflation is higher than national inflation (low case), annual growth is projected at 1.7 percent for the region and 2.0 percent for the city. Annual employment growth is projected from a high of 1.6 percent to a low of 0.7 percent for the SCA. The city growth range is narrower: 1.1 percent to 0.9 percent.

Projections of SCA income and employment by sector are presented in Table 8.3, and projections of NYC income and employment by sector are shown in Table 8.4. Both correspond to the "middle" case forecast. In the SCA, six of the seven sectors are projected to have growth in real income at average annual rates of 2 percent or better from 1983 to 1990. The exception is manufacturing, with forecasted growth in real income of 1.1 percent per year, 1983 to 1990.

The table compares actual growth between 1975 and 1983 to projected growth from 1983 to 1990. The forecast scenario indicates a slowdown in growth of total SCA real income (or output) from 2.6 percent per year from 1975 to 1983 to 2.1 percent per year from 1983 to 1990. That projected slowing can be attributed to three sectors which grew rapidly from 1975 to 1983 but are expected to have diminished growth rates through 1990 (that is, transportation etc., finance etc., and services).

Turning to SCA employment forecasts, growth in total employment from 1983 to 1990 (+1.1 percent per year) is expected to be about the same as the recent historical experience (+1.0 percent per year from 1975 to 1983). There are marked changes among sectors, however, with diminished growth rates in finance and services compared with recent history, and stronger growth in government. The manufacturing sector is the only one in which a significant decline in

Table 8.3
SCA Income and Employment by Sector, 1975, 1983 and Projected 1987, 1990ᵃ

	1975	1983	Projected		Average Annual Percent Change	
			1987	1990	1975–1983	Projected 1983–1990
Income (million 1972 $)						
Mining and construction	$ 2,791	$ 3,419	$ 3,900	$ 4,100	2.6	2.6
Manufacturing	16,824	18,164	19,250	19,600	1.0	1.1
Transportation, communication, and public utility	7,274	9,691	10,600	11,400	3.7	2.4
Wholesale and retail	13,058	14,725	16,500	17,000	1.5	2.1
Finance, insurance, and real estate	7,629	11,605	13,200	13,600	5.4	2.3
Services and miscellaneous	12,761	17,985	20,400	21,900	4.4	2.9
Government	11,179	12,353	13,550	14,200	1.3	2.0
Total	$71,516	$87,941	$97,400	$101,800	2.6%	2.1%
Employment (thousands)						
Mining and construction	197	216	233	227	1.1	0.7
Manufacturing	1,316	1,209	1,221	1,184	−1.1	−0.3
Transportation, communication, and public utility	458	458	469	472	—	0.4
Wholesale and retail	1,334	1,451	1,530	1,570	1.1	1.1
Finance, insurance, and real estate	578	697	747	765	2.4	1.3
Services and miscellaneous	1,322	1,748	1,925	2,045	3.6	2.3
Government	1,100	1,067	1,109	1,145	−0.4	1.0
Total	6,304	6,846	7,234	7,408	1.0%	1.1%

ᵃ Parts may not sum to totals due to rounding.
SOURCE: Employment for 1975 and 1983 from U.S. Department of Labor, Bureau of Labor Statistics, *Employment and Earnings, States and Areas, 1939–78*, 1980, and *Employment and Earnings*, March, 1984. Income and projections computed for this study.

Table 8.4
NYC Income and Employment by Sector, 1975, 1983 and Projected 1987, 1990[a]

	1975	1983	Projected 1987	Projected 1990	Average Annual Percent Change 1975–1983	Average Annual Percent Change 1983–1990
Income (million 1972 $)						
Mining and construction	$ 1,155	$ 1,411	$ 1,660	$ 1,760	2.5	3.2
Manufacturing	6,101	5,629	5,620	5,420	-1.0	-0.5
Transportation, communication, and public utility	4,265	4,950	5,420	5,740	1.9	2.1
Wholesale and retail	6,515	6,408	7,120	7,250	-0.2	1.8
Finance, insurance, and real estate	5,689	8,597	10,000	10,400	5.3	2.8
Services and miscellaneous	7,501	10,046	11,550	12,240	3.7	2.9
Government	5,911	6,097	6,600	6,890	0.4	1.8
Total	$37,137	$43,138	$47,770	$49,700	1.9%	2.0%
Employment (thousands)						
Mining and construction	82	89	99	100	1.1	1.7
Manufacturing	537	432	410	385	-2.7	-1.6
Transportation, communication, and public utility	269	236	242	240	-1.6	0.2
Wholesale and retail	634	608	635	634	-0.5	0.6
Finance, insurance, and real estate	420	494	543	560	2.1	1.8
Services and miscellaneous	770	967	1,061	1,128	2.9	2.2
Government	573	519	532	535	-1.2	0.4
Total	3,283	3,344	3,523	3,582	0.2%	1.0%

[a] Parts may not sum to totals due to rounding.
SOURCE: See Table 8.3.

employment is projected (-0.3 percent per year), but that is less than the recent manufacturing decline of -1.1 percent per year from 1975 to 1983.

The NYC long-term forecasts (Table 8.4) indicate significant growth of real income in all sectors except manufacturing. Construction, transportation etc., finance, and services are all projected to grow at rates above 2 percent per year, while trade, and government are projected to grow at rates between 1 percent and 2 percent per year.

The employment scenario for NYC indicates a change in pattern among sectors compared with recent history. The two strong growth sectors between 1975 and 1983, finance etc., and services, are expected to show some slowdown in growth (for finance, from 2.1 percent per year from 1975 to 1983 to 1.8 percent per year from 1983 to 1990; for services, from 2.9 percent per year between 1975 and 1983 to 2.2 percent per year from 1983 to 1990). However, the four sectors which showed declining employment between 1975 and 1983 are projected to show some positive growth between 1983 and 1990 (transportation etc., trade, and government) or a lessened rate of decline (manufacturing).

The choice of 1975 as the beginning year for the historical period to compare with the forecast period is not altogether arbitrary. Both SCA and NYC total income hit bottom in that year and then began to recover. However, SCA employment was at its low in 1976 and NYC employment bottomed out in 1977, having declined every single year since 1969. Consequently, it is also informative to compare the historical recovery of NYC employment between 1977 and 1983, with the NYC forecast scenario. The sector-by-sector comparison of historical and projected growth rates is shown in the accompanying table.

	Average Annual Percent Change in NYC Employment	
Sector	1977–1983	Projected 1983–1990
Mining and construction	5.2	1.7
Manufacturing	−3.6	−1.6
Transportation, communication, and public utilities	−1.5	0.2
Wholesale and retail trade	−0.3	0.6
Finance, insurance, and real estate	3.0	1.8
Services and miscellaneous	3.6	2.2
Government	0.4	0.4
Total	0.8%	1.0%

The more appropriate comparison shows that NYC total employment has risen 0.8 percent per year on average from its low in 1977 to 1983. That rise reflects very strong growth in finance etc., (3.0 percent per year) and services (3.6 percent per year), more than offsetting a steep decline in manufacturing jobs of −3.6 percent per year and declines in transportation etc., and trade jobs. The projected growth in finance and services is considerably lower than the past history.

8.3 SCA and NYC forecasts of employment by occupation

Using the industry-occupation matrices explained in Chapter 5, employment in each of 47 occupational categories for each of 53 industries has been projected from 1983 to 1990 for the region and the city. A summary of the forecast for broad occupational groups is presented in Table 8.5. The occupational employment forecasts have been generated for the "middle" projection only, not for the "high" or "low" projections. As noted in Section 8.1, total SCA employment is projected to rise +1.1 percent per year, from 1983 to 1990. Projected change among the eight occupational groups for the SCA

Table 8.5
Projections of Employment by Occupational Groups, SCA and NYC for 1983 and 1990 (thousands)

Occupational Groups	SCA			NYC		
	1983	1990	Average Annual Percent Change 1983–1990	1983	1990	Average Annual Percent Change 1983–1990
Professional	1,240	1,386	1.6	622	695	1.6
Managerial	842	919	1.3	441	480	1.2
Sales	472	519	1.4	221	236	0.9
Clerical	1,712	1,881	1.4	923	1,003	1.2
Crafts	732	777	0.9	308	322	0.6
Operatives	780	763	−0.3	308	290	−0.9
Services	822	912	1.5	421	455	1.1
Other labor	246	251	0.3	100	101	0.1
Total	6,846	7,408	1.1%	3,344	3,582	1.0%

SOURCE: Computed for this study.

ranges from a high of + 1.6 percent per year (professional and technical) to a low of − 0.3 percent per year (operatives). Of the four blue-collar occupations (crafts, operatives, services, and other labor), only two, services and crafts, are projected to have significant growth: + 1.5 and + 0.9 percent respectively. The service group is comprised of the occupations of cleaning, food, health, personal, and protection. Of the four white-collar occupations (professional and technical, managerial, sales and clerical), all are projected to rise from 1983 to 1990. The NYC projections show a similar pattern, except that the forecasted drop in operatives' jobs in the city is more severe: − 0.9 percent per year from 1983 to 1990.

The upshot of the occupational projection is that both the city and the region are expected to continue to generate far more higher-skill white-collar jobs than lower-skill blue-collar jobs, as shown below.

| | 1983–1990 Job Change (thousands) | |
	SCA	NYC
White-collar	+ 439	+ 207
Blue-collar	+ 123	+ 31
Total	+ 562	+ 238

8.4 Forecasts of New York City tax revenues

The tax revenue equations of the model (see Chapter 7) have been used to project revenues through FY 1988. Some of the revenue sources were forecast judgmentally because no acceptable equation has been estimated. Seven tax revenues have been forecast with equations (namely, the property tax, general sales tax, personal income tax, general corporation tax, utility tax, unincorporated business tax, and financial corporation tax).

Table 8.6 presents actual revenues by source for FY 1983. Forecasts for FY 1986 through FY 1988 are also shown. Total local revenues (that is, excluding state and federal transfers) are projected to grow 6.0 percent per year from FY 1983 to FY 1988, rising from $9917 million in FY 1983 to $13,291 million in FY 1988. For individual tax revenues, the projected growth rates differ substantially. The combination of expanding income and "bracket creep" (that is, inflation's pushing taxpayer's money income into higher tax brackets) results in projected growth of personal income tax revenues of 12.3 percent per year. The largest revenue source, the property tax, is projected to grow at only 4.2 percent per year between FY 1983 and FY 1988.

State and federal transfers, the nonlocal part of NYC revenues, represented about one-third of total revenues in FY 1983. Rather than forecast those transfers, the projections made by the city's Office of Management and Budget have

Table 8.6
NYC Government Projected Revenues by Source for Fiscal Years
1983–1988 (millions $)

Revenue Source	Actual FY 1983	Projected FY 1986	Projected FY 1987	Projected FY 1988	Projected Average Annual Percent Change 1983–1988
Property tax	$3,787	$4,126	$4.399	$4,649	+4.2%
General sales tax	1,515	1,823	1,061	2,116	+6.9
Personal income tax	1,334	1,879	2,117	2,384	+12.3
General corporation tax	767	1,053	1,164	1,279	+10.8
Stock transfer tax	171	118	118	118	−7.2
Commercial rent tax	334	420	451	490	+8.0
Financial corporation tax	107	177	182	188	+11.9
Utility tax	202	215	233	253	+4.6
Unincorporated business tax	145	226	258	292	+15.0
All other taxes[a]	343	394	398	402	+3.2
Fees and user charges	609	665	680	695	+2.7
Other local revenues[a]	603	425	424	425	−6.8
Total Local Revenues	$9,917	$11,521	$12,385	$13,291	+6.0%
State and Federal transfers[b]	5,814	6,238	6,307	6,415	+2.0
Total Revenues	$15,733	$17,759	$18,692	$19,706	+4.6%

[a] NYC Office of Management and Budget projections from *Message of the Mayor,* April, 1983.
[b] NYC Office of Management and Budget projections from *The City of New York Financial Plan Fiscal Years 1984–1988.*
SOURCE: Fiscal year 1983 from *Report of the Comptroller Fiscal Year 1983.* Fiscal years 1986–1988 projections computed for this study unless otherwise noted.

been accepted and included in Table 8.6. As shown, those intergovernmental transfers are expected to grow very slowly (2 percent per year).

The fiscal implications of those revenue forecasts are laid out in Table 8.7. Revenue and expenditure forecasts presented in the New York City Financial Plan of January, 1984, are compared with the author's model forecasts. Because local revenues only have been forecast with the model, the expend-

Table 8.7
NYC Government Projected Revenues, Expenditures, and Budget Gap for Fiscal Years 1986–1988

	FY 1986		FY 1987		FY 1988	
	Financial Plan	Author	Financial Plan	Author	Financial Plan	Author
Revenues						
Property tax	$ 4,378	$ 4,126	$ 4,586	$ 4,399	$ 4,811	$ 4,649
All other taxes	6,129	6,305	6,508	6,882	6,923	7,522
Other local revenues	1,249	1,090	1,247	1,104	1,249	1,120
Total local revenues	$11,756	$11,521	$12,341	$12,385	$12,983	$13,291
State and federal transfers	6,238	6,238	6,307	6,307	6,415	6,415
Total revenues	$17,994	$17,759	$18,648	$18,692	$19,398	$19,706
Expenditures						
Low Total expenditures, 2 percent wage increase (Financial Plan)	$18,639	$18,639	$19,266	$19,266	$19,867	$19,867
Middle Total expenditures, 4 percent annual wage increase	18,939	18,939	19,738	19,738	20,515	20,515
High Total expenditures, 6 percent wage increase	19,239	19,239	20,210	20,210	21,163	21,163
Budget Gap						
Low (Financial Plan)	– $ 645	– $880	– $ 618	– $ 574	– $ 469	– $ 161
Middle	– 945	– 1,180	– 1,090	– 1,046	– 1,117	– 809
High	– 1,245	– 1,480	– 1,562	– 1,518	– 1,765	– 1,457

SOURCE: Financial Plan projections of revenues and expenditures, including the cost-of-wage increases above 2 percent per year, from *The City of New York Financial Plan Fiscal Years 1984–1988*. Author's projections of revenues from Table 8.6.

itures and state- and federal-transfer forecasts of the Financial Plan are adopted for the model forecst.

Comparing the forecasts of total local revenues, the Financial Plan totals are higher than the author's for 1986 and lower for 1987 and 1988. However, the differences are not great, the largest being less than 2 percent for 1988.

The NYC government expenditure forecasts from the Financial Plan assume that wage increases will be limited to 2 percent per year through 1988. That seems unrealistic in the light of the fact that inflation is expected to average around 5 percent per year. Consequently, that expenditure scenario is labeled "Low" in Table 8.7. The "Middle" and "High" scenarios (computed by the author using the Financial Plan numbers on cost-of-wage increases above 2 percent per year) assume annual wage increases for city employees of 4 percent to 6 percent per year, respectively.

As shown in Table 8.7, the Financial Plan projections with a 2 percent annual wage boost (low case here) yield budget gaps that range from $645 million in FY 1986 to $469 million in 1988. The author's projections for the "Low" case (which differ from the Financial Plan only in the revenue projections) yield budget gaps that range from $880 million in FY 1986 to $161 million in FY 1988.

But more important (and worse) is the fiscal outlook which results from assuming a more realistic 4 percent annual rise in wages—the "Middle" case. There, the budget gap under the financial Plan projections ranges from $945 million in FY 1986 to $1117 million in FY 1988. And the author's "Middle" case budget gaps are of course similar: $1180 million in FY 1986, $1046 million in FY 1987, and $809 million in FY 1988. Clearly, the city cannot countenance actual budget gaps of that magnitude, but at the same time the solution does not lie in some vain hope of holding wage increases to 2 percent or less. The municipal work force, which bore so much of the burden of the fiscal crisis, will not allow their earnings to continue to stagnate viz-à-viz jobs in the private sector. Enhancing the quality and delivery of municipal services, an oft-stated goal of the mayor, is impossible with a disgruntled and demoralized work force.

PART II

POLICY ANALYSIS WITH THE MODEL

9

Prologue to Part II

The model has been laid out in the first part of this study. This second part attempts to achieve a few objectives, narrow and broad. The narrow, but important objective is to demonstrate the usefulness of this model, and by extension, similar models, for policy analysis. The policies explored relate to broad, not narrow issues. They are broad because they are issues central to all large metropolitan areas and cities, especially the older ones widely viewed as beset with problems. Because the models are necessarily specific to one place, the policy simulations performed are specific to one place, but the broader ramifications are described for all old and/or large urban areas.

The promise of the Introduction was that models for policy analysis can be useful in addressing the issues of urban economic development. Part I, if not directly, by implication fulfilled that promise by providing information on what has been happening to the economies of two old and large metropolitan areas, New York and Baltimore, especially the former. Key points brought out in Part I are

1. secular decline in goods production and distribution industries (manufacturing, wholesale trade, and rail and water transport)
2. exacerbation of that decline after 1969 in a period of slow national growth and high inflation

3. apparent high sensitivity of manufacturing industries to relative costs
4. favorable performance of finance and services industries
5. population loss
6. shifting composition of occupational employment to higher level occupation groups (professional and managerial) and with expected net gains for lower skilled workers only in service and clerical jobs
7. continuing fiscal problems of the adequacy of local government revenues to cover expected expenditures

The list is not unique for New York and Baltimore, as any informed observer of the contemporary urban scene knows. Consequently, it is quite appropriate to use the models developed to perform policy simulations, the results of which can be generalized to other urban places.

The dispersion of manufacturing away from large urban areas is a national phenomena. In the past two decades, the metropolitan areas of the Northeast and North Central States—the manufacturing belt of the nation—have collectively lost substantial numbers of their manufacturing jobs.[1] And the central cities of those Northeast and North Central metropolitan areas lost more heavily.[2]

The favorable performance of the services and financial industries is similarly part of a national trend and not a recent one. In a *Scientific American* article, Eli Ginzberg and George J. Vojta noted that in 1948 the goods producing sectors (agriculture, mining, construction, and manufacturing) accounted for 46 percent of the GNP but that their share dropped to 34 percent by 1978.[3] Thus the sectors collectively that do not produce goods have accounted for most of the employment expansion. Of the 45 million jobs added in the nonagricultural economy since 1950, 15 million have been in the finance and services sector compared with only 5 million more in manu-

Table 9.1
United States Nonagricultural Employment by Sector, 1950 and 1980 (thousands)

	1950		1980	
	Number	Percent Share	Number	Percent Share
Mining and construction	3,265	7.2	5,493	6.1
Manufacturing	15,241	33.7	20,365	22.5
Transportation, communication, and public utilities	4,034	8.9	5,155	5.7
Wholesale and retail trade	9,386	20.8	20,571	22.7
Finance, insurance, and real estate	1,888	4.2	5,162	5.7
Services	5,357	11.9	17,736	19.6
Government	6,026	13.3	16,171	17.8
Total	45,197	100	90,652	100

SOURCE: U.S. Department of Labor, Bureau of Labor Statistics, *Employment and Earnings, United States, 1909–78,* 1979, and *Employment and Earnings,* January 1981.

facturing. In that period government employment rose 10 million (mostly state and local) and trade rose 11 million (see Table 9.1). But the national gains in private sector employment did not show up in the large, old, central cities, although the change in mix did. The central cities of the Northeast and North Central States with populations over one-half million in 1970 have been losing population too, not just New York. The combination of fixed city boundaries and the filling in over time of open areas within the city, plus the long-standing inclusion of low-density living in what economists call the preference function of Americans, inexorably leads to population declines in large old central cities. The population of the largest, old, United States central cities east of the Mississippi peaked in 1950 and has been falling steadily since.[4] The birth rate could rise significantly and still not reverse the trend of population decline in the older filled-in central cities.

The changing occupational composition in New York City

and the wider region noted in Chapter 5 is also not unique but mirrors the national pattern. In 1970, 47 percent of all United States workers were in the white-collar occupations. Eight years later the white-collar share topped 50 percent. Gains in the highest level (in terms of training and pay) white-collar occupations, that is, professional, technical, and managerial, totaled 5.9 million and exceeded the gain of 5.7 million in all of the blue-collar occupations combined. In 1979 the number of computer specialists in the nation was 534,000, up 72 percent from 1974, exceeding the number of plumbers and pipefitters. Artists, writers, and entertainers were as numerous as auto mechanics (1.2 million of each). For every longshoreman and stevedore in the United States there were two economists (excluding those in teaching).[5]

Even with the rather upbeat model forecast presented in Chapter 8, the fiscal forecast for New York City indicated a substantial budget gap. Local governments in the other large, old central cities are not unfamiliar with New York's problem of finding revenues to cover expenditures.

Thus, the facts or information brought out in Part I are not peculiar to New York and Baltimore. Problems about central cities not brought out in Part I but widely perceived and known to be interwoven with those facts are

1. the high concentration of impoverished households, particularly minority households, living in deficient housing
2. deteriorating and undermaintained public infrastructure
3. the ruined areas of abandoned housing and other structures
4. high unemployment, especially among the young, unskilled, poorly educated

5. high crime, unsuccessful education, and deficient public services
6. a shrinking tax base as higher income households move out and businesses vanish (more fail than move)

In the best of possible worlds, urban economic development is supposed to make the horrors listed above go away. In the 1960s it was federal, state, and local programs that were supposed to make those horrors disappear (some, deteriorating infrastructure, deficient public services, and shrinking tax base, were not widely perceived then). Billions of dollars and billions of words were hurled at those urban ills, but the general perception is that they are still here and perhaps worse. But perceptions are often faulty because we have short memories and changing expectations. President Kennedy (beloved champion of the poor) would never have dreamed of proposing a comprehensive family income-support program as President Nixon (hated enemy of the poor) did. Its time had not yet come. There can be little doubt that the poor are better off than they were 20 years ago thanks to food stamps, medicare, medicaid, and expanded welfare programs, although they are worse off than in 1980, thanks to President Reagan and supply-side economics. To the extent that the food-stamp program has curbed malnutrition in this nation, which it certainly has, then it rivals the Salk vaccine as a major achievement of the public sector.

One problem about perception is the issue of capability. A popular sentence among those many hurled at our urban ills began: "If we can put a man on the moon, why can't we. . . ." There are many things government cannot do well, especially when they require interacting with other levels of government in our system. If the President ruled the United States of

America with carte blanche, many things which cannot be done well now would get done. To believe that urban economic development can make all those problems go away is just as unreal as the belief in public-spending programs as a panacea.

Now it is necessary to put some content into the phrase "urban economic development." Much has been written about it that is fluff (for a recent example see R. Vaughn and M. Willis, "Economic Development" in *Setting Municipal Priorities, 1982*). It is easier to say what it is not. First of all, it is not an income redistribution program such as AFDC or food stamps. Nor is a Keynesian-type public-works program with short-term multiplier effects. Those who view the long-fought Westway highway project in Manhattan primarily on such terms might as well argue for spending the money on a colossus of Mayor Koch straddling New York Harbor. The value of Westway is first in improving car and truck access to Manhattan and Long Island and second in clearing the debris from the Hudson waterfront so that something good might happen there (such as economic development). Economic development is not smoke-stack chasing, that is, aggressive luring of outside firms to move into a jurisdiction with individually tailored tax-abatement packages and state-subsidized financing. Some areas will win and some will lose in that sort of beggar-thy-neighbor approach. But even the winners cannot gain much with such a policy. An analysis at the Joint Center for Urban Studies has shown that the part of any state's employment increase (or decrease) due to firm relocation is tiny.[6] Also, such a policy is manifestly discriminatory toward firms already in the jurisdiction because they cannot qualify for the same benefits.

Good economic development policy for older metropolitan areas and their central cities is constrained by what is good economics and good public finance. Good economics means, among other things, recognizing some market forces as inexorable and thus not wasting resources on a fruitless attempt to reverse or stop them. Good public finance means, among other things, not designing an urban economic development program which fleeces the U.S. Treasury with outrageous equity outcomes.

One of the inexorable market forces which must be recognized in thinking about urban economic-development has been brought out above, namely, falling population density which in the older cities has resulted in absolute declines in population. Another is the dispersion of goods production and distribution activities. To reverse those trends would require another Great Depression. Those who long to see the abandoned and dilapidated neighborhoods of our old central cities filled up again with people, shops, and small factories should visit Warsaw or Seoul in the winter. That is how Milwaukee and Detroit looked in 1944. As noted before, low-density living appears to have a high priority among the preferences of most Americans, and as their real incomes have risen they have realized that preference. The fact that New York and other old cities have had substantial population declines in the past 20 years is not a sign of our failure. Many people do not want to live there and apparently do not have to. When the older cities were more populous, perhaps many residents did not want to live there either, but their incomes did not provide other options.

Every large, old American city has depopulated neighborhoods, and it is difficult to think of them as monuments to our success in raising real incomes because of the wasted structures and social pathology of those left behind. The social pathology is outside the scope of this study. The wasted buildings are also a monument to an external cost of our economic system, namely, that capitalism does not tidy up when it is finished. At any moment in time, the tremendous concentration of immobile capital in the form of private structures in cities represents the result of many individual investment decisions spread over the past century or more. The decisions were presumably rational in a profit-loss context when they were made in terms of that structure on that site. But now some may be technologically or locationally obsolete or devalued by the negative externalities of their location, while others may be greatly enhanced in value. In many cases the underlying land values would improve if the structures were gone, for, being useless themselves, the land cannot be reused without first demolishing the structures.

Keeping in mind the constraints of good economics and good public finance, economic development policy should be founded upon a central principle: Whatever improves the competitive advantage of the urban area viz-à-viz other places is good for economic development, and whatever worsens the competitive advantage is bad for economic development. Corrolaries to this principle would include one that indicates that the more pervasive any change which improves competitive position, the better. Narrow improvements targeted for a single segment of the economy should be eschewed if they are likely to cause offsetting deterioration in the competitive advantage of other segments.

The perspective in applying this principle in designing or appraising urban economic development policy will, of course, be different at different levels of government. But if they are informed by good economics and good public finance, the different roles of the different governments will be clearly sorted out and the separate policies will not be at cross purposes. Key questions which should always be asked include the following. (1) What is it that can realistically be done to improve competitive advantage? (2) Who should do it? (3) How much will it cost and who shall pay?

The chapters which follow attempt to apply the principle, to sort out the proper roles of different levels of government, to use the model either in simulations or simply to use the data of the model in exploring possible effects of different policies, and then to draw broad conclusions applicable to large urban areas.

Notes

1. U.S. Department of Labor, Bureau of Labor Statistics, *Employment, Hours, and Earnings, States and Areas, 1939–82,* 1984.
2. Peter Mieszkowski, "Recent Trends in Urban and Regional Development," *Current Issues in Urban Economics,* Peter Mieszkowski and Mahlon Straszheim editors, Baltimore: The Johns Hopkins University Press, 1979, p. 10.
3. Eli Ginzberg and George Vojta, "The Service Sector of the United States Economy," *Scientific American* Vol. 244, No. 3 (March 1981), pp. 32–39.
4. U.S. Department of Commerce, Bureau of the Census, *Statistical Abstract of the United States: 1972,* 93rd edition, Washington, 1972.
5. United States Department of Labor, Bureau of Labor Statistics, *The National Industry-Occupation Employment Matrix, 1970, 1978, and Projected 1990,* 1981.
6. David Birch and Peter Allaman, "Components of Employment Change for States by Industry Group 1970–72," *Working Paper No. 5,* Cambridge, Mass: Joint Center for Urban Studies, Harvard and M.I.T., September, 1975.

10

The Federal Role in Urban Economic Development

10.1 The McGill report

In *A National Agenda for the Eighties,* referred to as the McGill report after the chairman, William J. McGill, of the President's Commission for a National Agenda, there are recommendations on federal urban policy.[1] One which received much negative reaction in the press was the proposal that the federal government assist the unemployed to relocate from high unemployment areas to low unemployment areas. That notion quite naturally flows from the more central recommendation of the report on urban policy, namely that the federal government should shift to assisting people rather than places. Part of the basis presented for that view is the same argument presented here in Chapter 9, that is, inexorable market forces are dispersing people and jobs and making big central cities shrink, and government cannot change that. But migration assistance is not an urban economic-development policy. Thus, there is not really a recommended urban economic-development stance for the federal government in the McGill report, except to stop assistance to urban places.

The case for separating urban development from poverty programs was made very well by Gail Schwartz.

Federal policy should not confuse an urban development strategy with an antipoverty program. The fact that the cities of America house large concentrations of relatively poor persons is testimony of past history, not a requisite for future policy. The solution to urban poverty does not lie in maintaining permanet communities of the relatively disadvantaged in the urban settings where they happen to be currently trapped. It is easy to build a fence of government assistance around the urban poor, creating urban "reservations" that permanently isolate their residents from mainstream opportunities in the larger society. Although the problems of "distressed" people may properly be conceived of as place-linked problems, the solutions to them in the long run cannot be excusively placed linked.[2]

It is good public finance to assign full responsibility of income redistribution to the federal government, which would include medicaid, food stamps, and welfare. The president recently proposed one step forward (federal assumption of all medicaid) and two steps backward (shifting food stamps and AFDC to the states with only temporary funding from federal excise taxes). Income redistribution at lower levels of government has non-optimal impacts upon the location of economic activity and households, as Dick Netzer has pointed out.

By now the philosophic argument for this has gained very wide acceptance: it is difficult to find reasonable people who argue that the redistribution of income is a sensible role for state and/ or local governments in principle. Most agree with both the equity component of the argument—in an open society characterized by much geographic mobility of persons, the public sector costs associated with concentrations of low-income people ought to be borne nationally, not locally—and the efficiency component—local efforts to depart from the national consensus on the proper degree of income redistribution will generate inefficient shifts in the location of people and economic activity.[3]

Areas with large burdens of low-income households tend

to lose their tax base but not their low-income households, and so they tax more and lose more. A national standard of income maintenance fully funded by the federal government and wholly indifferent to the location of the eligible households (city, suburb, or rural) would be more equitable and location-ally neutral. It is not an economic-development policy, but it would make all the states more equal in their pursuit of economic development. Obviously, if such a national system were in place, there would not only be less need to induce the indigent to move to locations where employment opportunities were greater but the size of the public financial inducement could be smaller. With the present system, a high price is imposed on those who leave a state with high social benefits for one with low benefits in search of employment. The poor can hardly be blamed if they exhibit the same prudence as businessmen in evaluating risk in the face of uncertainty.

As will be noted below, there is in the McGill report a very clear-headed notion of what the federal government should do which would indirectly aid urban areas. But the recommended hands-off policy for direct federal involvement in urban economic development is short sighted. The McGill report correctly recognizes that markets work, markets respond, and that it is fruitless to get in the way of inexorable market forces. But the market is never visionary. On rare but momentous occasions the public sector, particularly the federal government, has been visionary and the market has responded. New York State built the Erie Canal and thus linked the rich trans-Appalachia farm lands to the markets of the seaboard and Europe. The federal government electrified rural America, greatly increasing the productivity of agriculture in the United States. The interstate highway system has transformed the nation and reduced access and transport costs. The federal dams in the West have made possible the tremendous population and economic growth of the arrid Southwest. The federal project to put a man on the moon has spun off the growth industries of mini- and microcomputers.

All of those ventures were either too big or too risky (or both, or not profitable) for the private sector to take on. The common thread is that they all were technically innovative, huge capital projects with enormous spillover benefits for the private sector. There could be such opportunities in the future with great spillover benefits for urban economies (or rural economies) but only the federal government could marshall the resources. It would be shortsighted in the extreme to rule out in advance any federal involvement in great leaps forward.

To summarize this section, there are two major points about the federal role in urban economic development. Income maintenance is not an urban economic development policy but it should be fully funded by the federal government and stand-ardized nationally to make the states more equal in their pursuit of economic development. Second, the federal government should be postured to exploit special opportunities through capital projects if they appear to have great spillover benefits and not rule them out if the spillover benefits accrue wholly to urban areas.

10.2 Macroeconomic policies

As in all the modern industrial democracies, our central government is charged with maintaining a full-employment economy, stable prices, and productivity growth. Setting aside the fact that neither our nor the other governments can deliver as charged, they do try. The aim of the Employment Act of 1946, which formally gave that mandate to the president, was not to help cities and metropolitan areas. But to the extent that the federal government can sometimes help make that happen, that is, full employment growth with low inflation, it is the best single thing it can do for the older urban areas of the nation. This point was well made in the McGill Report.

What should constitute a reasonable federal urban policy role in the light of domestic trends that are transforming this nation and transnational trends that are drawing us into closer community with the world?

The federal government can best assume the well-being of the nation's people and the vitality of the communities in which they live by striving to create and maintain a vibrant national economy characterized by an attractive investment climate that is conducive to high rates of economic productivity and growth and defined by low rates of inflation, unemployment, and dependency.[4]

In Chapter 6, the cyclical behavior of the New York City economy was described, using the data assembled for estimating the quarterly version of the model. The long economic decline in the city, from 1969 to 1977, was documented, and it was shown that the severe national recession from 1973 to 1975 had a particularly adverse effect upon the local economy.

The quarterly version of the New York City model has been used to simulate total income and employment in the city under the full-employment case and under the actual situation from 1973 to 1978. (The full-employment GNP and unemployment rate of the United States used in the simulation were taken from the *Economic Report of the President, 1979.* The results of the simulation are presented in Table 10.1.)

For the worst year of the national recession, 1975, total city income was about $4.4 billion, or 9 percent, lower than the estimated level if the United States economy had been at full employment. That translates into a city employment 157,000 below what it might have been with full employment. No economic development scheme ever dreamed of would generate a 5 percent job boost in a single year, but that is roughly what a national economy at full employment might

Table 10.1
Simulation of the Impact of the Full Employment of the United States Economy on the NYC Economy between 1973–1978

	NYC Income (million 1972 $)			NYC Employment (thousands)		
Year	Control	Full Employment	Control–Full Employment	Control	Full Employment	Control–Full Employment
1973	$48,054	$47,949	+ $ 105	3,551	3,571	− 20
1974	46,476	47,647	− 1,171	3,566	3,524	+ 42
1975	43,024	47,431	− 4,407	3,276	3,433	− 157
1976	44,396	47,697	− 3,301	3,245	3,382	− 137
1977	45,033	47,421	− 2,388	3,204	3,316	− 112
1978	46,027	47,355	− 1,328	3,251	3,280	− 29

SOURCE: Computed for this study.

have produced. In 1976 and 1977 the job loss due to less-than-full employment is also more than 100,000.

Using the fiscal part of the model, the simulation was extended to estimate the impact of the six economically sensitive city tax revenues. Because there were tax-rate and base changes over that period, it is not appropriate to look at dollar amounts of tax revenues for the control case and full employment case. Instead, the calculated percentage reductions in revenues from those six taxes due to less-than-full employment are compared with the actual collections.

Fiscal Year	Actual Revenues, Six Taxes[a] (million $)	Percent Reduction from Full Employment Revenues
1973	$1,408	+ 0.3%
1974	1,450	− 3.3
1975	1,771	− 12.6
1976	2,092	− 9.4
1977	2,304	− 6.8
1978	2,432	− 3.8

[a] Personal income, sales, general corporation, financial corporation, utility, and unincorporated business taxes.

Fiscal year 1975 (July 1974 to June 1975) shows the largest estimated loss in city tax revenues attributed to less-than-full employment: -12.6%. Estimated losses in 1976 and 1977 are also substantial.

Other large old cities suffer employment losses and tax revenue losses in periods of recession, especially cities with a heavy industry export base such as Cleveland and Detroit. Recession will continue to be the most serious short-term economic problem facing cities so long as the federal government cannot deliver on its charge to maintain a full employment economy.

One of the ill effects of recession (and inflation and high interest rates) which hits large cities more so than other places is the quickened demise of small firms and the slowed birth of new small firms. That is impossible to simulate with this model. Historically, around 50 percent of establishments in urban areas have fewer than 20 employees, but the national proportion of such small establishments is closer to 25 percent.[5] Regional and urban economists have long recognized that a key function of cities historically has been to serve as an incubator of new small firms, often with new products and technology. The external economies and agglomeration economies of cities continue to be conducive to high-risk, underfunded ventures. Such enterprises are highly sensitive to the business cycle. So the long-run productivity of the nation, linked as it is to technological innovations, can benefit from a lower death rate and higher birth rate of small firms. And cities that spawn them will benefit too. Thus, the full-employment economy (with low inflation and interest rates) serves not only the nation but the big cities in critical ways. Full-employment policies are not urban economic-development policies, but there is nothing the federal government could do in direct urban economic development that comes even close to matching the

short- and long-run benefits to the big cities from full-employment growth.

It must be pointed out, recalling inexorable market forces,
that a long period of full-employment growth would probably
make the old large cities shrink at a faster rate than they
otherwise would. In simulations performed by Glickman with
his Philadelphia city and region model he found such a tendency. "Thus it appears—at least for the Philadelphia region—
that a rapidly growing national economy will lead to a relative
expansion of the suburbs at the expense of the central city."[6]
Indeed, the simulation presented for New York city above in
Table 10.1 shows that with the full-employment case, real city
income is high but very stable over the six years. With faster
productivity growth in the full-employment scenario, city employment falls steadily (not precipitously) over the six years.
The net change in jobs from 1973 to 1978 in the control case is
−300,000, and in the full employment case it is −291,000,
almost identical. Whether our big cities get smaller is of no
consequence. What is of consequence is that real income per
capita or per household grow, in and out of cities, and a full-
employment growth path for the national economy can make
that happen.

In the Prologue it was noted that old cities are cursed with
neighborhoods almost depopulated but still very much full of
obsolete, abandoned, deteriorated structures. That is part of
the mess capitalism leaves behind. Whatever viable use the
land underneath may now have, those potential uses are constrained by the cost of clearing out the junk. And because of
the substantial externalities (positive and negative) character-
istic of urban land and structures, no single plot in the midst
of such devastation appreciates by just demolishing its structure; rather, it appreciates by demolishing all of the structures.

Since investors and the public benefit from the mobility

of capital in our system, it is inequitable to impose the external cost of all that used-up immobile capital upon the people who happen to live in the older cities where it is concentrated. Thus it is sound economics to place the burden for demolition and clearing squarely upon the federal government. Sound public finance suggests a federal excise tax upon investment in structures, residential (other than farm) and nonresidential, to be used solely for demolition and clearing of abandoned structures. In 1983, investment spending on those two types of capital was $257 billion. A tax of three-quarters of 1 percent would yield about $1.9 billion annually. Of course that is not enough to make a substantial dent in the national inventory of devestated areas in one year, but over many years it could do the job. All of the legal work and paperwork necessary prior to demolition should be strictly in the hands (and hair) of the cities and states. The federal role should be limited to paying contractors for demolition and clearing. Nor should the federal government have any involvement in what happens to the land after it is cleared. Its reuse is best left either to the market or to local government or to both. Admittedly that is not an activist stance by Washington in urban economic development, but since no one knows how to make such development happen, it is appropriate to use public resources to simply remove impediments and allow market forces to respond.

To summarize this section, there are two key points about macroeconomic policy. Facilitating a full-employment national economy is the best single thing Washington can do for the cities, and if the big cities shrink faster as a result, so be it. Second, the federal government should assume responsibility for the physical clearing out of the devestated areas of older cities and then walk away, allowing the market and the locality to determine the land's reuse.

10.3   Microeconomic policies

By microeconomic policies here is meant those aimed at specific industries, specific places, or special technological opportunities (such as those past ones noted in the Prologue). The latest idea in this arena for federal urban economic development is the Kemp-Garcia bill, endorsed by the president in his 1982 State of the Union address, which proposes urban enterprise zones. Ten to 25 zones would be designated each year for three years. To qualify, an area must have characteristics such as very high unemployment, a large proportion of poverty households, and recent population loss. The federal government would give tax incentives to businesses in the zone in the form of tax credits, capital gains tax forgiveness, and exclusion of a part of gross income from taxation, the exclusion diminishing over time. Tax credits would also be given to employees, and local government must participate by also giving tax reductions to zone businesses, improved services, and simplified regulation. A minimum population of 4000 would be required to be eligible for zone designation. Clearly, an upper limit will be set on the size of a zone, and therein lies the rub. One analyst in New York has calculated that 26 community districts in the city, containing 2 million residents and 825,000 (or half) of the city's low-income population, would qualify for designation as urban-enterprise zones. With at most 25 zones to be designated nationally each year for three years and with New York having about 3 percent of the nation's poor, he concludes New York might be entitled to one zone per year or a total of three zones.[7] If the upper limit set on the size of a zone is as generous as 75,000 residents (unlikely), then only three of the 26 community districts qualifying could receive designation. And if New York can get three zones in three years, Philadelphia, Cleveland, Baltimore, and Detroit could probably each get one zone in three years. Bridgeport and Terre Haute might get none. It is not that the zones are so few, but inevitably because of fiscal prudence they will be so small as to affect a slight proportion of the eligible residents and businesses.

Thus the urban enterprise zone concept is not a sound urban economic development program, it is a federal sweepstakes. Some few would receive windfall gains, while the majority of the eligible businesses and areas would receive nothing. But some few businesses would also receive penalties if they were in competition with firms suddenly hit by the lightning of urban enterprise zone designation. It might effectively accelerate the decline in eligible areas near a winning area. This is pork-barrel legislation at its worst, with the only sure winners being lobbyists and law firms which are lucky enough to assist in getting designation for some public-private local coalition.

Because it is so selective, and arbitrary, in who receives benefits, it is bad economics. This type of tax expenditure financing is bad public finance too because the cost is unknown. "For one, it is difficult to predict the price in foregone taxes the policy (Urban Enterprise Zones) or program will engender, since the indirect dollar costs will depend on how well the policy succeeds as an incentive for private capital to participate."[8]

Presumably, a premise behind the urban enterprise zone is the notion that businesses in distressed urban areas are at a competitive disadvantage. By giving them an offsetting advantage and stimulating other firms to move into the distressed area, employment in the area would hopefully expand, absorbing the unemployed residents of the area.

The premise of a competitive disadvantage is not a bad one. The model equations presented in Chapter 3 show that

Table 10.2
Price Elasticities of Output for Manufacturing Industries in SCA and NYC

	Regional Relative Price Elasticity	
Manufacturing Industry	SCA	NYC
Food	−3.3	−8.8
Tobacco	[a]	−13.9
Lumber	+2.9[b]	+2.9
Furniture	−2.4	−4.7
Paper	+1.6	−2.1
Chemicals[c]	−0.8	−4.5
Rubber	−3.0	−1.0
Stone	[d]	−5.7
Primary metals	+3.2	−2.9
Fabricated metals	+2.6	−2.6
Machinery	+0.5[b]	−5.7
Electrical machinery	−1.7	−5.2
Transportation equipment	−3.4	−5.2
Instruments[c]	−1.2	−4.9

[a] No equation estimated.
[b] Not statistically significant.
[c] Export industry for the SCA but not NYC.
[d] Relative price variable not in the equation.
Source: Computed for this study from industry-output equations in Appendix Tables 2, 4, and 5.

for many industries in the SCA and New York City, particularly the goods-producing industries, industry output is inversely related to the regional relative price variable (the region's CPI divided by the United States CPI). The same is true for the equations for the Baltimore model in Chapter 4.

The model equations for the SCA and New York City have been used to calculate the regional relative price elasticity of industry output for all manufacturing industries which are presumed to be local (rather than export) industries. The elasticities for corresponding city and SCA industries are compared in Table 10.2

Of the 14 industries shown, 13 of the city industries have negative price elasticities (as would be expected), and they tend to be exceedingly large (12 are larger than 2.0). This indicates very great sensitivity to changes in regional relative prices (recall that the price variable measures the relative rate of price changes in the area versus price changes in the nation). Further, 12 of the 14 city industries show greater inverse sensitivity than do their regional counterparts. In fact, in a few cases where the city's industry elasticity is negative, it is positive in the SCA. That curiosity may be due to a tendency to shift output from city firms to firms outside the city (but within the SCA) in periods of differentially higher inflation (that is, when the relative price variable is rising).

Although some of the city elasticities appear unbelievably high, the consistent pattern of greater price sensitivity in the city than in the SCA suggests that manufacturing firms inside big cities are, *ceteris paribus,* more sensitive to changes in their competitive position than are firms in the same industry and region but not in the city. That inference from the model, rather than doing violence to our qualitative impressions, tends to support them.

The implication for federal urban economic policy is to do something evenhanded to lower costs (or slow their rate of increase) for *all* manufacturing industries in *all* cities. A simple, straightforward policy of modest cost would be to "forgive" two percentage points of the employer's share of the social security tax on manufacturing establishments inside central cities. Using 1980 data, the average annual earnings of manufacturing workers was $15,000.[9] Two percentage points off the employer's share would lower the annual cost of labor by $300 per person. A firm with 20 employees would save $6000 in labor costs. If roughly 4 million of the 20 million manufacturing work force is in central cities, the annual cost to the U.S. Treasury would be $1.2 billion. That could be pared down by limiting the cut in the social security tax to blue-collar workers, or to workers with annual earnings less than some maximum. It should not be pared down by limiting the two percentage point tax forgiveness to small establishments. A firm contemplating moving a city plant with 400 workers to a noncity site would face an immediate $120,000 rise in labor costs after the move, if the policy were in place and it applied to all city manufacturing establishments. The reverse would hold for a firm contemplating shifting a plant into a city.

The Urban Development action Grant (UDAG) program is a good urban economic development program because it provides limited federal assistance to key central city projects which have private sector backing. The passive role of the federal government is appropriate in that it should not be involved in choosing the projects. The critical issues is finding the right projects, and that falls to local government and private-sector interests in cities. The chapter on the role of local government in urban economic development addresses the issue of identifying the worthy projects.

Notes

1. President's Commission for a National Agenda for the Eighties, *A National Agenda for the Eighties* Washington, D.C.: U.S. Government Printing Office, 1980.

2. Gail Schwartz, *Bridges to the Future: Forces Impacting Urban Economics,* Economic Development Administration, U.S. Department of Commerce, p. 1978.

3. Dick Netzer, "Public Sector Investment Strategies in the Mature Metropolis," *The Mature Metropolis,* Charles L. Levin (ed.), Lexington, Mass.: Lexington Books, 1978, p. 240.

4. President's Commission for a National Agenda for the Eighties, op. cit., p. 167.

5. Schwartz, *op. cit.,* p. 15.

6. Norman Glickman, *Econometric Analysis of Regional Systems,* New York: Academic Press, 1977, p. 190.

7. David Grossman, "What Kemp-Garcia Would do for New York City," *City Almanac* (June, 1981).

8. Regina Armstrong, "The Enterprise Zone Concept: Fiscal and Urban Policy Issues," *City Almanac* (June, 1981).

9. U.S. Department of Commerce, *Survey of Current Business,* (April, 1981), pp. 5–12.

The Local Government Role in Urban Economic Development

11.1 Saving jobs versus creating jobs

Given the historical fact that large central cities have high concentrations of jobs and that they tend to lose jobs over time as economic activity and households become more dispersed, then policies aimed at saving city jobs (that is, slowing the rate of loss) would seem more productive than policies aimed at creating jobs. There are two problems about creating jobs. The first is that job creation is a mysterious process not well understood, least of all by local government. To prescribe that local governments formulate policies to create jobs is tantamount to prescribing that the Supreme Court reduce street crime. Both lack the knowledge and the power to deliver on such a charge. Of course local government is expert at creating local government jobs, even in the face of shrinking demand for their output, but that is part of the reason for their difficulties, as will be shown below.

The second problem about creating jobs in the private sector relates to how state and local governments have tended to pursue that objective, namely by the smoke-stack chasing noted in the Prologue. As stated there, even if one locality is successful in luring in firms, the overall effect is tiny and the tax and other advantages given the new arrivals is inequitable treatment of resident businesses.

In order to formulate policies for local government to save jobs that exist requries an understanding of the little that is known about how private sector jobs get created and destroyed. Changes in technology can both create and destroy jobs. The tendency is to create more higher-skill jobs and destroy more lower-skill jobs. The dynamics of the individual firm have much to do with job creation and destruction. First, consider the single-establishment firm (all their jobs at one site). An expanding national economy (with low inflation and low interest rates thrown in for good measure) will increase the birth rate of new firms, lower the death (failure) rate of existing firms, and prompt more existing firms to grow rather than contract and thus increase jobs. A contracting national economy (with high interest rates and high inflation) will do all the opposite things and thus reduce jobs. Since new firms tend to be small, and small firms tend to be vulnerable (they are overrepresented among firm failures), and small firms are more concentrated in central cities, then this process of national economic expansion (especially with low interest and inflation) is a great blessing for employment in cities. The process of national economic contraction (especially with high interest and inflation) is a great curse for cities.

The multiestablishment firm (with jobs at two or more sites), tends to be larger than the single-establishment firm. The births and failures of firms play less important roles in total job creation and destruction by large firms. The oldest are usually the least efficient (that is, highest cost) of the firm's establishments, and those tend to be cut back (or closed down) in an economic contraction. And the oldest establishments tend to be inside central cities. In an economic expansion, the oldest establishments will be more fully utilized. For most types of manufacturing operations there is a state-of-the-art, optimal size for any establishment that is most cost effective. That optimal size, although varying greatly across industries, has tended to rise over time. So, when a firm chooses to expand, it may increase the size of one of its existing establishments or build a new one at a new site. Given the filled-in and built-up character of central cities, chances are that the establishment in the central city will not be the one chosen for expansion to optimal size because the adjacent space is not available or its cost (purchase plus demolition of existing structures) is too high compared with noncentral-city sites. And chances are a new establishment will not be built in the central city for lack of sites with desirable characteristics. In an expanding economy, over the long run, the multiunit manufacturing firm will phase out of use its older, too small, less efficient establishments. And those tend to be in central cities. So even in a long-run, full-employment growth economy (with low inflation and interest rates) some kinds of goods production, and the associated jobs, will tend to disappear from central cities even without the trauma of overblown "moveouts." They simply wither away.

In all of these scenarios, there are two key economic forces at play: the state of the national economy (expansion or contraction of aggregate demand) and relative costs. There is absolutely nothing local government can do about the national economy. It can have an effect upon relative costs, marginally, for good or for ill.

Saving jobs already in the city requires that local government recognize that relative costs (that is, the costs of operating in the city relative to operating somewhere else) are of major long-run importance. Recognizing their importance, every local program, new or old, every controllable expenditure item, every law and regulation should be scrutinized in terms of the effect (if any) of each upon relative costs of operating in the city by private sector organizations. Those that appear to make relative costs higher viz-à-viz other places should be evaluated in terms of possible offsetting benefits. If acceptable tradeoffs can be made, then the law or program or expenditure should be altered in the effort to improve competitive position at the margin.

This is *not* to suggest a dismantling of what Peter Bearse defines as urbanization. "By urbanization I mean much more than inreasing population and city size. I mean the panoply of institutions and behavior associated with urban life such as interest groups, unionization, social welfare programs and higher expectations regarding the 'quality of life.' "[1] Of course, every large, old city with state help could dramatically lower its relative costs by abolishing unemployment insurance, workmens' compensation, and unions, by closing its public high schools, and by allowing firms to dump raw waste into the rivers and belch black smoke into the air. Firms would be attracted from South Carolina and South Korea. As Bearse also points out, it is impossible (and undesirable) to turn back the clock. Rumania (sans planners) or South Korea cannot be re-created in Lower Michigan or New Jersey or Maryland. Planners may try in South Carolina, but to the extent that they are successful in industrialization, then urbanization, as defined by Bearse, will certainly follow.

The Baltimore metropolitan area has been used to simulate the employment effects of a charge in relative costs. The ratio of the Baltimore consumer price index to the United States consumer price index is the variable in the model which represents relative costs. When that ratio rises, it means consumer prices in the Baltimore area are rising faster than consumer prices in the nation (or falling more slowly, which hardly ever happens). To the extent that consumer prices reflect the underlying cost pressures from wages, intermediate and primary goods, rents, taxes, and transport costs, than the ratio

Table 11.1
Simulation of Increase in Relative Price Variable, Baltimore SMSA[a]

Industry	Change in Income Due to 1 Percent Rise in BCPIUS (million 1972 $)	VAPE 1978	Change in Employment, 1978
Textiles	−$ 1.7	$ 9,320	−182
Apparel	−6.6	7,450	−886
Furniture	−2.1	9,358	−224
Printing	−6.6	13,208	−500
Communication and electric and gas utilities	−11.7	23,872	−490
Retail trade	−26.4	7,003	−3,770
Total	−$55.1		−6,052
Percent of 1978 level	−0.5%		−0.7%

[a] *Variables*
BCPIUS = Consumer price index for Baltimore ÷ Consumer price index for United States
VAPE = Value added per employee, 1972 $.
SOURCE: Computed using Baltimore industry equations in Appendix Tables 8 and 9.

does represent an aggregate measure of relative costs. Table 11.1 shows the simulated loss in income and employment, for 1978, in the Baltimore SMSA assuming a rise of 1 percent in the relative cost variable. The simulated job loss is about 6000 or −0.7 percent down from the 1978 level of 882,000. A 1 percent fall in the relative cost variable would have the opposite effect, that is, a simulated gain of 6000 jobs, *ceteris paribus.* Even in a metropolitan area as large as Baltimore, a rise of 6000 in employment could lower the area unemployment rate from 7.0 to 6.4 percent.

Other than scrutinizing its programs, regulations, and laws for opportunities to improve the competitive position of the central city (without unraveling the urban quality of life), the main chance for such improvement within the domain of local government is to put its own fiscal house in order.

11.2 Fiscal difficulties of local government as barriers to an improved competitive position

With the fanfare that accompanied the near bankruptcy of Newark, New York, Detroit, and Cleveland there has developed an increased public awareness that those cities are not alone in their fiscal difficulties. Many of the older cities, large and small, face a chronic difficulty in raising sufficient revenues to cover expenditures.

In Part I, the model economic forecast presented for New York City included a forecast of city tax revenues which was compared with the revenue and expenditure forecast made by the city government in its Financial Plan (see Table 8.7). Both the city's own projections and the model projections anticipate a budget gap for FY 1986 through FY 1988. In the annual Financial Plan, the city is required to set forth a program to close any anticipated gap. The program often includes three basic components: reductions in expenditures through workforce cutbacks, anticipated increases in state and/or federal aid, and increases in local taxes.

Although other central cities are not required to prepare such a financial plan, their mayors and budget directors face the same problem of expenditures tending to rise faster than own-source revenues. The bailout for most of them in recent history has been the sharp increases in federal and state assistance. Netzer has shown that from the late 1960s to the mid-1970s the local government expenditures of the ten largest cities in the northeast and north central states (excluding New York city) rose about 60 percent. Over the same period, their various revenue sources grew as shown in the table. The three own-source revenue items increased at a much slower rate than the 60 percent rise in expenditures. The very rapid rise in federal and state revenue sources made it possible to cover expenditures.

Revenue Source	Percent Increase, 1969–1970 to 1974–1975, for Local Government Units in Ten Cities[a]
Federal government sources	208
State government sources	115
Property taxes	27
Other local taxes	52
User charges	28

[a] Baltimore, Boston, Chicago, Cleveland, Detroit, Milwaukee, Minneapolis, Philadelphia, Pittsburgh, and St. Louis.

SOURCE: Dick Netzer, "Public Sector Investment Strategies in the Mature Metropolis," *The Mature Metropolis* Chas. L. Leven (ed.), p. 232.

Given the low likelihood of the federal government properly assuming full responsibility for income redistribution programs (Medicaid, and aid to families with dependent children), no matter what the outcome of the New Federalism, local government should anticipate that combined total state and federal aid will no longer be a growth industry. That, in turn, narrows from three to two the options for bringing budgets into balance: cutting expenditures and raising own-source revenues (taxes and user charges). If expenditures are cut by reductions in work force and corresponding reductions in the level of services, and revenues are raised by increasing tax rates and adding new taxes, then local government will be a key contributor to further erosion of the competitive position of the locality. Raising tax burdens and diminished local services can accelerate the disappearance of the tax base, which necessitates further tax increases, and so the dismal downward spiral continues.

A downward spiral need not be the outcome. Local government in big cities could be much more cost effective in performing its functions and could dispense with some functions altogether. The fact that New York City sharply reduced its numbers of police and firemen during the fiscal emergency but objective measures of performance or output for those services showed that they did not deteriorate suggests that the labor-intensive functions of local government in big cities could be cut back without a curtailment of public services.[2] And if the methods of delivering some services by local government utilized the technology and the management methods widely used in some organizations which are forced to be cost conscious by competition, it might even be possible to improve the level of some public services with fewer public employees. Management in local government is no better (and no worse) than in other large organizations. Good management emerges in organizations so harried by competition that survival seems precarious. On the one hand, it is difficult to imagine local government initiating changes in its mode of operation. On the other hand, the worst possible response of state and federal government would be to bail out big-city governments with operating subsidies. It is the worst because it rewards inertia and inefficient operations.

A modest proposal for forcing reform in operations down the throats of big-city governments, and thus striking a blow for an improved competitive position of those cities, would be a federal law requiring an intensive degree of external scrutiny and disclosure through auditing firms. Each city which sells municipal bonds would have to be audited annually and the auditing firm (or other firm chosen by the auditor) would be required to perform a management analysis of operations with recommendations for overhaul the first year of the audit. In subsequent years the auditors would be required to report on progress (or lack thereof) in the internal reform of operations. The hope would be that the bond rating agencies (not to mention the mayor's opposition) and the investment banks would be influenced by the progress reports, and the city governments would feel external pressure to reform.

To sum up this section, the New York City budget gap forecast with the model is not a unique case. Given the likelihood of reduced growth in combined state and federal assistance to cities, hard times lie ahead. If business as usual prevails at city halls, tax burdens will rise, services and their quality will decline, and local government, rather than being an agent for gaining on improved competitive position, will be a major force in its deterioration. This bleak outlook, combined with some good advice, has been expressed well by Dick Netzer.

> If urban governments are not rescued from without and do *not* make major changes in their conventional modes of operation, the prospects for the mature city are indeed dismal. Public expenditure will be reduced in the manner it has been in the cities hit by fiscal crises, like New York, Detroit, Cleveland and Newark, more or less across-the-board, with all conventional activities continued by marginally smaller, but considerably more superannuated workforces doing the same old things, only much more inadequately.
>
> But the fact is that *none* of the major services provided by local governments are performed in ways that differ significantly from the methods and approaches used fifty years ago. Police patrol, refuse collection and disposal, schooling, health services, street repair, park maintenance, library operations and transit operations have actually changed a lot less in the past fifty years than they did in the previous half century. . . .
>
> Obviously, if things have changed so little in fifty years, change must be difficult indeed. And so it is, so much so that I conclude that the approach often urged on local governments, the application of "modern management methods" to ordinary operations, is a fruitless one. Instead, what is necessary is the stripping away of functions and activities of marginal value, leaving them to private entrepreneurial initiatives or leaving them entirely undone. It is foolish to expensively sweep city streets if the result is to reduce street litter by less than 5 percent; it is preposterous to deploy firefighters to rescue cats from trees; it is pointless to maintain hospital clinics to treat the common cold; it is wasteful in the extreme to use municipal government money to subsidize commercial sports.
>
> In short, governments in the mature metropolis must learn

to combine tight-fistedness and an unwillingness to do all sorts of "good things" with an eye for the main chance, that is, the spending of public money on things that actually, *not allegedly*, foster the competitive position of the area, things that range from the prosaic (like replacement of essential elements of infrastructure) to the way-out (like becoming the locus for large-scale experiments in new waste management technologies). And governments must also learn how to stay out of the way of the entrepreneurial energies and initiatives of residents, firms and nonprofit institutions; the potential supply of these energies and initiatives in the mature city remains very large.[3]

11.3 Indirect and direct roles for local government in urban economic development

The indirect role for local government in urban economic development is of major importance. And that is in doing the routine jobs traditional to local government, namely, delivering services, maintaining and replacing public infrastructure. But as was made clear in Section 11.2, it is critical for the long-run competitive position of the mature city that local government do those things more efficiently than it has in the past.

The importance of the maintenance and replacement of the infrastructure for old cities in holding or improving their competitive position is brought out in considering the analysis of New York City's export base, discussed in Chapter 3. With the transformation of the New York City economy, its export industry jobs have become primarily office jobs. Those jobs are highly concentrated in the 286 million square feet of office space in midtown and downtown Manhattan.[4] That concentration requires the continued operation of the network of suburban commuter trains and subway lines (not all of them). If that mass-transit network collapsed under the weight of accumulated neglect, the long-run impact upon New York's export base would be devastating. It is unlikely to collapse completely, but if its diminished performance in recent years (insufficient capacity, late trains, frequent breakdowns, and long waits) holds steady, than the export base of New York city will be hurt.

Not all the older cities, of course, have mass-transit systems, but they do not have other types of aging infrastructure, the contined efficient functioning of which is critical for the long-run competitive position of the city. Highways and streets must be maintained and improved because good access and lowered congestion are important components in the competitive position of any city. The smaller cities of the 1940s which were passed by in both jet airport service and interstate highway links have become backwater places. But not all the infrastructure has to be maintained. The substantial population losses of most large, old central cities in the past 20 years have resulted in excess capacity. Underutilized schools, fire stations, and police stations could be shut down, and the students and personnel redistributed.

The direct role for local government in urban economic development is of minor importance. It is minor because it pales before the tasks set out above which do have a long-run, but indirect, impact upon the competitive position of any city. The direct role includes seizing special opportunities, usually a key capital project, and assisting in making it go forward. The urban development action grants (UDAG) program of the federal government is the best current example in which local government initiative (or response to private interests in the city) plays a direct role in urban economic development. The critical issue, especially with development resources so scarce, is to pick the right projects and not to throw the money away on something worthless or give it away on projects which private backers would have fully financed without any public assistance.

In New York one of the best examples of a good use of

UDAG funds is the Portman Hotel project. The nature of New York's export base described earlier is such that it is importantly served and enhanced by ancillary activities such as restaurants, hotels, theaters, and convention facilities.

In the late 1970s as the city's economy improved and visitors, particularly foreign, both business and tourist, flooded in, some flaws or holes in the local economic fabric became more evident.

1. lack of a convention center with capacity to handle the largest conventions
2. shortage of first-class hotel rooms
3. sleezy and threatening environment in the theater district on the west side of midtown Manhattan

Construction of a convention center began on the west side. New and renovated hotels were in the making, but all were situated in the prime office tower area on the east side of Manhattan, or no further west than the Avenue of the Americas.

The Portman Hotel project, a 2000 room convention hotel assisted with UDAG funds, is to be built in the Times Square area in the heart of the theater district. It will be closer to the new convention center than other large hotels. The likely spillover benefits in terms of upgrading the surrounding buildings and shops could be substantial. Theater patrons may be attracted to linger rather than flee the area, and an improved ambience cannot hurt the theaters. Considering where all the other new hotels have been built, public assistance with UDAG funds seems appropriate because the private developers face a greater risk on that site and the spillover benefits for the public could be great if the hotel results in an upgrading of the area.

Baltimore provides one of the best examples of local public and private initiative seizing special opportunities for economic development. In the 1960s a major technological change, the containerization of nonbulk ocean cargo, transformed some United States ports (the ones that have survived). Containerization makes it possible to load or unload a ship in 20 percent of the time formerly required, with great reductions in breakage and pilferage. Containers can be transferred to trains or to trucks. A port worker can move 600 tons of freight per week with the new system versus 32 tons formerly. Ships designed especially for container cargo are much larger and it is far more cost effective for them to stop at a single port rather than to meander along the coast before returning across the ocean.[5] The Port of Baltimore (a public organization) spent $125 million in construction, mostly on port container facilities, over the past twenty years.[6]

But the full advantages of containerization were not reaped by eastern ports at first because the heavy regulation of railroads and trucking provided no incentive for land cariers to develop attractive rates to move containers to distant inland points. The Canadian railroads were not so burdened. Integrated through service at attractive rates from Chicago and Detroit through Canada to the new container port at Halifax diverted both Midwest exports and imports from eastern United States ports. Halifax is more than one day closer to European ports than United States eastcoast ports.[7]

In the late seventies more-rational rate setting in rail and truck transport has changed that situation, and the benefits have abounded to the port of Baltimore, which is closer to some large midwestern export sources and import destinations than New York. Further investment of $75 million on the port is slated to be completed by 1985. As a result, Baltimore's share of North Atlantic general cargo in the past 20 years has moved up from 12 percent to about 18 percent, while in the same period New York's share fell from 62 percent to 46 percent. In addition, the tremendous export demand for coal from the United States, which is separate from general cargo, that has developed since the advent of OPEC in 1973 has greatly increased activity in the Port of Baltimore.[8]

In the same period, Baltimore managed to win the new Social Security Administration headquarters, to revitalize its downtown waterfront, to rescue a neighborhood of deteriorating old houses with $1 sales and sweat equity, and to host a first-rate medical center at Johns Hopkins University. All of this plus the port represent direct economic development activity, if not initiated at least fostered by the local public sector. What it all adds up to in terms of jobs is impossible to say. As noted before, the creation of private sector jobs is a mysterious process. The symbiotic connection between greatly increased foreign trade through Baltimore and all other economic activity in the city is impossible to measure. But history suggests that there is a link. In 1800, Charleston, South Carolina was the fifth largest city in the nation, slightly smaller than Baltimore, which ranked third, and both were major ports.[9] Charleston is no longer a major port, nor is it a major city. Baltimore, however, continues to rank among the ten largest cities of the nation.

Notes

1. Peter J. Bearse, "Government as Innovator: A New Paradigm for State Economic Development Policy," *The New England Journal of Business and Economics,* Vol. 2, No. 2 (Spring, 1976), p. 46.

2. Dennis C. Smith, "Police"; Peter Kolesar and Kenneth L. Rider, "Fire," *Setting Municipal Priorities, 1982,* C. Brecher and R. Horton, editors, New York: Russell Sage Foundation, 1981, pp. 229–290.

3. Dick Netzer, "Public Sector Investment Strategies in the Mature Metropolis," *The Mature Metropolis,* Charles L. Leven (ed.), Lexington, Mass.: Lexington Books, 1978, pp. 248–249.

4. Matthew Drennan, "The Local Economy and Local Revenues," *Setting Municipal Priorities, 1984,* C. Brecher & R. Horton (editors), New York: New York University Press, 1983, p. 32.

5. William D. Middleton, "True-Train Tip-Off," *Trains* (March 1971), p. 24.

6. "The Great Port War," *Forbes* (October 16, 1978), p. 170.

7. "An End Run Around U.S. Ports," *Business Week* (March 16, 1970).

8. "The Great Port War," op. cit.

9. Matthew Drennan, "Economy," *Setting Municipal Priorities, 1982,* op. cit., p. 57.

12

Local Taxes and Economic Development Policy

12.1 Introduction

In the previous chapter on the role of local government in urban economic development, it was noted that the taxes imposed by local government have an impact upon the competitive position of the locality, but the matter of specific types of taxes on various activities was not addressed. The analysis in Part I of New York and the SCA would suggest that, as a general rule, the weakest or most vulnerable industries be taxed less than the stronger parts of the economy. In the case of New York city, the weakest industries—measured by their severe shrinkage in employment—are the goods production and distribution part of the export base, plus all the other manufacturing industries. Again, the case of New York is not unique among old, large central cities because collectively they have all lost manufacturing jobs.

The New York City model presented in Part I (along with a further extension of it) has been used to analyze the employment effects of changes in some local tax rates. The elaborate simulation described was originally performed for the city's Office of Economic Development. Following the simulation, the ramifications for other large central cities are summarized.

12.2 New York City taxes and industry output

The fiscal soundness of New York City government ultimately rests upon the health and vitality of the city's economy. And the city's economy is not unaffected by the local tax structure. Roughly two-thirds of city government revenues are from its own sources (city taxes, fees, and charges), primarily taxes. From the viewpoint of economic development, the fundamental question about the existing structure and mix of city taxes is how they affect the city's economy. Specifically, how responsive is employment in New York to specific tax rate and base changes, and what changes in tax rates would have the most favorable employment effects?

In order to address the questions posed above, an alternative set of annual industry-output equations have been estimated for New York. Those equations link output and, indirectly, employment in city industries to past changes in the rate and base of relevant city taxes. That is, they attempt to measure the sensitivity of output by industry to city tax rates. The estimated equations, which necessarily include variables other than tax rates alone, are then used to simulate the employment effects of possible future changes in city tax rates.

For most of the 21 city export industries, time-series equations have been estimated. The dependent variable is always the constant-dollar measure of output for that industry. To review the calculation of the output measure,

$$CY_{it} = (VAPE_{it})CE_{it}$$

where,

CY_{it} = city output of industry i in year t, in 1972 dollars
$VAPE_{it}$ = national value added per employee of industry i in year t, in 1972 dollars
CE_{it} = city employment in industry i and year t

For this analysis, the appropriate city tax rate was introduced as one of the independent variables in each of the export industry equations. The purpose is to determine if and to what extent the output of a city export industry is sensitive to changes in city tax rates. The a priori expectation is that industry output is inversely related to the city tax rate imposed on that industry. In the case of highly monopolistic or oligopolistic industries, that may not be the case. For five export industries, no equations are presented because either no city tax rate appeared relevant to output in that industry (such as social services and nonprofit membership organizations, S.I.C. 83 and 86), or statistically acceptable equations could not be estimated. The list of excluded export industries is shown below.

S.I.C.

83 and 86	social services and nonprofit membership organizations
84 and 89	miscellaneous services, museums, zoos, and botanical gardens
64	insurance agents and brokers
63	insurance carriers
78	motion pictures

The output equations presented below, for both the export industries and the local industries, are used in the following section to measure the employment effects of hypothetical changes in tax rates. Any industry-output estimate, or change in output, can be used to derive an industry-employment estimate, or change in employment as follows.

$$CE_{it} = \frac{CY_{it}}{\text{VAPE}_{it}}$$

The equations estimate or predict CY (city output) for each industry. Separate equations have been estimated for predicting VAPE (a national variable) for each industry (see Chapter 3). Consequently, having a forecast of CY for any industry and any year, VAPE can also be forecast for that industry and year, and so the corresponding industry employment forecast can be calculated for that year using the above identity.

Table 12.1 presents the estimated equations for the city export industries. They are all annual time-series equations estimated for 1958 to 1977. The dependent variable in each equation is output, in millions of 1972 dollars, of the industry named. Each equation has at least one city tax rate among the independent variables, the tax rate which is assumed to be most germane for that industry. The other independent variables are mostly national because it is assumed that export industries are responsive to the national economy. The explanatory power of the equations ranges from quite good (seven have adjusted R^2 values above .90) to mediocre (four have adjusted R^2 values below .80).

Of the tax-rate variables, 10 have the expected negative sign and six have positive signs. Only five of the 10 tax-rate variables with negative coefficients are statistically significant at the .10 level (see the t statistics below each coefficient). However, the absence of statistical significance in the other five is not necessarily due to weak or nonexistent correlation with the dependent variable but rather due to multicolinearity (that is, high correlation among independent variables in the same equation which increases the size of the standard errors of the partial regression coefficients and thus reduces the calculated t statistic).

Among the 16 export industries with estimated equations, eight have the general corporation tax rate as the relevant tax variable. Only the banking equation has the financial corporation tax rate as a variable, and it is negative and highly significant. Only the real estate equation has the commercial rent tax rate as a variable, and it too is negative and highly

Table 12.1
NYC Export Industry Equations (n = 20)[a]

Equation Number	S.I.C. Code	Dependent Variable	Constant	Independent Variables, Coefficients, and t Statistics (in parentheses)	Adjusted R^2	Durbin-Watson	Standard Error (million $)
CXT 1	23	CYAPP =	6,437	−14.61 CTXRGB − 77.37 UUNEMPR − 4,482 SCPIUS (2.3) (7.8) (4.9)	.928	1.4	$ 56.7
CXT 2	27	CYPRNT =	2,899	−2.907 CTXRGB − 83.64 UUNEMPR − 1,061 SCPIUS (0.4) (7.9) (1.1)	.804	1.6	60.5
CXT 3	31	CYLETH =	1,224	−0.1882 CTXRGB − 21.47 UUNEMPR − 909.8 SCPIUS (0.1) (9.3) (4.3)	.896	1.4	13.2
CXT 4	39	CYMMAN =	2,469	−4.292 CTXRGB − 31.92 UUNEMPR − 1,652 SCPIUS (1.3) (6.1) (3.4)	.861	1.9	29.9
CXT 5	44	CYWATT =	4,877	−8.457 CTXRGB − 47.37 UUNEMPR − 3,961 SCPIUS (1.7) (6.1) (5.6)	.918	1.5	44.3
CXT 6	45	CYAIRT =	−292.9	−7.033 CTXRGB − 24.83 UUNEMPR + 1.107 UGNP (1.1) (4.3) (10.2)	.975	1.4	32.1
CXT 7	47	CYTSRV =	115.3	+1.519 CTXRGB − 6.680 UUNEMPR + 0.1565 UGNP (0.6) (2.8) (3.6)	.887	1.7	12.9
CXT 8	48	CYCOMM =	411.3	+46.00 CTXRUT − 26.57 UUNEMPR + 0.9863 UGNP (0.6) (2.1) (8.1)	.914	1.4	64.1
CXT 9	50 & 51	CYWHOL =	3,726	−11.36 CTXRGB + 95.97 UUNEMPR + 0.6162 UGNP (0.8) (7.0) (2.4)	.793	1.6	75.3
CXT 10	60	CYBANK =	646.2	−54.37 CTXRFIN + 420.1 DUM66 + 1.008 UGNP (3.1) (2.6) (1.9)	.686	0.9	171.0
CXT 11	62	CYSEC =	2,317	+173.4 CTXRUB − 197.8 UUNEMPR + 0.1586 USTOCKV − 173.3 UTRSBLL (2.2) (3.2) (1.7) (3.3)	.753	2.0	217.6
CXT 12	65 & 66	CYRELC =	−440.1	−73.07 CTXRCMR − 70.49 CTXRUB + 2.845 SCPIUS (2.5) (1.9) (0.8)	.717	0.9	166.1
CXT 13	73	CYBSRV =	494.4	+1.576 CTXRUB − 38.35 UUNEMPR + 6.009 UGEXT (0.1) (4.0) (5.6)	.944	1.2	54.7
CXT 14	80	CYMED =	−397.1	+14.83 CTXRUB + 1.817 UGNP (0.8) (10.6)	.967	0.9	72.2
CXT 15	81	CYLEGL =	52.09	+4.862 CTXRUB + 0.7502 UGNP (0.3) (5.9)	.897	0.5	53.8
CXT 16	82	CYEDUC =	−42.23	−19.03 CTXRPI − 10.98 UUNEMPR + 0.5646 UGNP (0.8) (3.5) (4.9)	.908	1.2	30.6

[a] Each dependent variable is output, in millions of 1972 $, of industry named.

significant. The other tax rates which appear as explanatory variables are the utility tax, the unincorporated business tax, and the personal income tax. Those three always have either the wrong sign (positive) or are insignificant, or both. It is most interesting that some of the strongest industries in New York's export base are ones in which the tax rate variable is positive or insignificant or both (such as, communication, transportation services, securities, business services, legal services, and health services).

The local industry equations are presented in Table 12.2. Although there are 32 local industries identified in the model, equations for seven of them are not presented either because no city tax rate seemed relevant or statistically significant equations could not be estimated. The list of excluded local industries is shown below.

S.I.C.

10–14	mining
29	petroleum and coal products
41	local passenger transit
7–9	agricultural services, forests, and fisheries
61	credit agencies, excluding banks
91	federal government
92, 93	state and local government

Of the 25 local industry equations shown, the general corporation tax rate appears as an explanatory variable in the first 18 (mostly manufacturing industries). It has the correct sign (negative) in 15 of those 18 equations, but it is not always significant. One equation, electric and gas utilities, includes the utility tax rate as a variable and it is positive and insignificant. The remaining six equations all include the sales-tax rate as an explanatory variable and it is negative in only one equation (hotels) but far from significant.

Table 12.2
NYC Local Industry Equations ($n = 20$)[a]

Equation Number	S.I.C. Code	Dependent Variable	Constant	Independent Variables, Coefficients, and t Statistics (in parentheses)	Adjusted R^2	Durbin-Watson	Standard Error (million $)
CLT 1	15–17	CYCNST	= 319.6	−27.09 CTXRGB − 95.18 UUNEMPR + 1,498 UDPICNST + 4.933 SNEWHST (1.4) (4.5) (3.2) (2.6)	.641	1.4	$108.9
CLT 2	20	CYFOOD	= −904.6	+1.698 CTXRGB − 13.53 UUNEMPR + 417.8 CPOPPCT (0.2) (2.1) (5.3)	.927	1.2	37.1
CLT 3	21	CYTOBA	= 28.19	+0.5181 CTXRGB + 0.01874 CYBANK (1.2) (2.6)	.452	0.8	5.7
CLT 4	22	CYTEXT	= 250.3	−0.4446 CTXRGB − 18.21 UUNEMPR + .003176 CALLY (0.3) (4.2) (1.3)	.868	1.7	11.8
CLT 5	24	CYLUMB	= 18.47	−.01257 CTXRGB − 2.185 UUNEMPR + .001196 CALLY (0.0) (2.3) (2.1)	.807	1.8	2.6
CLT 6	25	CYFURN	= 109.3	−1.104 CTXRGB − 11.44 UUNEMPR + 24.43 CPOPPCT (1.1) (12.0) (2.1)	.939	1.9	5.4
CLT 7	26	CYPAP	= 1,417	−1.522 CTXRGB − 10.49 UUNEMPR − 1,027 SCPIUS (1.2) (5.4) (13.4)	.908	2.1	11.2
CLT 8	28	CYCHEM	= 3,172	−6.217 CTXRGB − 34.35 UUNEMPR − 2,252 SCPIUS (2.0) (6.9) (4.9)	.918	1.9	28.3
CLT 9	30	CYROBB	= 629.1	+2.205 CTXRGB − 9.999 UUNEMPR − 461.7 SCPIUS (3.3) (9.4) (4.7)	.858	1.9	6.1
CLT 10	32	CYSTON	= −123.7	−2.760 CTXRGB − 4.187 UUNEMPR + 523.8 CPOPSCA (3.1) (4.7) (3.5)	.956	2.1	4.7
CLT 11	33	CYPMET	= 381.1	−2.171 CTXRGB − 12.10 UUNEMPR − 126.6 SCPIUS (1.6) (5.6) (0.6)	.740	0.9	12.3
CLT 12	34	CYFMET	= 1,754	−5.911 CTXRGB − 21.51 UUNEMPR − 1,173 SCPIUS (3.0) (6.9) (4.1)	.921	2.0	17.7

CLT 13	35	CYMACH = 1,868 − 8.105 CTXRGB − 23.20 UUNEMPR − 1,330 SCPIUS	.938	1.6	18.5
		(3.9) (7.1) (4.5)			
CLT 14	36	CYELMA = 2,515 − 6.169 CTXRGB − 33.32 UUNEMPR − 1,748 SCPIUS	.894	1.5	28.8
		(2.9) (6.6) (3.8)			
CLT 15	19 & 37	CYTRQO = 1,183 − 5.983 CTXRGB − 5.968 UUNEMPR − 942.7 SCPIUS	.908	1.6	14.2
		(3.8) (2.4) (4.1)			
CLT 16	38	CYINST = 1,673 − .7083 CTXRGB − 28.66 UUNEMPR − 1,231 SCPIUS	.883	1.6	19.8
		(0.3) (8.3) (3.9)			
CLT 17	40	CYRR = 391.7 − 18.43 CTXRGB − 3.484 UUNEMPR − .1179 CYAIRT	.930	0.6	24.3
		(4.6) (0.7) (1.7)			
CLT 18	42	CYTRCK = −240.0 − 5.218 CTXRGB − 1.188 UUNEMPR + .01822 CALLY	.844	0.7	18.1
		(2.4) (0.2) (4.7)			
CLT 19	49	CYELGS = −450.6 + 57.75 CTXRUT + 490.5 UDPIELGS + 1.691 CYTSRV	.610	2.0	34.8
		(1.4) (3.6) (3.8)			
CLT 20	52–59	CYRETL = 7,060 + 11.01 CTXRSAL − 133.9 UUNEMPR − 3,241 SCPIUS	.736		121.1
		(0.2) (5.7) (2.8)			
CLT 21	70	CYHOTL = 1,291 − 2.128 CTXRSAL − 12.00 UUNEMPR − 996.7 SCPIUS	.886	0.9	11.3
		(0.3) (5.5) (9.2)			
CLT 22	72	CYPSRV = 3,227 + 6.571 CTXRSAL − 40.96 UUNEMPR − 2,572 SCPIUS	.867	1.1	34.8
		(0.3) (6.1) (7.8)			
CLT 23	75	CYAREP = −186.2 + 15.81 CTXRSAL + .008364 CALLY	.766	0.4	11.4
		(2.8) (0.8)			
CLT 24	76	CYMREP = 32.41 + 7.376 CTXRSAL − 1.757 UUNEMPR + .002127 CALLY	.503	1.2	6.3
		(2.1) (1.1) (2.9)			
CLT 25	79	CYAMUS = −34.32 + 4.275 CTXRSAL + .004872 CALLY	.737	1.7	7.1
		(1.2) (7.4)			

[a] Each dependent variable is output, in millions of 1972 $, of industry named.

The upshot of the regression results is that a broad simulation (that is, one including many industries) of the impact of tax rate changes is only feasible for the general corporation tax. None of the other tax rates used are consistently negative and significant.

12.3 Model simulations of the employment and revenue effects of tax rate changes

The simulation of employment and revenue effects following from hypothetical changes in city tax rates is a five-step process.

1. Industry equations (Tables 12.1 and 12.2) are used to calculate the output effect of a given change in a specific tax rate.
2. The output effects, expressed in millions of 1972 dollars, are converted into employment effects by dividing the output change in each industry by the VAPE for that industry and year.
3. Employment effects are translated into *indirect* tax revenue effects (such as, the impact of more or less city employment on sales-tax revenues and personal income tax revenues).
4. *Direct* revenue effects of the initial change in a specific tax rate are calculated using tax revenue equations in which the tax rate appears as an independent variable.
5. Net overall tax revenue effects are calculated by combining the direct revenue effect with the indirect revenue effects (which will always be of opposite signs). That is, in this system, when a tax rate is reduced, the direct revenue effect is negative, and the indirect revenue effect is positive. The simulation requires the selection of specific year or years because of Step 2. in which

output effects are converted into employment effects
for each industry by using the identity

$$CE_{it} = \frac{CY_{it}}{VAPE_{it}}$$

The years 1980 and 1981 have been chosen for this
exercise.

The simulation also requires the use of tax revenue equations in which the tax rate appears as an independent variable
in order to estimate direct revenue effects (Step 4.). The tax
revenue equations presented in Chapter 7 and used to make
tax revenue forecasts in Chapter 8 are not acceptable for use
in the simulation because they do not contain the tax rate as
an independent variable. Consequently, another set of tax
revenue equations has been estimated to use in this simulation.
In those equations (Table 12.3) the tax rate appears as an
independent variable. Of course, the expected sign on the tax
rate variables is positive, reflecting the obvious truth (contrary
to Reaganomics) that an increase in a tax rate, *ceteris paribus,*
will increase revenues from that tax.

The simulation of the general corporation tax assumes a
two percentage point reduction in that tax rate. The estimated
output and employment effects (Steps 1. and 2. of the simulation procedure) are presented in Table 12.4. Column 1 includes the industry equations in which the general corporation
tax rate variables appear. Column 2 shows the partial regression coefficient on that tax rate variable in each equation (the
equations are shown in Tables 12.1 and 12.2). Because the
dependent variable in each of those equations is industry output in millions of 1972 dollars, each partial regression coefficient in column 2 can be interpreted as the estimated output
effect (in millions of 1972 $) of a one percentage point change

Table 12.3
Tax Revenue Equation for Use in Simulation

Dependent Variable	Constant	Independent Variables, Coefficients, and t Statistics (in parentheses)	Adjusted R^2	Standard Error
ACTXVPIUB =	−3,244	+ 41.56 CTXRPI + .05773 CALLY + 9.401 SCPI (0.5)　　　　(1.5)　　　　(2.6)	.848	70.1
ACTXVSAL =	−432	+ 163.0 CTXRSAL + 3.452 SCPI (13.0)　　　　(16.1)	.997	9.6
ACTVGB72 =	90.23	+ 22.91 CTXRGB (−1) (5.1)	.746	26.0
LACTXVFIN =	1.792	+ 1.229 LCTXRFIN (46.3)	.834	0.3

Dependent Variables

ACTXVPIUB = Actual city tax revenues, personal income and unincorporated business taxes.
ACTXVSAL　= Actual city sales tax revenues.
ACTVGB72　= Actual city general corporation tax revenues in 1972 $.
LACTXVFIN = Actual city financial corporation tax revenues, log.

Independent Variables

CTXRPI　　= Personal income tax rate.
CALLY　　 = Total city output in millions 1972 $.
SCPI　　　 = Regions consumer price index, 1967 = 100.
CTXRSAL　= Sales tax rate.
CTXRGB　 = General corporation tax rate.
LCTXRFIN = Financial corporation tax rate, log.

Table 12.4
Computation of Estimated Output and Employment Effects of Change in the General Corporation Tax Rate

Industry	Regression Coefficients on General Corporate Tax Rate	VAPE, 72 $		Employment Effect	
		1980	1981	1980	1981
CYAPP	− 14.61	$ 7,333	$ 7,470	+ 1,992	1,956
CYPRNT	− 2.907	12,897	13,054	+ 225	223
CYLETH	− 0.1882	7,948	8,048	+ 24	23
CYMMAN	− 4.292	10,250	10,341	+ 419	+ 415
CYWATT	− 8.457	14,089	14,368	+ 600	+ 589
CYAIRT	− 7.033	17,347	17,840	+ 405	+ 394
CYTSRV	+ 1.519	11,728	11,886	− 130	− 128
CYWHOL	− 11.36	15,648	15,892	+ 726	+ 715
CYCNST	− 27.09	14,451	14,711	+ 1,875	+ 1,841
CYFOOD	+ 1.698	14,081	14,317	− 120	− 119
CYTOBA	+ 0.5181	27,095	27,814	− 19	− 18
CYTEXT	− 0.446	9,100	9,307	+ 49	+ 48
CYLUMB	− 0.01257	12,898	13,289	+ 1	+ 1
CYFURN	− 1.104	9,090	9,263	+ 121	+ 119
CYPAP	− 1.522	15,864	16,121	+ 96	+ 94
CYCHEM	− 6.217	19,164	19,465	+ 324	+ 319
CYFUBB	+ 2.205	11,980	12,090	− 184	− 182
CYSTON	− 2.760	12,920	13,030	+ 214	+ 212
CYPMET	− 2.171	17,368	17,618	+ 125	+ 123
CYFMET	− 5.911	13,348	13,530	+ 443	+ 437
CYMACH	− 8.105	15,008	15,375	+ 540	+ 527
CYELMA	− 6.169	12,909	13,129	+ 478	+ 470
CYTRQO	− 5.983	18,577	19,105	+ 322	+ 313
CYINST	− 0.7083	13,694	14,042	+ 52	+ 50
CYRR	− 18.43	16,956	17,314	+ 1,087	+ 1,064
CYTRCK	− 5.218	13,937	14,218	+ 374	+ 367
Total	− 134.75			10,039	9,853

in the general corporation tax rate. For example, in the first equation (CYAPP, apparel industry output) the partial regression coefficient is − 14.61. A one percentage point reduction in the tax rate would yield an increase of $14.61 million in real output in the apparel industry, *ceteris paribus;* that is, − 14.61 (− 1.0) = + 14.61. The sum of the coefficients in column 2,

− 134.75, thus represents the estimated output effect over all industries of a one percentage point change in the general corporation tax rate. So, a one percentage point reduction in the rate yields an estimated $134.75 million increase in total city real output; for example, − 134.75 (− 1.0) = + 134.75. Similarly, a one percentage point increase in the tax rate yields an estimated drop of $134.75 million in total city real output; for example, − 134.75 (+ 1.0) = − 134.75. This estimating procedure with coefficients from linear equations is valid for small changes in either direction. Hence, a reduction of two percentage points in the tax rate would yield an estimated $269.5 million increase in total city real output (that is, $134.75 × 2).

Columns 3 and 4 show the annual value added per employee (VAPE) in 1972 dollars for 1980 and 1981 for each industry. Columns 5 and 6 are the calculated employment effects by industry of a one percentage point reduction in the general corporation tax rate. The calculation uses the identity,

$$CE_{it} = \frac{CY_{it}}{VAPE_{it}}$$

Using the apparel industry as an example again,

$$CYAPP = -14.61\,(-1.0)$$

$$CYAPP = +\$14.61 \text{ million}$$

$$EAPP_{80} = \frac{\$14.61 \text{ million} (1972\,\$)}{\$7333\,(1972\,\$)}$$

$$EAPP_{80} = 1992$$

For 1981,

$$EAPP_{81} = \frac{\$14.61 \text{ million} (1972\,\$)}{\$7470\,(1972\,\$)}$$

$$EAPP_{81} = 1956$$

The sums of columns 5 and 6 represent the estimated total employment increases over all industries of a one percentage point drop in the general corporation tax rate. The effects are not cumulative. That is, the estimated employment increase of 9853 shown for 1981 is not in addition to the estimated 1980 increase of 10,039. The two columns simply show that the employment effect in 1981 would likely be slightly smaller than that in 1980 because of the increased VAPE.

The overall output and employment effects of a hypothetical change in the general corporation tax rate are summarized below.

Hypothetical Change in General Corporation Tax Rate	Estimated Change in Total City Output (million 1972 $)	Estimated Change in Total City Employment	
		1980	1981
− 2.0 points	+ $269.5	+ 20,078	+ 19,706
+ 2.0 points	− 269.5	− 20,078	− 19,706

SOURCE: Calculated from Table 12.4.

Step 3 of the simulation procedure is to translate output and employument effects into indirect revenue effects. An increase in city output and employment can be expected to increase city tax revenues from the sales tax and the personal income tax. The equation for the revenue from the personal income tax in Table 12.3 is used to estimate the impact of increased city output on revenues from that tax. One of the independent variables in that equation is total city output (CALLY) in millions of 1972 dollars. Its partial regression coefficient is + .05773. So,

$$\begin{bmatrix} \text{Change in Revenues, Personal} \\ \text{Income, and Unincorporated} \\ \text{Business Taxes (million \$)} \end{bmatrix} = +.05773 \begin{bmatrix} \text{Change in} \\ \text{CALLY} \end{bmatrix}$$

Assuming a rise in CALLY of $269.5 million (the estimated

effect of a two-point cut in the general corporation tax rate shown above), the change in personal income tax and unincorporated business tax revenues is

$+.05773$ ($269.5 million 1972 $) $= +15.6$ million (current $)

It was not possible to estimate an acceptable sales-tax-revenue equation in which either total city output or total city employment appear as an independent variable. Thus to estimate the effect upon sales tax revenues of a rise (or decline) in city employment requires the use of simple averages. In 1978, the average sales tax revenues (in constant 1972 $) per employee in the city was $193. So this calculation of the sales tax revenue effect is,

$$\begin{bmatrix} \text{Change in Sales} \\ \text{Tax Revenues} \\ \text{(current \$)} \end{bmatrix}_t = \begin{bmatrix} \text{Sales Tax} \\ \text{Revenues per} \\ \text{Employee} \end{bmatrix}_t$$

$$\times \begin{bmatrix} \text{Change in} \\ \text{Employment} \end{bmatrix}_t \times \begin{bmatrix} \text{Consumer} \\ \text{Price Index} \\ (1972 = 100) \end{bmatrix}_t$$

$\$7.1$ million $= (\$193) \times (20,078)_{1980} \times (1.833)$

The estimated direct revenue effect of a 2-percentage point reduction in the general corporation tax rate is calculated using the general corporation revenue equation in Table 12.3. The partial regression coefficient on the tax rate variable is $+22.91$. So the estimated revenue effect is

$$22.91 \, (-2.0) = -45.8 \text{ million 1972 \$}$$

Inflating the revenue change to a 1980 current dollar basis,

$$(-\$45.8) \, (1.833) = -\$84.0 \text{ million}$$

Table 12.5
Summary of General Corporation Tax Simulation

	Tax Decrease	Tax Increase
Hypothetical change in general corporate tax rate	− 2.0 points	+ 2.0 points
Estimated change in total city output (million 1972 $)	+ $269.5	− $269.5
Estimated change in total city employment		
1980	+ 20,078	− 20,078
1981	+ 19,706	− 19,706
Indirect revenue effect sales tax	(millions)	
1980	+ $7.1	− $7.1
1981	+ $7.6	− $7.6
Personal income and Unincorporated business tax		
1980	+ $15.6	− $15.6
1981	+ $15.6	− $15.6
Direct revenue effect general corporate tax		
1980	− $84.0	+ $84.0
1981	− $91.1	+ $91.1
Net revenue effect		
1980	− $61.3	+ $61.3
1981	− $67.9	+ $67.9

SOURCE: Computed for this study.

The final step of estimating the net revenue effect of the tax rate change is shown in the simulation summary, Table 12.5.

Considering a rate reduction of two points, Table 12.5 shows that in 1980 the direct revenue effect is a reduction of $84.0 million in revenues from the general corporation tax. But the indirect revenue effects are to raise sales tax revenues an estimated $7.1 million and to raise personal income tax and unincorporated business tax revenues an estimated $15.6 million. Hence the net revenue effect of the two-point rate reduction is an estimated revenue loss of $61.3 million.

The simulation presented here does not reflect all of the indirect offsets to direct revenue losses from tax cuts. Other offsets can be named, but they cannot be quantified at this point. The hypothetical cut in the general corporation tax rate is estimated to increase real output in the city $270 million in 1972 dollars (or $495 million in inflated dollars). An increase in output of that magnitude would necessarily generate an increase in the capital base, which with some lag would add to property tax revenues and thus contribute to offsetting the direct revenue loss from the initial tax cut. Also, 20,000 additional jobs would surely take some households off of welfare rolls, providing an offset on the expenditure side. Another revenue offset would be the increase in commercial rent tax revenues which would rise with 20,000 additional jobs.

This exercise has important implications for tax policy as it relates to economic development. Three of the tax revenues analyzed here are quite naturally tied to inflation (personal income, sales, and utility). They are projected to grow much faster than the other tax revenues through 1990 and even faster than inflation (see Chapter 8). The industry-output equations presented in which the sales tax rate or the utility tax rate was included as a plausible variable (the personal income tax rate, on a priori grounds, does not make sense as an explanatory variable for industry output and so was almost never included), did not show significant negative effects upon output.

Revenues from the general corporation tax are not tied to inflation, and that tax rate does appear to have a significant negative impact on output in many city industries. The evidence also shows that the financial corporation taxes are not strongly linked to inflation, and although there is no evidence presented here, that tax is reportedly easy to avoid. The banking-industry equation does indicate a significant negative impact of that tax on banking output in the city, but it must be remembered that the equation is not very good.

The policy conclusion, then, is that if the city has leeway to cut taxes, by say, $70 million, it should not throw away an economic-development opportunity by parceling out tiny cuts of numerous taxes. Instead the city should "spend" its $70 million in cutting one tax: the general corporation tax. And it should spend more than $70 million on the cut because of the offsets explained above.

12.4 Ramifications for other places

Few cities have local tax structures approaching the complexity of that of New York. Some do have a tax on the income of corporations, but in more cases it is only the state which taxes corporate income. Given the shift in economic activity in cities away from goods production, most large cities should analyze their tax revenue base (and that of the state within the city) in terms of how much is paid by various industry groups and how that compares with city employment in each industry group. It may be true that local (and state) taxes fall disproportionately hard on goods-producing industries. And if the findings for New York can be generalized, those are the industries most sensitive to local taxes. Perhaps the state-local tax impact on cities should be adjusted to shift (slightly) more tax liability upon nongoods-producing industries and lighten taxation of goods-producing industries, as Netzer has suggested.

"The ideal revenue system for the mature metropolis is one that reaches the aspects of the local economy most likely to be expanding, without choking off the expansion. But the mature city needs to emphasize damage-minimizing tactics, where there is a conflict between taxing growth and not impeding that growth. Concretely, the appropriate policies include the following:

1. General taxes—on property, sales and business income—should be revised to reduce the impact on manufacturing and other goods-handling activities, because they are declining activities in the mature central cities and because they appear to be especially sensitive to tax increases and tax dif-

ferentials (which is a consequence of the central city's lack of attractiveness as a location for such activities).

2. For other types of economic activity, a given central city may maintain substantial locational attractiveness and thus it may be able to tax such activities more heavily without damage. However, it is difficult to be wildly optimistic on this score for the long run. A cautious policy would be one that refrains from heavier taxation of such activities per se, but does not extend to them the benefits of the de-emphasis urged in (1), above.[1]

Note

1. Dick Netzer, "Public Sector Investment Strategies in the Mature Metropolis," *The Mature Metropolis,* Charles L. Leven (ed.), Lexington, Mass.: Lexington Books, 1978, p. 246.

13

Changing Occupational Structure and Local Economic Development

13.1 Job training

In the prior chapters of Part II, a clear distinction is made between which levels of government are or should be responsible for which tasks that have a bearing, direct or indirect, upon urban economic development. Here the task is quite clear, training for jobs, but the responsibility for doing it does not fall on any one level of government. Historically, federal and local government have been jointly involved in job training programs. Because job training is an extension of public education and because the labor force is so mobile, it seems appropriate that all levels of government be involved.

The economic argument for a public subsidy of job training and retraining is difficult to dispute. To the extent that changes in technology (such as containerization) benefit the entire society but bring in their wake shrinkage of some occupations (for example, longshoremen) and consequent employment dislocations, then society should assist those who suffer job loss. But society should also assist the low-skilled new entrant whose range of job opportunities is much reduced compared with a generation ago because of the same technological forces. Job training and retraining is necessarily an activity closely related to the location because areas differ in their combinations of industry and occupation and requirements and in the size and needs of their underutilized labor force.

It is, of course, critically important that people be taught skills necessary for the "right" jobs, that is, those that now need or soon will need filling in the local area. For if people are trained for the "wrong" jobs, or occupations that will not be in demand within the local area when training is completed, three types of waste are created. First, funds used on the training program are wasted; second, the time spent on the program is wasted—and with it the time that could have been used to train for jobs that will be in demand; and third, the willingness of people to undergo training or retraining might be lost. While this last factor may not be measurable in monetary terms, one must consider it a severe problem vis-à-vis the waste of human resources. Often people who are the subjects of training or retraining programs find themselves in this situation out of sheer desperation and look to the program as a promise of future stable employment. Finding themselves unemployed after making such an effort is devastating, and the likelihood of such people breaking out of the unemployed ranks is further diminished.

Thus, an occupational picture of present and future employment needs for a local area can be of great value to all of the various institutions involved with the educating and training of people. The historical industry-occupation matrices for New York City and the SCA explained in Chapter 5 provide the essential data base for analyzing occupational trends in the city and region. They thus represent an indispensible tool for establishing area wide policies on the allocation of job training funds. The forecasts of industry-occupation matrices developed here as an integral part of the forecasting models provide the basis for planning allocation of training effort and training funds.

The following section uses the occupational component of the SCA and New York City models presented in Part I to explore the occupational trends of the local area from 1970, and to draw out the training policy implications of the forecast for 1983 to 1990. Finally, the implications for all large urban areas are addressed.

13.2 Local area historical trends in employment by occupation

In Chapter 3, the unprecedented losses of jobs in the region and the city since 1969 are documented. There the employment changes are shown by sector (groupings of industries), which is the standard manner in which employment data is published and analyzed. Viewing employment changes in the region and city from an occupational perspective rather than an industry perspective adds a new dimension to understanding the transformation of the area economy.

In 1970, blue-collar occupations represented 41.4 percent of all jobs in the SCA. From 1970 to 1977 total jobs declined by 348,000 and most of that loss—287,000—was in blue-collar occupations. The only white-collar occupation which suffered a substantial drop in the region for that period was clerical, down by 82,000 jobs. Total regional employment turned up in 1977, but most of the gain since then has been in white-collar jobs. Consequently, by 1983, the share of blue-collar jobs in the SCA was down to 37.8 percent. From 1970 to 1977, only two occupation groups in the SCA had gains in employment: professional and managerial (see Table 13.1). The largest decline, in number and percent, was in operatives, which fell 157,000 or 16.0 percent from 1970 to 1977.

In the recovery from 1977 to 1983, the SCA added 508,000 jobs, of which 414,000 were white collar. The largest gains were in clerical jobs (up 167,000) and professional and tech-

Table 13.1
SCA Employment by Occupation Group, 1970–1983 (thousands)

Occupation Group	Employment			Change in Employment	
	1970	1977	1983	1970– 1977	1977– 1983
Professional and technical	1,069	1,100	1,240	+31	+140
Managerial	754	766	842	+12	+76
Sales	464	441	472	−23	+31
Clerical	1,627	1,545	1,712	−82	+167
Total white-collar	3,914	3,852	4,266	−62	+414
Crafts	777	683	732	−94	+49
Operatives	982	825	780	−157	−45
Services	757	748	822	−9	+74
Other labor	257	230	246	−27	+16
Total blue-collar	2,773	2,486	2,580	−287	+94
Total occupations	6,686	6,338	6,846	−348	+508

[a] Figures may not add to totals due to rounding.
SOURCE: Computed for this study based on unpublished Occupational Employment Survey data from U.S. Department of Labor, Bureau of Labor Statistics.

nical jobs (up 140,000). Among the blue-collar group, only the operative jobs continued to decline.

The employment decline in New York City from 1970 to 1977 was 558,000 or 14.9 percent. The loss was by no means concentrated in blue-collar jobs. Every one of the eight occupation groups showed declines from 1970 to 1977. Sales jobs fell 17 percent (84,000), operative jobs fell 26 percent (124,000), craft jobs fell 22 percent (86,000) as did other labor (25,000). The single largest occupational group, clerical, lost 141,000 jobs, a 14.1 percent decline. Only two of the eight occupation groups fell by less than 10 percent from 1970 to 1977: professional, down 43,000 or 7 percent and managerial, down 41,000 or 9 percent (see Table 13.2).

The New York City pattern of decline is thus not neatly described in terms of the white-collar and blue-collar dichotomy, because the drops in sales and clerical jobs, both white-collar occupations, were larger than the drop in services, a

Table 13.2
NYC Employment by Occupation Group, 1970–1983 (thousands)[a]

Occupational Group	Employment			Change in Employment	
	1970	1977	1983	1970–1977	1977–1983
Professional and technical	597	554	622	−43	+68
Managerial	455	414	441	−41	+27
Sales	265	219	221	−46	+2
Clerical	997	856	923	−141	+67
Total white collar	2,314	2,043	2,207	−271	+164
Crafts	384	299	308	−85	+9
Operatives	482	358	308	−124	−50
Services	443	392	421	−51	+29
Other labor	121	96	100	−25	+4
Total blue collar	1,430	1,145	1,137	−285	−8
Total occupations	3,745	3,187	3,344	−558	+157

[a] Figures may not add to totals due to rounding.
SOURCE: See Table 13.1.

blue-collar vocation. The service group includes health-service workers, which increased almost 10 percent from 1970 to 1977. If the health jobs are excluded, the services group shows a decline of 15 percent similar to the drop in clerical jobs. The detailed occupations which comprise each occupational group are listed in Appendix Table 10.

From 1977 to 1983 job expansion in New York City was heavily concentrated in white-collar categories. Professional and technical jobs increased 68,000; clerical jobs rose 67,000. In the blue-collar groups, services jobs rose 29,000, while operatives declined 50,000.

The net result of the changes from 1970 to 1983 are brought out in the changes in relative shares of occupation groups (see Table 13.3). Every blue-collar occupation group in the region and city has diminished in the number of jobs available (excepting services). Every white-collar occupation group in the region and city has increased in the number of jobs (excepting sales.)

Table 13.3
SCA and NYC Percent Distribution of Occupational Groups,
1970 and 1983

	SCA		NYC	
Occupation Group	1970	1983	1970	1983
	(percent)		(percent)	
Professional and technical	16.0	18.1	15.9	18.6
Managerial	11.3	12.3	12.1	13.2
Sales	6.9	6.9	7.1	6.6
Clerical	24.3	25.0	26.6	27.6
Crafts	11.6	10.7	10.3	9.2
Operatives	14.7	11.4	12.9	9.2
Services	11.3	12.0	11.8	12.6
Other Labor	3.8	3.6	3.2	3.0
Total	100.0	100.0	100.0	100.0

SOURCE: See Table 13.1.

The upshot of this analysis is that the region and the city have come to offer more high-skill, white-collar jobs and fewer low-skill jobs. Training of the local hard-to-employ unskilled cannot, of course, prepare them for professional and managerial jobs. Of the feasible occupations such people could enter, the message from the 1970s experience is that service jobs would have been the least unpromising. The most unpromising, of course, were operative jobs, and some crafts jobs.

13.3 Training for jobs in the 1980s

The projections of employment by broad occupational groups for the region and the city from 1983 to 1990 were shown in Chapter 8 (Table 8.5). In both the region and city the trend of relatively better growth in white-collar groups than in blue-collar groups is expected to continue. The only blue-collar group projected to show significant increases is the services.

In this the SCA is projected to have a net gain of 55,000 jobs, of which 17,000 are expected to be in New York City. Clerical jobs in the region are expected to rise by 98,000 from 1983 to 1990. Much of that projected gain (42,000) is in the city. Professional jobs are also projected to go up as well as managerial jobs. But managerial and professional jobs are not filled from the ranks of the minimally skilled and minimally educated segment of the labor force. Indeed they hardly depend upon the local labor force at all, drawing applicants from a national and even international labor pool. So, focusing upon jobs for which local people should be trained, two occupational groups deserve futher scrutiny: clerical and service jobs.

In light of the huge numbers of unemployed young blacks and Hispanics in the city now and those who will be entering the local labor force after 1983, a net gain of 42,000 clerical jobs and 17,000 service jobs is not sufficient to absorb them, considering that they will be competing with new entrants to the labor force that are not from minority groups and with females returning to the labor force. But net job gains over time mask the churning which goes on in labor markets. Because of retirements, deaths, promotions, job-switching, resignations, and firings, there is a continual turnover in jobs even when the total remains stable. Turnovers increase in good times and decrease in bad times. Although local data on turnovers is not readily available, the long-run national average of new hires (that is, adding people not previously employed at an establishment) in the manufacturing sector is 3 percent, with a low of 2.0 percent (1975) and a high of 3.9 percent (1973). Using the more conservative 2 percent figure and applying it to New York's largest occupational group, clerical jobs, there could easily be 18,000 to 19,000 new openings for clerical workers each year, between 1983 and 1990. No other occupational group which offers a feasible opportunity for the minimally skilled and inexperienced promises such a large volume of jobs. Applying the 2 percent assumption to service jobs, annual new hires could be 8000 to 9000.

Training or directing people to the service occupations requires more specific industry targeting than is the case for clerical occupations. Clerical jobs are to be found in every sector in significant numbers. That is not the case with the services occupational group. Only eight industries out of 53 have more than 10,000 service group jobs. Those eight industries account for almost 90 percent of the service jobs in the city. The projected net gain of 17,000 service jobs is concentrated in four of those eight industries: health (private sector), business services, hotels, and personal services.

APPENDIX

Table 1
Industries and SIC Codes

Code Name	Industries	Actual SIC Code(s)	Export	
ALL	ALL INDUSTRIES	7–93		
MC	Mining and Construction	10–17		
MIN	Mining	10–14		
CNST	Construction	15–17		
MF	Manufacturing	19–39		
FOOD	Food and Kindred Products	20		
TOBA	Tobacco Products	21		
TEXT	Textile Mill Products	22		
APP	Apparel and Related Products	23	C	S
LUMB	Lumber and Wood Products	24		
FURN	Furniture and Fixtures	25		
PAP	Paper and Allied Products	26		
PRNT	Printing and Publishing	27	C	S
CHEM	Chemicals and Allied Products	28		S
PETR	Petroleum and Coal Products	29		
RUBB	Rubber and Plastics Products	30		
LETH	Leather and Leather Products	31	C	S
STON	Stone, Clay, and Glass Products	32		
PMET	Primary Metal Industries	33		
FMET	Fabricated Metal Products	34		
MACH	Machinery, Except Electrical	35		
ELMA	Electrical Machinery	36		
TRQO	Transportation Equipment and Ordnance	19, 37		
INST	Instruments and Related Products	38		S
MMAN	Miscellaneous Manufacturing	39	C	S
TC	Transportation, Communication, and Public Utilities	40–49		
RR	Railroad Transportation	40		
LOCT	Local Passenger Transit	41		
TRCK	Trucking and Warehousing	42		
WATT	Water Transportation	44	C	S
AIRT	Air Transportation	45	C	S
TSRV	Transportation Services	47	C	S
COMM	Communication	48	C	S
ELGS	Electric, Gas, and Sanitary Systems	49		
WR	Wholesale and Retail	50–59		
WHOL	Wholesale Trade	50, 51	C	S
RETL	Retail Trade	52–59		
FI	Finance, Insurance, and Real Estate	60–67		
BANK	Banking	60	C	S
CRED	Credit Agencies	61		
SEC	Security Brokers and Services	62	C	S
INSC	Insurance Carriers	63	C	S
INSA	Insurance Agents and Services	64	C	S
RECH	Real Estate and Miscellaneous Financial	65–67	C	S

Table 1 (Continued)
Industries and SIC Codes

Code Name	Industries	Actual SIC Code(s)	Export	
SV	Services and Miscellaneous	70–89, 7–9		
HOTL	Hotels and Other Lodging Places	70		
PSRV	Personal Services	72		
BSRV	Business Services	73	C	S
AREP	Auto Repair and Services	75		
MREP	Miscellaneous Repair Services	76		
FILM	Motion Pictures	78	C	S
AMUS	Amusement Services	79		
MED	Health Services	80	C	S
LEGL	Legal Services	81	C	S
EDUC	Educational Services	82	C	S
MEMB	Social Services and Nonprofit Organizations	83, 86	C	
MSVM	Miscellaneous Services and Museums	84, 89	C	S
AGSV	Agricultural Services, Forests and Fisheries	7–9		
GV	Government	91–93		
FED	Federal Government	91		
STLO	State and Local Government	92, 93		

1. Each of the seven broad industry sectors (Mining and Construction; Manufacturing; Transportation, Communication, and Public Utilities; Wholesale and Retail; Finance, Insurance, and Real Estate; Services and Miscellaneous; Government) is a composite of the individual industries which follow it. The "ALL" industry group is a composite of all 53 individual industries or, equivalently, a composite of all seven broad industry sectors.

2. In the "Export" column, a "C" designates an export industry for NYC; an "S" designates an export industry for the SCA. For a given region, all industries not considered "export" are considered "local." Several aggregate income variables in the data base measure total export and total local income. Only the 53 individual industries (*not* the broad industry sectors) have been designated "export" or "local."

3. Standard Industrial Classification (SIC) codes are widely used to classify numerically the many types of economic activities that go on in the United States. The *Standard Industrial Classification Manual, 1972,* published by the Office of Management and Budget, Executive Office of the President, describes this classification system in full. Briefly, all economic activities are separated into 84 major groups, each of which is assigned a two-digit code number, ranging from 1 to 99. Each major group is subcategorized by the addition of a third and, in many cases, a fourth digit for the purpose of identifying specific subgroups within each major group. For example, the two-digit SIC code, 36, is assigned to all businesses dealing in the manufacture of electrical machinery; a firm specializing in manufacturing radios and televisions would be assigned the four-digit SIC code, 3662. Table 1 presents the actual two-digit SIC codes applicable to the different industries and broad industry sectors under the heading, "Actual SIC Code(s)."

Table 2
SCA Export Industry Equations, 1958–1978 (n = 21)

Industry S.I.C. Code	Dependent Variable	Constant	Independent Variables, Partial Regression Coefficients, and t Statistics (in parentheses)			Adjusted R^2	Durbin-Watson	Standard Error (million 1972 $)
23	SYAPP =	4,637	− 1651SCPIUS (1.6)	− 111.9UUNEMPR (9.6)	− 0.4764UGNP (4.0)	.910	1.84	$ 67.7
27	SYPRNT =	3,107	− 1064UWPIPAP (1.3)	− 79.76UUNEMPR (4.6)	+ .3521UGNP (4.0)	.783	1.13	73.7
28	SYCHEM =	3,035	− 2076SCPIUS (1.6)	− 40.34UUNEMPR (2.8)	+ 1.740UGNP (12.0)	.940	1.60	83.6
31	SYLETH =	657.5	− 153.4SCPIUS (0.5)	− 27.84UUNEMPR (8.4)	− 0.09482UGNP (2.8)	.852	1.25	19.2
38	SYINST =	2,444	− 1183SCPIUS (1.9)	− 49.77UUNEMPR (4.4)		.547	1.51	66.3
39	SYMMAN =	2,557	− 1299SCPIUS (1.8)	− 48.89UUNEMPR (6.2)	− 0.06152UGNP (0.8)	.758	1.92	46.0
44	SYWATT =	1,250	− 17.80YEARRANK (6.2)	− 58.93UUNEMPR (4.4)		.784	0.81	77.7
45	SYAIRT =	−382.9	+ 1.220UGNP (30.6)	− 19.46UUNEMPR (3.0)		.979	1.14	37.8
47	SYTSRV =	8,100	+ 0.3107UGNP (11.7)	− 3.062UUNEMPR (0.7)		.872	0.90	25.1
48	SYCOMM =	48.99	+ 2.027UGNP (27.5)			.974	1.35	70.9

50,51	$SYWHOL = 1{,}729 + 4.131UGNP$ (18.4)		.944	0.81	216.2

$$50{,}51 \quad SYWHOL = 1{,}729 + \underset{(18.4)}{4.131}\,UGNP \qquad\qquad .944 \quad 0.81 \quad 216.2$$

$$60 \quad SYBANK = -397.5 + \underset{(5.8)}{1.761}\,UGNP + \underset{(3.5)}{97.95}\,UPROFITF \qquad .925 \quad 0.95 \quad 165.2$$

$$62 \quad SYSEC = 3{,}337 + \underset{(6.1)}{0.3807}\,USTOCKV - \underset{(5.4)}{331.0}\,UUNEMPR - \underset{(2.8)}{180.4}\,UTRSBLL \qquad .734 \quad 1.40 \quad 282.7$$

$$63 \quad SYINSC = 880.9 + \underset{(8.2)}{68.62}\,UPROFITF - \underset{(1.6)}{18.28}\,UUNEMPR - \underset{(3.3)}{38.54}\,UTRSBLL \qquad .789 \quad 0.99 \quad 64.9$$

$$65{,}66{,}67 \quad SYRECH = 9{,}636 - \underset{(8.5)}{7685}\,SCPIUS - \underset{(5.8)}{81.48}\,UUNEMPR + \underset{(2.6)}{0.1619}\,UNEWHST \qquad .881 \quad 1.15 \quad 78.4$$

$$64 \quad SYINSC = -13.05 + \underset{(12.3)}{.4325}\,UGNP + \underset{(6.5)}{16.05}\,UPROFITF - \underset{(3.5)}{11.70}\,UTRSBLL \qquad .983 \quad 1.05 \quad 14.5$$

$$73 \quad SYBSRV = -653.9 + \underset{(14.9)}{14.02}\,UGEXT \qquad\qquad .917 \quad 1.17 \quad 152.7$$

$$78 \quad SYFILM = 141.1 + \underset{(5.7)}{2.006}\,UPROFITN - \underset{(2.8)}{9.727}\,UUNEMPR \qquad .686 \quad 1.00 \quad 20.6$$

$$80 \quad SYMED = -1{,}226 + \underset{(23.4)}{3.709}\,UGNP \qquad\qquad .965 \quad 0.41 \quad 152.4$$

$$81 \quad SYLEGL = -3{,}561 + \underset{(6.5)}{3961}\,SCPIUS - \underset{(2.2)}{14.78}\,UUNEMPR + \underset{(11.6)}{0.7837}\,UGNP \qquad .976 \quad 1.85 \quad 38.8$$

$$82 \quad SYEDUC = 41.26 + \underset{(11.9)}{0.8579}\,UGNP - \underset{(3.8)}{44.79}\,UUNEMPR \qquad .877 \quad 1.57 \quad 68.7$$

$$84{,}89 \quad SYMSVM = -254.8 + \underset{(15.9)}{7.175}\,UGEXT - \underset{(1.8)}{22.63}\,UUNEMPR \qquad .927 \quad 0.86 \quad 73.4$$

Table 3
NYC Export Industry Equations, 1958–1978 (n = 21)

Industry S.I.C. Code	Dependent Variable		Constant	Independent Variables, Partial Regression Coefficients, and t Statistics (in parentheses)			Adjusted R^2	Durbin-Watson	Standard Error (million 1972 $)
23	CYAPP	=	4,100	− 1675SCPIUS (2.3)	− 82.89UUNEMPR (10.2)	− 0.5301UGNP (6.4)	.946	1.91	47.3
27	CYPRNT	=	2,214	− 215.4SCPIUS (0.2)	− 86.09UUNEMPR (7.7)	− 0.1606UGNP (1.4)	.781	1.45	65.4
31	CYLETH	=	539.2	− 123.3SCPIUS (0.5)	− 23.02UUNEMPR (8.7)	− 1029UGNP (3.8)	.880	1.24	15.4
39	CYMMAN	=	1,838	− 893.4SCPIUS (2.0)	− 31.66UUNEMPR (6.3)	− 0.1452UGNP (2.9)	.850	2.07	29.3
44	CYWATT	=	3,309	− 2052SCPIUS (2.8)	− 50.69UUNEMPR (6.2)	− 0.3878UGNP (4.7)	.911	1.09	47.4
45	CYAIRT	=	−199.7	+ 1.001UGNP (31.4)	− 27.80UUNEMPR (5.4)		.980	1.27	30.2
47	CYTSRV	=	112.4	+ 0.1930UGNP (11.5)	− 9.031UUNEMPR (3.3)		.869	1.33	15.9
48	CYCOMM	=	469.6	+ 1.025UGNP (15.3)	− 26.50UUNEMPR (2.4)		.921	1.24	63.6
50,51	CYWHOL	=	3,679	+ 0.560UGNP (8.2)	− 82.7UUNEMPR (8.4)		.877	1.69	56.2

60	CYBANK =	$-20.82 + 0.7390$UGNP (2.3)	$+ 82.73$UPROFITF (3.7)	$+ 50.40$UTRSBLL (1.6)	.902 0.95 133.1
62	CYSEC =	$3,345 + 0.3628$USTOCKV (5.6)	$- 336.9$UUNEMPR (5.3)	$- 179.2$UTRSBLL (2.7)	.705 1.35 291.6
63	CYINSC =	$1,026 + 30.80$UPROFITF (5.1)	$- 36.87$UUNEMPR (4.6)	$- 46.16$UTRSBLL (5.5)	.699 1.06 46.4
65,66,67	CYRECH =	$6,152 - 4685$SCPIUS (5.7)	$- 50.91$UUNEMPR (4.1)	$+ 2.558$LSNEWHST (3.9)	.899 1.65 66.2
64	CYINSA =	$155.8 + .1207$UGNP (4.9)	$+ 10.56$UPROFITF (6.1)	$- 5.393$UTRSBLL (2.3)	.943 0.76 10.2
73	CYBSRV =	$290.9 + 6.913$UGEXT (14.3)	$- 31.42$UUNEMPR (2.4)		.912 1.68 78.9
78	CYFILM =	$149.2 + 1.379$UPROFITN (5.2)	$- 11.39$UUNEMPR (4.3)		.722 1.23 15.4
80	CYMED =	$-367.1 + 1.755$UGNP (23.0)			.964 0.53 73.2
81	CYLEGL =	$-2,746 + 3180$SCPIUS (6.5)	$- 12.35$UUNEMPR (2.3)	$+ 0.4340$UGNP (8.0)	.962 1.50 31.4
82	CYEDUC =	$152.3 + 0.4132$UGNP (7.7)	$- 32.73$UUNEMPR (3.8)		.762 1.29 50.7
84,89	CYMSVM =	$263.9 + 3.206$UGEXT (10..3)	$- 30.93$UUNEMPR (3.6)		.855 1.13 50.7
83,86	CYMEMB =	$65.91 + 0.4417$UGNP (11.5)			.867 0.38 17.0

Table 4
SCA Local Industry Equations, 1958–1978 ($n = 21$)

Industry S.I.C. Code	Dependent Variable	Constant	Independent Variables, Partial Regression Coefficients, and t Statistics (in parentheses)	Adjusted R^2	Durbin-Watson	Standard Error
15–17	SYCNST =	2,441	− 191.4UUNEMPR (5.7) + .0160L2SALLY (1.0) + 505.9DUM7075 (1.6) + 5.093SNEWHST	.803	2.22	$175.7
20	SYFOOD =	2,309	− 33.38UUNEMPR (3.1) − 399.1SCPIUS (0.4) − 0.4170UGNP (3.9)	.762	1.27	61.8
21	SYTOBA =	Prior year's value (Identity)				
22	SYTEXT =	520.1	− 34.69UUNEMPR (8.0) + .002249SALLY (3.2)	.806	0.97	25.4
24	SYLUMB =	−305.0	− 1.510UUNEMPR (0.6) + .001347SALLY (2.3) + 324.1L2SCPIUS (1.7) − 14.57DUM7075 (3.0)	.724	1.98	8.4
25	SYFURN =	850.5	− 19.43UUNEMPR (6.6) + .0004462SALLY (0.6) − 536.2L2SCPIUS (2.4)	.917	1.90	10.3
26	SYPAP =	−751.4	− 4.937UUNEMPR (0.9) + .004705SALLY (3.5) + 1196L2SCPIUS (2.7) − 57.67DUM7075 (5.2)	.868	1.40	19.4
29	SYPETR =	−167.0	+ .003837SALLY (3.0) + 418.1UWP101L (11.0)	.893	1.80	45.0
30	SYRUBB =	1116	− 6.580UUNEMPR (1.7) + .0109SALLY (11.3) − 1368L2SCPIUS (4.4) − 39.66DUM7075 (5.0)	.950	1.26	13.9
32	SYSTON =	436.0	− 14.48UUNEMPR (6.5) − .0004633SALLY (1.3)	.667	1.47	13.0
33	SYPMET =	−209.3	− 73.13UUNEMPR (10.0) + .01134SALLY (6.4) + 2056L2SCPIUS (3.6)	.909	1.31	25.5
34	SYFMET =	−1,987	− 44.56UUNEMPR (3.8) + .005330SALLY (1.9) + 3031L2SCPIUS (3.3) − 65.15DUM7075 (2.8)	.840	2.68	41.2
35	SYMACH =	120.6	− 63.95UUNEMPR (4.8) + .01381SALLY (4.3) + 647.5L2SCPIUS (0.6) − 89.32DUM7075 (3.4)	.897	2.14	46.1
36	SYELMA =	5,229	− 109.1UUNEMPR (5.9) + .007083SALLY (1.6) + 3210L2SCPIUS (2.3)	.900	1.87	64.4

	Equation							
19, 37	SYTRQO = 5,228	− 69.18UUNEMPR (2.5)	+ .002386SALLY (0.4)	− 3725L2SCPIUS (1.7)	− 178.7DUM7075 (3.3)	.816	1.61	95.0
10–14	SYMIN = Prior year's value (Identity)							
40	SYRR = 4,028	− 3721L2SCPIUS (3.6)	+ .1483SYWATT (1.0)			.790	0.45	58.8
41	SYLOCT = −223.3	− 3.201UUNEMPR (1.1)	− .04194SPOP (5.8)			.666	1.45	16.0
42	SYTRCK = −3,390	− 4.296UUNEMPR (0.9)	+ .01720SALLY (14.0)	+ 3299SCPIUS (7.8)		.986	1.46	25.4
49	SYELGS = −2,304	+ 1346UDPIELGS (4.8)	+ .02986SALLY (8.2)			.829	1.15	60.2
61	SYCRED = 334.0	+ 0.4185ULOANS	− 11.87UUNEMPR	− 9.963UTRSBLL		.560	0.97	24.0
52–59	SYRETL = 934.0	+ 59.89UUNEMPR (1.7)	+ .07921SALLY (9.4)	+ 1.515SPOPCH (3.2)		.902	1.80	162.7
70	SYHOTL = 969.5	− 14.68UUNEMPR (3.6)	− 736.9L2SCPIUS (3.9)	+ .01156CEXPI (2.4)		.871	1.87	14.2
72	SYPSRV = 1,059	+ 59.81UUNEMPR (6.7)	+ .4535SPOPCH (5.0)	− 18.58DUM7075 (0.7)		.863	1.60	48.2
75	SYAREP = −318.4	+ 14.07UUNEMPR (7.1)	+ .008319SALLY (26.1)			.972	1.46	11.6
76	SYMREP = 342.5	+ 5.301UUNEMPR (2.3)	+ .004815SALLY (8.5)	− 462.8SCPIUS (2.4)		.873	0.85	11.6
79	SYAMUS = 18.69	− 1.486UUNEMPR (0.7)	+ .004407SALLY (12.3)			.887	1.19	13.0
83, 86	SYMEMB = −13.94	+ .7616UGNP (24.6)				.968	0.79	29.7
7–9	SYAGSV = −57.59	+ 3.887UUNEMPR (2.6)	+ .001913SALLY (8.1)			.767	1.21	8.6
91	SYFED = 670.4	+ .035636SALLY (10.7)				.850	0.75	123.4
92, 93	SYSTLO = −3,343	+ 9.073UGNP (17.5)	− 599.0DUMFC (2.2)			.957	0.85	381.7

Table 5
NYC Local Industry Equations, 1958–1978 ($n = 21$)

Industry S.I.C. Code	Dependent Variable	Constant	Independent Variables, Partial Regression Coefficients, and t Statistics (in parentheses)	Adjusted R^2	Durbin-Watson	Standard Error
15–17	CYCNST =	881.7	− 73.84UUNEMPR (2.8) + .0108L2CALLY (0.5) + 229.1DUM7075 (2.1) + 5.446SNEWHST (4.4)	.787	1.71	$104.6
20	CYFOOD =	3,871	− 2835L2SCPIUS (4.1) − 0.3482UGNP (4.0)	.953	.75	30.0
22	CYTEXT =	365.0	− 24.25UUNEMPR (7.5) + .00085CALLY (0.6)	.834	1.29	14.9
24	CYLUMB =	−118.4	− 3.660UUNEMPR (2.6) + .0005231CALLY (0.8) + 169.9L2SCPIUS (2.9)	.653	2.01	4.1
25	CYFURN =	798.2	− 9.791UUNEMPR (3.9) + .0005589CALLY (0.5) − 627.9L2SCPIUS (6.0)	.923	1.19	7.3
26	CYPAP =	1,175	− 12.26UUNEMPR (3.7) − .003307CALLY (2.1) − 649.7L2SCPIUS (4.7) − 29.84DUM7075 (5.3)	.936	2.10	9.4
29	CYPETR =	Prior year's value (Identity)				
28	CYCHEM =	3,017	− 25.68UUNEMPR (3.2) − 2027L2SCPIUS (2.0) − 0.1563UGNP (1.3)	.883	1.04	35.9
30	CYRUBB =	127.2	− 3.341UUNEMPR (1.7) − .003280CALLY (3.5) − 116.5L2SCPIUS (1.4) − 16.64DUM7075 (5.0)	.877	1.98	5.5
32	CYSTON =	907.1	− 7.227UUNEMPR (3.1) − .003480CALLY (6.4) − 626.4L2SCPIUS (6.4) + 3.810DUM7075 (1.0)	.910	1.40	6.6
33	CYPMET =	−255.6	− 15.50UUNEMPR (6.6) + 663.3L2SCPIUS (2.2) − 0.1479UGNP (4.3)	.856	.86	10.6
21	CYTOBA =	Prior year's value (Identity)				
34	CYFMET =	1,890	− 26.30UUNEMPR (3.3) − .005954CALLY (1.6) − 1075L2SCPIUS (3.3)	.828	1.53	22.7
35	CYMACH =	2,874	− 30.31UUNEMPR (3.9) − .008631CALLY (2.3) − 1991L2SCPIUS (6.1)	.918	1.42	22.5

No.	Equation	R^2	DW	SEE
36	CYELMA = 3,422 − 32.07UUNEMPR − .003948CALLY − 2538L2SCPIUS (3.7) (1.0) (7.0)	.929	1.73	25.1
19, 37	CYTRQO = 1,512 − 19.94UUNEMPR − .009162CALLY − 860.3L2SCPIUS (4.3) (4.1) (4.5)	.923	1.31	13.1
38	CYINST = 1,590 − 20.15UUNEMPR + .0008188CALLY − 1234L2SCPIUS (2.3) (0.2) (3.4)	.801	1.04	24.9
10–14	CYMIN = Prior year's value (Identity)			
40	CYRR = 1,908 − 1815L2SCPIUS + .2270CYWATT (2.3) (1.8)	.798	0.62	39.6
41	CYLOCT = Prior year's value (Identity)			
42	CYTRCK = 140.6 − 10.88UUNEMPR + .009509CALLY (2.5) (4.8)	.777	0.76	20.3
49	CYELGS = .5*SYELGS (Identity)			
52–59	CYRETL = −2,575 − 99.07UUNEMPR + .8048CPOP (5.1) (6.9)	.884	1.89	97.9
61	CYCRED = .5*SYCRED (Identity)			
70	CYHOTL = 1,327 − 15.84UUNEMPR − 1021L2SCPIUS (7.4) (8.7)	.933	1.63	10.9
72	CYPSRV = 3,481 − 26.15UUNEMPR − 2891L2SCPIUS − 9.104DUM7075 (3.9) (7.1) (0.5)	.892	0.81	33.4
75	CYAREP = −255.9 + 10.28UUNEMPR + .009651CALLY (5.9) (12.2)	.884	1.23	8.1
76	CYMREP = 159.5 − .07448CPOPCH + .002495SCALLY − 127.4SCPIUS (2.8) (3.1) (1.2)	.414	1.22	8.5
79	CYAMUS = −.1352 + .004169CALLY (5.5)	.700	1.23	7.8
7–9	CYAGSV = −50.75 + 2.287UUNEMPR + .001437CALLY (5.8) (8.2)	.767	1.26	1.8
91	CYFED = 262.3 + .04507CALLY + .6977CPOPCH (5.2) (2.4)	.611	0.80	101.1
92, 93	CYSTLO = −1,431 + 4.569UGNP − 729.7DUMFC (13.2) (4.0)	.912	0.81	254.6

Table 6
United States Value Added per Employee Equations, by Industry, 1958–1978 (n = 21)

Industry S.I.C. Code	Dependent Variable		Constant	Independent Variables, Partial Regression Coefficients, and t Statistics (in parentheses)	Adjusted R^2	Durbin-Watson
10–14	UVAEMIN	=	9,519.678	+ 447.2616 YEARRANK (8.0)	.761	.62
15–17	UVAECNST	=	−10,010.62	+ 1.511581 UGNPPE (14.0)	.907	1.15
20	UVAEFOOD	=	9,449.729	+ 190.0894 YEARRANK (10.4)	.844	1.31
21	UVAETOBA	=	13,848.39	+ 576.3982 YEARRANK (8.3)	.774	.87
22	UVAETEXT	=	3,036.091	+ 3.56 UINVPE (8.1) − 47.469 UUNEMPR (0.8)	.797	1.23
23	UVAEAPP	=	−2,283.35	+ 0.7667 UYPE (16.4)	.930	.78
24	UVAELUMB	=	6,570.312	+ 396.0339 YEARRANK (11.9)	.875	1.60
25	UVAEFURN	=	5,313.084	+ 0.3869 UYPE (3.9) − 233.674 UUNEMPR (4.5)	.648	1.42
26	UVAEPAP	=	10,636.84	+ 228.2687 YEARRANK (12.3)	.883	.82
27	UVAEPRNT	=	−3,256.866	+ 1.2986 UYPE (22.8)	.963	1.46
28	UVAECHEM	=	−1,676.958	+ 1.6621 UYPE (7.4)	.727	.86
29	UVAEPETR	=	2,235.717	+ 1024.145 YEARRANK (6.6) + 24235.45 UWPIOIL (7.1)	.936	2.23
30	UVAERUBB	=	2,256.33	+ 0.7925 UYPE (7.7)	.745	1.62
31	UVAELETH	=	−389.642	+ 0.6903 UYPE (8.3) − 991.0532 UUNEMPR (2.1)	.788	1.54
32	UVAESTON	=	10,729.73	+ 141.0342 YEARRANK (7.8)	.749	1.15
33	UVAEPMET	=	12,385.52	+ 205.8444 YEARRANK (5.9)	.627	.77

#	Equation	R²	DW
34	UVAEFMET = 9,922.833 + 226.1656 YEARRANK (10.3) − 17.5309 UUNEMPR (0.3)	.841	1.42
35	UVAEMACH = −5,542.482 + 1.6537 UYPE (15.8) + 22.1488 UUNEMPR (0.4)	.926	1.03
36	UVAEELMA = −1,644.888 + 1.1354 UYPE (9.6) + 45.6425 UUNEMPR (0.2)	.820	1.26
37	UVAETRQO = −12,431.06 + 2.4136 UYPE (6.2) − 55.1948 UUNEMPR (0.6)	.649	.82
38	UVAEINST = −2,989.233 + 1.4733 UYPE (7.8)	.750	1.76
39	UVAEMMAN = 6,264.936 + 134.6839 YEARRANK (5.8) + 2163.98 UWPIMISC (0.6)	.769	1.85
40	UVAERR = 9,975.471 + 317.5354 YEARRANK (14.1)	.909	1.25
41	UVAELOCT = 4,551.303 + 0.431 UYPE (4.7) − 111.0373 UUNEMPR (2.2)	.575	1.37
42	UVAETRCK = 9,299.105 + 264.3986 YEARRANK (18.3)	.944	1.47
44	UVAEWATT = 9,523.813 + 230.7763 YEARRANK (14.2)	.910	1.06
45	UVAEAIRT = −28,713.85 + 3.6994 UYPE (10.3)	.841	.90
47	UVAETSRV = −299.9645 + 1.0339 UYPE (4.8) − 23.6481 UUNEMPR (0.2)	.513	.88
48	UVAECOMM = −17,580.2 + 2.9971 UYPE (10.7)	.849	.48
49	UVAEELGS = −52,905.2 + 5.1842 UYPE (8.4) + 15243.66 UDPIELGS (3.8)	.816	1.21
50, 51	UVAEWHOL = 10,675.36 + 226.2111 YEARRANK (11.8)	.874	.82
52–59	UVAERETL = 8,449.612 − 191.1264 UUNEMPR (4.9)	.534	1.76
60	UVAEBANK = 15,763 − 352.8 UUNEMPR (2.5) + 304.0 UPROFITF (3.8)	.490	0.60
61	UVAECRED = Prior year's value (Identity)		
62	UVAESEC = Prior year's value (Identity)		
63	UVAEINSC = −1,898.994 + 1.0678 UYPE (4.4)	.480	.93

Continued

Table 6 (Continued)
United States Value Added per Employee Equations, by Industry, 1958–1978 ($n = 21$)

Industry S.I.C. Code	Dependent Variable		Constant	Independent Variables, Partial Regression Coefficients, and t Statistics (in parentheses)		Adjusted R^2	Durbin-Watson
64	UVAEINSA	=	−2,717.68	+ 1.696 UYPE (11.1)	− 67.5457 UUNEMPR (0.8)	.862	1.16
65, 66, 67	UVAERECH	=	17,037.47	− 125.4145 YEARRANK (3.8)	− 547.0255 UUNEMPR (3.5)	.621	.59
70	UVAEHOTL	=	1,965.209	+ 0.4658 UYPE (4.4)	− 242.4587 UUNEMPR (4.3)	.663	1.30
72	UVAEPSRV	=	3,255.908	+ 0.4494 UYPE (7.5)	− 73.58 UUNEMPR (2.3)	.758	1.79
73	UVAEBSRV	=	Prior year's value (Identity)				
75	UVAEAREP	=	1,544.292	+ 0.5784 UGNPPE (12.1)		.880	1.07
76	UVAEMREP	=	3,736.023	+ 0.8186 UYPE (7.5)	− 92.3691 UUNEMPR (1.6)	.749	1.58
78	UVAEFILM	=	−4,664.979	+ 1.1853 UYPE (6.5)	− 188.195 UUNEMPR (1.9)	.697	.88
79	UVAEAMUS	=	6,886.784	+ 0.1174 UYPE (1.6)	− 177.7366 UUNEMPR (4.7)	.546	1.89
80	UVAEMED	=	8,130.339	+ 0.2183 UYPE (4.3)	− 66.751 UUNEMPR (2.3)	.548	1.28
81	UVAELEGL	=	Prior year's value (Identity)				
82	UVAEEDUC	=	−8,420.588	+ 1.2351 UYPE (8.0)	+ 24.6381 UUNEMPR (0.3)	.756	1.73
83, 86	UVAEMEMB	=	1,805.286	+ 0.248 UGNPPE (6.3)	− 36.703 UUNEMPR (1.4)	.668	.47
84, 89	UVAEMSVM	=	6,388.175	+ 0.859 UYPE (8.6)	− 115.8419 UUNEMPR (2.2)	.802	1.17
7–9	UVAEAGSV	=	8,276.325	+ 57.3089 YEARRANK (6.2)		.654	1.99
91	UVAEFED	=	−12,406.23	+ 2.1087 UGNPPE (10.7)		.849	.44
92, 93	UVAESTLO	=	6,299.665	+ 132.9848 YEARRANK (15.2)		.920	.39

Guide to Equation Tables 2 through 6

Dependent Variables

The prefix SY indicates SCA income in millions of 1972 dollars.

The prefix CY indicates NYC income in millions of 1972 dollars.

The prefix UVAE indicates United States value added per employee in 1972 dollars.

All dependent variables in Tables 2 through 6 begin with one of those three prefixes followed by an industry abbreviation name.

For example, SYAPP = SCA income in millions of 1972 $ of apparel industry.

To identify the full industry name of any dependent variable, note the S.I.C. Code and refer to Appendix Table 1.

Independent Variables

The prefix U always indicates a national variable, S always indicates an SCA variable, and C always indicates a NYC variable. The independent variables are defined below in alphabetical order.

CALLY	Total income, all industries, in NYC, millions of 1972 dollars
CEXP1	Export component income of all city export industries, millions 1972 $
CPOP	NYC population in thousands
CPOPCH	Annual change in population of NYC, in thousands

CTXRGB   Rate of NYC general corporation tax on net income of corporations located partly or wholly in the city

DUM7075   Dummy variable for the period of the city depression equals 1 for 1970 to 1975, and zero for all other years

DUMFC   City fiscal emergency dummy variable, equals 1 for 1975 to 1978 and zero for all other years

L2CALLY   Total income, all industries in NYC in millions of 1972 $, lagged two years

L2SALLY   Total income, all industries in the SCA in millions of 1972 $, lagged two years

L2SCPIUS   Consumer price index for SCA divided by United States consumer price index, lagged two years

LSNEWHST   Total new housing starts in the SCA, in thousands of units, lagged one year

SALLY   Total income, all industries in the SCA in millions of 1972 dollars

SCPIUS   Consumer price index for SCA divided by United States consumer price index

SNEWHST   Number of residential building permits issued in the SCA, in thousands

SPOP   Population of the SCA, in thousands

SPOPCH   Annual change in population of the SCA, in thousands

UDPIELGS   United States price deflator, electricity and gas, divided by GNP implicit price deflator

UGEXT   Government expenditures component of United States GNP in billions of 1972 dollars

UGNP   United States GNP in billions of 1972 dollars

UGNPPE   United States GNP per employee in 1972 $

UINVPE	United States nonresidential investment expenditures per employee, in 1972 $
UNEWHST	Total new housing starts in the United States, thousands of units
UPROFITF	Profits of United States financial corporations in billions of 1972 dollars
UPROFITN	Profits of United States nonfinancial corporations, in billions of 1972 $
USTOCKV	Annual volume of transactions on the N.Y. Stock Exchange in millions of shares
UTRSBLL	Rate of intrest on three-month U.S. Treasury bills
UUNEMPR	United States unemployment rate
UWPIMISC	Wholesale price index for miscellaneous manufacturing, divided by all-items wholesale price index
UWPIOIL	Wholesale price index for oil, divided by all-items wholesale price index
UWPIPAP	Wholesale price index for paper, divided by all-items wholesale price index
UYPE	United States national income per employee in 1972 $
YEARRANK	Time trend: 1958 = 1, 1959 = 2, etc.

Table 7
Industries and Their S.I.C. Codes for the Baltimore SMSA Model

	Abbreviated Industry Name	Industries	S.I.C. Codes
1	MIN	Mining	10, 11, 12, 13, 14
2	CNST	Construction	15, 16, 17
	(S.I.C. 19–39)	*MANUFACTURING*	
3	FOOD	Food and Kindred Products	20
4	TEXT	Textile Mill Products	22
5	APP	Apparel and Related Products	23
6	LUMB	Lumber and Wood Products	24
7	FURN	Furniture and Fixtures	25
8	PAP	Paper and Allied Products	26
9	PRNT	Printing and Publishing	27
10	CHEM	Chemical and Allied Products	28
11	PETR	Petroleum and Coal Products	29
12	RUBB	Rubber and Plastics Products	30
13	STON	Stone, Clay, and Glass Products	32
14	PMET	Primary Metal Industries	33

15	FMET	Fabricated Metal Products	34
16	MACH	Machinery, Except Electrical	35
17	ELMA	Electrical Machinery	36
18	TRQO	Transportation Equipment	37, 19 (phased out in 1972)
19	INST	Instruments and Related Products	38
(S.I.C. 40—47)		*TRANSPORTATION, COMMUNICATION, AND PUBLIC UTILITIES*	
20	RR	Railroad Transportation	40
21	TRAN	All Other Transportation	41, 42, 44, 45, 46, 47
22	CMEG	Communication; and Electric, Gas and Sanitary Services	48, 49
		WHOLESALE AND RETAIL	
23	WHOL	Wholesale Trade	50, 51
24	RETL	Retail Trade	52, 53, 54, 55, 56, 57, 58, 59
25	FIRE	*FINANCE, INSURANCE, AND REAL ESTATE*	60, 61, 62, 63, 64, 65, 66, 67
26	SERV	*SERVICES AND MISCELLANEOUS*	70, 72, 73, 75, 76, 78, 79, 80, 81, 82, 83 (New in 1975), 84, 86, 89, 7, 8, 9
		GOVERNMENT	
27	FED	Federal Government	91
28	STLO	State and Local Government	92, 93

Table 8
Baltimore SMSA Export Industry Equations, 1958–1976 ($n = 19$)[a]

S.I.C. Codes	Dependent Variable	Constant	Independent Variables, Coefficients, and t Statistics (in parentheses)	Adjusted R^2	Durbin-Watson	Standard Error (million 1972 $)
15–17	BYCNST	= −1,036	+ 0.423 UGNP − 19.03 UUNCMPR + 1246 BCPIUS (1.9) (3.0) (1.0)	.909	1.0	28.5
27	BYPRNT	= 724.1	+ 0.107 UGNP − 4.31 UUNEMPR − 662.4 BCPIUS (11.9) (4.0) (3.2)	.937	1.7	4.8
28	BYCHEM	= 152.7	+ 0.0755 UGNP − 5.54 UUNEMPR (7.8) (4.0)	.799	1.0	7.9
33	BYPMET	= 662.1	+ 0.0322 UGNP − 27.1 UUNEMPR (0.6) (3.7)	.401	1.0	41.4
40	BYRR	= 195.1	− 0.2540 LBYTRAN − 1.204 UUNEMPR (11.1) (2.1)	.886	2.3	3.1
41–47	BYTRAN	= 167.7	+ 0.169 UGNP − 2.587 UUNEMPR (16.1) (1.7)	.935	1.0	8.6
48–49	BYCMCG	= 1,170	+ 0.3823 UGNP − 1168 BCPIUS (26.6) (4.0)	.984	2.0	8.5
50–51	BYWHOL	= −172.9	+ 0.6986 UGNP (21.3)	.962	0.4	26.8
52–59	BYRETL	= 2,747	+ 0.795 UGNP − 2638 BCPIUS (18.1) (3.0)	.965	1.0	26.1
60–67	BYFIRE	= 155.0	+ 0.3356 UGNP (10.1)	.849	0.7	27.2
70–86, 89, 7–9	BYSERV	= −457.9	+ 1.552 UGNP (38.2)	.988	0.8	33.3

[a] Each dependent variable is income, in millions of 1972$, of industry named.

Table 9
Baltimore SMSA Local Industry Equations, 1958–1976 ($n = 19$)[a]

S.I.C. Code	Dependent Variable		Constant	Independent Variables, Coefficients, and t Statistics (in parentheses)	Adjusted R^2	Durbin-Watson	Standard Error (million 1972 $)
10–14	BYMIN	=	(Identity) Prior year's value				
20	BYFOOD	=	(Identity) Prior year's value				
22	BYTEXT	=	186.2	− 0.3986UUNEMPR − 170.7BCPIUS (1.1) (3.3)	.504	1.2	$ 1.8
23	BYAPP	=	797.2	− 6.946UUNEMPR − 655.8BCPIUS (9.5) (6.4)	.931	1.6	3.7
24	BYLUMB	=	−19.06	+ 0.004491BALLY + 0.8895UUNEMPR (7.5) (1.5)	.757	0.9	3.3
25	BYFURN	=	268.6	− 3.818UUNEMPR − 209.9 BCPIUS (11.7) (4.6)	.937	2.7	1.6
26	BYPAP	=	−17.44	+ 0.01355BALLY (14.1)	.917	1.0	5.2
29	BYPETR	=	−8.313	+ 0.01178UGNP + 29.57UWPIOL (2.1) (6.1)	.788	1.4	4.1
30	BYRUBB	=	108.3	− 7.808 UUNEMPR + 0.001742 BALLY (5.7) (1.2)	.639	1.0	7.8
32	BYSTON	=	52.45	+ 0.004036 BALLY (5.9)	.653	1.6	3.7
34	BYPMET	=	(Identity) Prior year's value				
35	BYMACH	=	33.37	+ 0.02151 BALLY − 8.869 UUNCMPR (17.4) (7.5)	.952	1.4	6.7
36	BYELMA	=	(Identity) Prior year's value				
37 & 19	BYTRQO	=	(Identity) Prior year's value				
38	BYINST	=	80.80	− 5.765 UUNEMPR (8.8)	.810	1.6	3.7
91	BYFED	=	−223.1	+ 0.5873 UGNP (21.6)	.963	0.5	22.3
92 & 93	BYSTLO	=	−688.8	+ 1.400 UGNP (22.0)	.964	0.5	52.1

Each dependent variable is income, in millions of 1972 $, of industry named.

Guide to Equation Tables 8 and 9

Dependent Variables

The prefix BY indicates Baltimore SMSA income in millions of 1972 dollars. All dependent variables in Tables 8 and 9 begin with this prefix followed by an industry abbreviated name. For example, BYCNST = Baltimore SMSA income in millions of 1972 $ of construction industry. To identify the full industry name of any dependent variable, note the S.I.C. Code and refer to Appendix Table 7.

Independent Variables

The prefix U always indicates a national variable, and the prefix B always indicates a Baltimore SMSA variable. The independent variables are defined below in alphabetical order.

BALLY	Total income, all industries, in the Baltimore SMSA in millions of 1972 dollars.
BCPIUS	Consumer price index for Baltimore SMSA divided by United States consumer price index.
LBYTRAN	Baltimore SMSA income in millions of 1972 dollars, of All Other Transportation industry *lagged one year.*
UGNP	United States GNP in billions of 1972 dollars.
UUNEMPR	United States unemployment rate.
UWPIOIL	Producer price index for refined petroleum, divided by all-items producer price index.

Table 10
Occupations

Code Name	Occupations[a]
ALL	ALL OCCUPATIONS
PROF	PROFESSIONALS
PENG	Technical Engineers
PSCI	Life and Physical Scientists
PMTH	Math and Computer Specialists
PSOS	Social Scientists
PDOC	Doctors and Dentists
PRNS	Registered Nurses
PMED	Other Medical Professionals (NEC)
PTEC	Technicians, Except Medical
PELT	Elementary and Preschool Teachers
PHST	High-school Teachers
PCLT	College and Other Teachers
PWRI	Authors, Reporters, and Public Relations Specialists
PART	Artists, Performers, and Other Writers (NEC)
PACC	Accountants
PLAW	Lawyers and Judges
PPER	Personnel and Labor Relations Specialists
POTH	Other Professionals (NEC)
MNGR	MANAGERS, OFFICIALS, AND PROPRIETORS
MBUY	Buyers, Sales, and Finance Managers
MADM	Administrators and Public Inspectors
MOTH	Other Officials, Proprietors, and Managers (NEC)
SALE	SALES WORKERS
SFIN	Brokers, Insurance, and Advertising Sales Workers
SOTH	Other Sales Workers (NEC)
CLER	CLERICAL WORKERS
CSEC	Secretarial Workers
CMAC	Office Machine Operators
CBKK	Bookkeepers, Billing, and Payroll Clerks
CAPP	Appraisers, Estimators, and Investigators
COTH	Other Clerical Workers (NEC)
CRAF	CRAFTS AND RELATED WORKERS
RCRP	Carpenters and Apprentices
RINC	Inside Construction Workers
ROTC	Outside Construction Workers
RSUP	Blue-collar Supervisors
RMET	Metal Workers, Except Mechanics
RCAR	Auto Mechanics

Continued

Table 10 (Continued)
Occupations

Code Name	Occupations[a]
RMEC	Mechanics, Except Auto
RTYP	Printing Workers
RUTL	Public Utility and Transit Craft Workers (NEC)
ROTH	Other Craft Workers (NEC)
OPER	OPERATIVES
OTRN	Transport Equipment Operatives
OMET	Metal, Textile, and Packing Operatives
OOTH	Other Operatives (NEC)
SERV	SERVICE WORKERS
VCLE	Cleaning Service Workers
VEAT	Food Service Workers
VMED	Health Service Workers
VPER	Personal Service Workers
VCOP	Protective Service Workers
OTHL	OTHER LABORERS (NEC)
LFRT	Freight and Material Handlers
LOTH	Other Laborers, Except Freight Handlers

[a] Each of the eight broad occupational groups (Professionals; Managers; Officials and Proprietors; Sales Workers; Clerical Workers; Crafts and Related Workers; Operatives; Service Workers; Other Laborers) is a composite of the individual occupations which follow it. The "ALL" occupational group is a composite of all 47 individual occupations or, equivalently, a composite of all eight broad occupational groups.

Table 11
SCA Industry—Occupation Matrix (1978)

Occupation	MIN	CNST	FOOD	TOBA	TEXT	APP	LUMB	FURN	PAP	PRNT	CHEM	PETR	RUBB	LETR	STON
PEGT	66.	4448.	1140.	32.	184.	313.	86.	67.	815.	314.	5720.	622.	897.	74.	552.
PLES	75.	2182.	2059.	2.	286.	444.	98.	101.	980.	517.	18421.	934.	1288.	100.	400.
PMCP	23.	132.	640.	33.	59.	110.	8.	63.	240.	1049.	1815.	393.	143.	5.	46.
PSOS	11.	165.	619.	66.	37.	32.	39.	53.	519.	322.	1628.	471.	270.	0.	133.
PDRD	0.	0.	0.	0.	0.	0.	0.	0.	0.	0.	133.	6.	0.	0.	0.
PRNS	0.	3.	126.	13.	0.	9.	0.	0.	19.	18.	148.	3.	0.	0.	44.
POMD	0.	0.	0.	1.	0.	0.	0.	0.	0.	22.	437.	9.	0.	0.	12.
PTEH	4.	91.	47.	0.	2.	0.	0.	0.	0.	15.	234.	10.	0.	0.	69.
PELT	0.	0.	0.	0.	0.	0.	0.	0.	0.	0.	0.	0.	0.	0.	0.
PHST	0.	0.	0.	0.	0.	0.	0.	0.	0.	0.	0.	0.	0.	0.	0.
PAOT	0.	0.	0.	0.	0.	11.	0.	0.	0.	17.	31.	0.	0.	0.	91.
PAEP	38.	93.	354.	53.	124.	397.	0.	16.	270.	19999.	885.	160.	238.	31.	91.
PADW	0.	766.	320.	0.	1048.	6925.	130.	448.	1073.	7732.	1690.	52.	383.	382.	274.
PACC	193.	711.	1140.	212.	174.	755.	95.	73.	581.	1216.	1947.	707.	251.	39.	335.
PLAW	19.	59.	299.	16.	4.	76.	0.	36.	78.	144.	855.	235.	16.	0.	95.
PPER	40.	159.	316.	21.	154.	206.	7.	36.	199.	420.	569.	128.	181.	15.	138.
PAOP	51.	414.	683.	0.	112.	157.	44.	148.	421.	817.	3045.	271.	128.	31.	140.
MBUY	88.	797.	1875.	117.	990.	3585.	306.	417.	1655.	2560.	4097.	288.	986.	484.	358.
MADM	0.	7.	0.	0.	0.	0.	0.	0.	0.	0.	0.	0.	0.	0.	0.
MAOM	271.	17234.	7277.	380.	5080.	17401.	758.	2136.	4249.	16575.	9989.	1507.	2170.	1608.	1358.
SADI	0.	0.	122.	0.	0.	8.	0.	0.	63.	2284.	62.	0.	0.	0.	0.
SADS	18.	1245.	2816.	238.	3142.	12636.	322.	1286.	3650.	7484.	4750.	194.	1907.	1311.	700.
CSEC	400.	4935.	4045.	686.	2129.	5907.	488.	720.	2937.	14727.	10479.	1710.	1912.	618.	881.
COMC	29.	198.	1050.	170.	186.	893.	29.	67.	792.	1793.	1861.	199.	243.	38.	162.

Continued

Table 11 (Continued)
SCA Industry—Occupation Matrix (1978)

Occupation	MIN	CNST	FOOD	TOBA	TEXT	APP	LUMB	FURN	PAP	PRNT	CHEM	PETR	RUBB	LET	STON
CBKK	164.	3622.	3281.	228.	1647.	8765.	511.	933.	2784.	6908.	4906.	407.	767.	1081.	436.
CAPP	8.	2580.	61.	0.	179.	127.	40.	47.	262.	690.	653.	28.	76.	9.	141.
CADC	222.	3370.	4108.	244.	2439.	9500.	185.	891.	4493.	16832.	12055.	982.	2367.	1428.	1142.
RCPT	39.	19302.	143.	0.	47.	68.	1198.	2198.	77.	106.	558.	49.	81.	81.	49.
RINC	22.	43379.	1058.	0.	57.	122.	84.	111.	469.	319.	3605.	252.	381.	13.	312.
ROTC	161.	14072.	66.	0.	5.	7.	37.	19.	19.	17.	290.	2.	9.	0.	214.
RBLC	66.	6663.	2375.	74.	1508.	7215.	469.	962.	2249.	4000.	6495.	469.	1838.	1197.	766.
RMET	34.	3026.	1057.	5.	90.	441.	167.	217.	1049.	370.	2204.	169.	1660.	123.	865.
RAMC	21.	400.	361.	0.	0.	11.	20.	0.	168.	50.	197.	32.	39.	0.	120.
ROMC	57.	6694.	2338.	12.	1100.	583.	67.	277.	2215.	1295.	4568.	261.	1385.	88.	912.
RPRT	0.	98.	220.	7.	579.	333.	25.	0.	4.	29208.	595.	25.	301.	61.	25.
RTRN	0.	672.	107.	0.	0.	34.	0.	0.		128.	122.	3.	0.	0.	0.
RADC	68.	4996.	5956.	0.	238.	8238.	667.	4320.	294.	439.	1070.	248.	311.	1619.	870.
OSSK	96.	1974.	8060.	48.	12226.	9888.	368.	745.	4287.	2896.	11881.	409.	5636.	1543.	2423.
OONT	281.	6283.	11761.	219.	10654.	111711.	1932.	4388.	9991.	7684.	20847.	1003.	12111.	10428.	3401.
OTRN	173.	3217.	10323.	12.	664.	1682.	409.	898.	2357.	1805.	3906.	466.	1555.	168.	2482.
VCLN	15.	792.	1215.	6.	276.	761.	57.	73.	375.	666.	2235.	58.	396.	127.	147.
VFOD	2.	49.	420.	0.	10.	96.	2.	29.	0.	162.	595.	27.	0.	27.	5.
VHLT	0.	0.	0.	0.	0.	0.	0.	0.	0.	0.	0.	0.	0.	0.	0.
VPER	5.	280.	99.	2.	36.	409.	0.	19.	71.	97.	266.	0.	94.	4.	0.
VPTC	9.	390.	214.	0.	78.	221.	7.	10.	182.	182.	1057.	85.	173.	0.	60.
LFRT	82.	287.	1943.	0.	220.	953.	104.	330.	1178.	904.	2383.	210.	605.	49.	487.
LAOL	51.	23716.	1104.	1.	435.	772.	345.	502.	591.	316.	2412.	117.	501.	218.	355.
Totals	2900.	179499.	81200.	2900.	46200.	211799.	9100.	22600.	53400.	153699.	151699.	13200.	41300.	23000.	21000.

Table 11 (Continued)
NY-NJ SCA Industry—Occupation Matrix (1978)

Occupation	PMET	FMET	MACH	ELMA	TRCO	INST	MMAM	RR	LOCT	TRCK	WATT	AIRT	TSRV	COMP
PEGT	816.	1944.	4430.	7430.	7626.	2902.	405.	57.	576.	306.	312.	408.	389.	4625.
PLES	1208.	2184.	3607.	6900.	2956.	4368.	625.	16.	233.	441.	179.	440.	120.	3232.
PMCP	156.	362.	3054.	1012.	666.	403.	124.	16.	28.	336.	146.	452.	180.	1137.
PSOS	99.	607.	1272.	646.	263.	335.	29.	5.	10.	0.	21.	271.	36.	387.
PDRD	4.	0.	0.	0.	0.	39.	0.	0.	1.	0.	0.	24.	0.	32.
PRNS	48.	32.	28.	54.	56.	71.	18.	0.	3.	0.	41.	31.	0.	15.
POMD	7.	0.	9.	62.	0.	478.	0.	7.	4.	29.	0.	5.	0.	2.
PTEH	0.	22.	129.	141.	170.	144.	0.	0.	38.	88.	22.	5978.	0.	749.
PELT	0.	0.	0.	0.	0.	0.	0.	0.	0.	0.	0.	0.	0.	0.
PHST	0.	0.	0.	0.	0.	0.	0.	0.	0.	0.	0.	0.	0.	0.
PAOT	0.	18.	67.	83.	34.	10.	0.	0.	0.	0.	0.	100.	0.	26.
PAEP	28.	142.	268.	682.	153.	373.	127.	17.	6.	111.	72.	275.	154.	2512.
PAOW	54.	560.	995.	1646.	568.	624.	1869.	10.	46.	0.	153.	158.	73.	1603.
PACC	324.	608.	1066.	1043.	589.	739.	542.	262.	101.	495.	906.	917.	875.	1716.
PLAW	35.	150.	226.	485.	46.	116.	187.	65.	37.	124.	12.	90.	63.	476.
PPER	74.	386.	812.	642.	189.	315.	134.	49.	127.	392.	223.	438.	117.	1086.
PAOP	298.	527.	1209.	931.	739.	1006.	61.	50.	30.	129.	96.	303.	185.	503.
MBUY	610.	2247.	2620.	3050.	531.	2006.	1178.	168.	25.	729.	341.	648.	412.	619.
MADM	0.	0.	0.	0.	0.	0.	0.	0.	0.	0.	0.	0.	0.	0.
MAOM	1651.	5955.	5606.	7505.	3941.	3950.	5253.	2645.	813.	7211.	6235.	4087.	12681.	12619.
SADI	19.	11.	34.	98.	4.	13.	40.	0.	25.	0.	19.	73.	11.	672.
SAOS	458.	1976.	2120.	2386.	595.	1257.	3562.	99.	171.	1163.	250.	555.	1247.	790.
CSEC	1250.	3182.	5356.	6748.	2698.	4268.	4743.	542.	379.	4210.	2562.	2985.	4225.	10465.
COMC	318.	804.	1289.	1713.	469.	1179.	568.	54.	126.	698.	132.	472.	531.	1767.

Continued

Table 11 (Continued)
NY-NJ SCA Industry—Occupation Matrix (1978)

Occupation	PMET	FMET	MACH	ELMA	TRCO	INST	MMAM	RR	LOCT	TRCK	WATT	AIRT	TSRV	COMM
CBKK	1054.	3024.	2302.	3643.	1122.	1925.	3841.	463.	617.	3469.	1870.	1568.	2358.	5745.
CAPP	182.	536.	639.	593.	184.	330.	73.	28.	82.	639.	311.	164.	288.	1931.
CAOC	2056.	5137.	7317.	9392.	3207.	4459.	4428.	2021.	4090.	8712.	5837.	13942.	6035.	32370.
RCPT	197.	1103.	162.	254.	1189.	144.	887.	82.	110.	239.	268.	52.	15.	246.
RINC	844.	1611.	994.	1468.	1545.	527.	266.	747.	1225.	291.	160.	335.	145.	1064.
ROTC	260.	102.	25.	61.	54.	0.	0.	33.	16.	40.	25.	49.	0.	0.
RBLC	1150.	3454.	2337.	3381.	1922.	1563.	3646.	433.	842.	2755.	682.	1164.	335.	3953.
RMET	2248.	8000.	9390.	6328.	2924.	2454.	1550.	181.	146.	99.	23.	153.	44.	1.
RAMC	47.	91.	108.	56.	510.	0.	19.	3.	2227.	1637.	30.	192.	50.	185.
ROMC	1084.	3863.	5772.	3699.	2704.	1708.	359.	1039.	230.	560.	570.	7379.	166.	991.
RPRT	65.	771.	654.	193.	141.	452.	445.	33.	0.	5.	24.	4.	41.	196.
RTRN	25.	26.	59.	4195.	11.	22.	26.	637.	154.	0.	0.	0.	14.	38034.
RADC	1035.	621.	642.	581.	817.	2948.	6361.	333.	671.	999.	308.	118.	145.	490.
OSSK	4185.	13437.	14614.	19303.	4935.	6378.	4164.	69.	64.	1177.	112.	98.	156.	31.
OONT	6509.	15688.	14128.	32573.	8624.	10637.	19811.	279.	240.	546.	2947.	1416.	124.	243.
OTRN	1124.	2697.	1230.	1443.	1051.	464.	1321.	1151.	26179.	34750.	1305.	791.	474.	478.
VCLN	443.	654.	1052.	1391.	607.	628.	392.	500.	669.	588.	276.	703.	396.	633.
VFOD	20.	66.	121.	334.	204.	86.	48.	148.	43.	93.	466.	513.	104.	148.
VHLT	0.	0.	0.	0.	0.	20.	0.	0.	0.	0.	0.	42.	0.	0.
VPER	23.	74.	64.	179.	4.	0.	81.	165.	121.	418.	219.	8017.	294.	210.
VPTC	132.	303.	280.	539.	432.	135.	121.	222.	801.	308.	302.	507.	210.	286.
LFRT	347.	1451.	1330.	1778.	393.	423.	263.	751.	22.	11952.	9144.	2753.	849.	332.
LAOL	812.	2877.	1081.	1159.	527.	798.	229.	1220.	2470.	2562.	202.	928.	358.	102.
Totals	31300.	87300.	98500.	135799.	55400.	60700.	72200.	14600.	43800.	88300.	36800.	59600.	33900.	132699.

Table 11 (Continued)
NY-NJ SCA Industry—Occupation Matrix (1978)

Occupation	ELGS	WHOL	RETL	BANK	CRED	SEC	INS	RECH	HOTL	PSRV	BSRV	APEP	MREP	FILM
PEGT	1618.	4802.	644.	226.	12.	120.	793.	420.	69.	25.	7259.	0.	35.	90.
PLES	1553.	2653.	743.	0.	0.	9.	336.	171.	0.	15.	5372.	0.	79.	371.
PMCP	271.	2348.	1804.	2548.	303.	969.	5264.	62.	12.	0.	8673.	125.	0.	84.
PSOS	94.	2091.	498.	1816.	336.	753.	474.	163.	22.	6.	4035.	0.	0.	7.
PDRD	14.	0.	101.	6.	0.	5.	145.	10.	2.		22.	0.	0.	8.
PRNS	13.	113.	169.	43.	13.	0.	141.	10.	90.	41.	21.	0.	3.	0.
POMD	27.	209.	11168.	3.	0.	0.	63.	13.	54.	45.	71.	0.	0.	18.
PTEH	93.	485.	209.	0.	0.	19.	32.	56.	76.	131.	656.	19.	14.	185.
PELT	0.	0.	0.	0.	0.	0.	0.	0.	0.	0.	0.	0.	0.	0.
PHST	0.	0.	0.	0.	0.	0.	0.	0.	0.	0.	0.	0.	0.	0.
PAOT	0.	149.	608.	14.	0.	0.	27.	0.	80.	10.	153.	1370.	23.	72.
PAEP	213.	1822.	1820.	367.	74.	183.	682.	182.	92.	44.	8072.	66.	0.	1631.
PADW	148.	3987.	7366.	251.	0.	59.	129.	97.	251.	4155.	14647.	21.	52.	8361.
PACC	386.	4787.	3776.	5173.	1345.	1852.	3179.	1241.	373.	122.	4521.	181.	93.	236.
PLAW	60.	453.	670.	370.	299.	228.	2533.	459.	0.	11.	375.	36.	0.	87.
PPER	308.	1419.	2085.	1402.	294.	666.	1000.	199.	60.	81.	14679.	76.	30.	54.
PAOP	244.	1714.	820.	2262.	168.	1146.	1122.	192.	1201.	105.	4446.	113.	0.	67.
MBUY	196.	29250.	43437.	45967.	6412.	1066.	1437.	714.	129.	240.	5114.	312.	100.	263.
MADM	0.	0.	0.	0.	0.	0.	0.	0.	0.	0.	0.	0.	0.	0.
MAOM	1906.	71572.	115872.	949.	2538.	11417.	19336.	26237.	3386.	8806.	43058.	4621.	1262.	5696.
SADI	0.	125.	571.	1609.	524.	17855.	35197.	23262.	10.	27.	5691.		0.	8.
SAOS	365.	83179.	207358.	267.	203.	4.	0.	0.	181.	625.	5184.	234.	175.	357.
CSEC	1512.	48273.	21454.	22469.	4203.	10487.	33927.	8767.	1209.	773.	42502.	1273.	491.	2193.

Continued

Table 11 (Continued)
NY-NJ SCA Industry—Occupation Matrix (1978)

Occupation	ELGS	WHOL	RETL	BANK	CRED	SEC	INS	RECH	HOTL	PSRV	BSRV	AREP	MREP	FILM
COMC	692.	6923.	6135.	10155.	486.	2646.	5711.	383.	86.	118.	10205.	205.	40.	207.
CBKK	1784.	36393.	28035.	10034.	2809.	7787.	13460.	4057.	1061.	1199.	15706.	1066.	411.	792.
CAPP	863.	2071.	4585.	5517.	2888.	780.	17955.	951.	12.	88.	3871.	287.	92.	33.
CAOC	3679.	52564.	108996.	66279.	5830.	15845.	23294.	4667.	3950.	4406.	42963.	2102.	1032.	2329.
RCPT	271.	536.	1447.	28.	0.	17.	192.	589.	191.	63.	325.	0.	69.	252.
RINC	1670.	2438.	2744.	52.	0.	10.	193.	2422.	604.	18.	940.	221.	252.	187.
ROTC	375.	214.	72.	0.	0.	0.	0.	238.	17.	0.	11.	0.	27.	48.
RBLC	3082.	8860.	6927.	250.	46.	387.	736.	1033.	76.	361.	4326.	291.	209.	193.
RMET	1777.	1572.	406.	0.	0.	0.	0.	208.	0.	22.	572.	31.	622.	58.
RAMC	638.	2877.	23834.	0.	0.	4.	21.	6.	18.	22.	628.	20678.	215.	2.
ROMC	3997.	13244.	12530.	394.	2.	40.	190.	1996.	185.	332.	5680.	252.	10851.	202.
RPRT	13.	878.	496.	132.	2.	110.	295.	12.	7.	20.	626.	0.	0.	62.
RTRN	2376.	698.	100.	17.	0.	25.	0.	0.	0.	8.	1552.	0.	33.	0.
RAOC	3515.	7110.	24198.	69.	22.	17.	529.	862.	307.	2451.	3041.	375.	2694.	1210.
OSSK	463.	10260.	10085.	0.	0.	0.	0.	87.	0.	321.	890.	60.	1068.	16.
OONT	1655.	16824.	35053.	308.	164.	93.	184.	631.	661.	12495.	11908.	2612.	638.	1293.
OTRN	3230.	30255.	22777.	210.	7.	382.	151.	437.	166.	2541.	3145.	3413.	224.	137.
VCLN	515.	2404.	9696.	2008.	134.	357.	1645.	24150.	9265.	1039.	49515.	128.	144.	664.
VFOD	144.	588.	139856.	497.	36.	41.	466.	160.	6066.	108.	54.	2.	4.	160.
VHLT	0.	0.	54.	0.	0.	0.	0.	0.	156.	0.	140.	0.	0.	0.
VPER	38.	1196.	5375.	140.	18.	28.	220.	10172.	5963.	25236.	2391.	11.	84.	2020.
VPTC	265.	443.	3254.	4501.	135.	208.	430.	2795.	349.	109.	22621.	56.	13.	158.
LFRT	375.	6607.	4103.	0.	0.	5.	103.	106.	70.	57.	543.	0.	42.	546.
LAOL	11561.	11114.	36370.	363.	0.	80.	210.	5283.	292.	324.	1887.	1155.	579.	41.
FARM	0.	0.	0.	0.	0.	0.	0.	0.	0.	0.	0.	0.	0.	0.
Totals	52000.	475499.	908299.	186699.	29300.	75699.	171799.	123499.	36800.	66600.	358099.	41400.	21700.	30400.

Table 11 (Continued)
NY-NJ SCA Industry—Occupation Matrix (1978)

Occupa-tion	AMUS	MED	LEGL	EDUC	MEMB	MSVM	AGSV	FED	STLO	STLO CNST	STLO LOCT	STLO ELGS	STLO MED	STLO EDUC	Totals
PEGT	0.	512.	14.	286.	521.	7296.	48.	1888.	1841.	1285.	1365.	1613.	286.	773.	81396.
PLES	0.	2707.	3.	836.	226.	7419.	285.	1679.	1146.	630.	551.	1545.	1512.	2258.	86497.
PMCP	0.	777.	0.	377.	415.	2611.	39.	621.	513.	38.	66.	271.	434.	1019.	42478.
PSOS	0.	2590.	0.	737.	686.	826.	0.	831.	952.	48.	25.	94.	1447.	1992.	28864.
PDRD	175.	40191.	10.	203.	294.	47.	0.	181.	156.	0.	3.	14.	22449.	548.	64830.
PRNS	95.	41190.	3.	332.	287.	43.	2.	240.	197.	1.	8.	13.	23007.	898.	67752.
POMD	74.	31038.	0.	947.	490.	299.	784.	272.	345.	0.	11.	27.	17336.	2559.	66943.
PTEH	0.	59.	0.	225.	13.	286.	0.	3227.	680.	26.	91.	93.	33.	607.	15185.
PELT	0.	37.	0.	24590.	628.	0.	0.	25.	38.	0.	0.	0.	21.	66430.	91845.
PHST	0.	0.	0.	19658.	0.	0.	0.	0.	0.	0.	0.	0.	0.	53106.	72764.
PAOT	2603.	1329.	0.	9927.	2270.	479.	0.	75.	314.	0.	0.	0.	742.	26819.	47460.
PAEP	629.	388.	46.	331.	2613.	3246.	2.	636.	587.	27.	15.	212.	217.	895.	52766.
PAOW	5355.	289.	72.	673.	4208.	13101.	319.	1411.	710.	221.	108.	148.	161.	1817.	97696.
PACC	468.	1151.	472.	363.	2592.	20498.	28.	4895.	3622.	205.	239.	385.	643.	981.	82418.
PLAW	41.	519.	34053.	70.	901.	211.	5.	1582.	4296.	17.	88.	60.	290.	189.	51909.
PPER	153.	900.	44.	2633.	1755.	522.	5.	1505.	2365.	46.	300.	308.	503.	7112.	48076.
PAOP	2045.	8046.	416.	5056.	50666.	7817.	370.	1535.	5056.	120.	71.	243.	4494.	13660.	125723.
MBUY	148.	832.	29.	426.	856.	679.	34.	574.	335.	230.	59.	195.	465.	1149.	174431.
MADM	0.	9753.	0.	4872.	0.	0.	0.	14314.	12625.	2.	0.	0.	5447.	13161.	60180.
MAOM	7142.	2485.	436.	3036.	22990.	5116.	502.	440.	728.	4979.	1925.	1901.	1388.	8202.	550073.
SADI	0.	0.	0.	0.	88.	28.	0.	0.	0.	0.	60.	0.	0.	0.	88615.
SAOS	357.	154.	0.	126.	1358.	792.	146.	65.	39.	360.	405.	364.	86.	341.	361045.
CSEC	2405.	29608.	18392.	9382.	35855.	8653.	570.	9749.	13704.	1426.	897.	1508.	16538.	25246.	479753.
COMC	112.	860.	140.	609.	1393.	2526.	43.	618.	1054.	57.	299.	690.	480.	1646.	72352.
CBKK	1419.	8261.	923.	1759.	9260.	3863.	374.	4223.	6641.	1046.	1461.	1779.	4614.	4751.	244407.
CAPP	52.	437.	56.	71.	693.	570.	0.	2308.	2040.	745.	193.	861.	244.	192.	59337.

Continued

Table 11 (Continued)
NY-NJ SCA Industry—Occupation Matrix (1978)

Occupation	AMUS	MED	LEGL	EDUC	MEMB	MSVM	AGSV	FED	STLO	STLO CNST	STLO LOCT	STLO ELGS	STLO MED	STLO EDUC	Totals
CAOC	4483.	28962.	2663.	17141.	18092.	4121.	402.	78572.	12098.	973.	9685.	3669.	16177.	46305.	750539.
RCPT	491.	892.	0.	265.	519.	61.	56.	105.	672.	5576.	260.	270.	499.	717.	43306.
RINC	729.	2844.	0.	397.	1212.	156.	15.	487.	1594.	12532.	2901.	1665.	1588.	1073.	100352.
ROTC	159.	54.	0.	39.	2.	31.	148.	72.	316.	4065.	37.	374.	30.	105.	22017.
RBLC	479.	566.	72.	155.	564.	168.	155.	1310.	1360.	1925.	1993.	3074.	316.	418.	103296.
RMET	30.	373.	0.	99.	0.	172.	0.	119.	219.	874.	346.	1772.	209.	266.	54767.
RAMC	124.	224.	12.	52.	73.	52.	35.	421.	879.	116.	5274.	636.	125.	140.	63672.
ROMC	1800.	1548.	21.	423.	238.	252.	81.	1555.	1316.	1934.	545.	3986.	864.	1142.	117963.
RPRT	28.	108.	0.	88.	269.	197.	0.	389.	156.	28.	0.	13.	60.	237.	40493.
RTRN	0.	7.	19.	2.	0.	1.	0.	22.	89.	194.	365.	2369.	4.	5.	52140.
RAOC	250.	4755.	0.	245.	287.	234.	29.	315.	731.	1443.	1589.	3505.	2656.	662.	108527.
OSSK	14.	190.	9.	10.	146.	15.	41.	220.	114.	570.	152.	462.	106.	26.	156519.
CONT	450.	4942.	27.	739.	1165.	671.	26.	555.	1075.	1815.	568.	1650.	2760.	1997.	429400.
OTRN	337.	2103.	53.	293.	535.	181.	74.	2158.	2251.	929.	61989.	3221.	1175.	791.	247712.
VCLN	2855.	18660.	0.	4251.	8411.	415.	102.	1486.	4051.	229.	1585.	514.	10423.	11484.	182313.
VFOD	5382.	7876.	29.	5657.	2306.	91.	0.	276.	180.	14.	101.	143.	4399.	15283.	193706.
VHLT	22.	90366.	32.	368.	695.	112.	19.	52.	192.	0.	0.	0.	50474.	995.	143736.
VPER	5230.	4325.	54.	4205.	10633.	170.	0.	347.	1365.	81.	286.	38.	2416.	11358.	104626.
VPTC	681.	3180.	0.	515.	483.	446.	5.	4031.	87812.	113.	1897.	265.	1776.	1390.	145232.
LFRT	0.	155.	0.	78.	295.	52.	26.	9181.	81.	83.	52.	374.	86.	212.	64751.
LAOL	4884.	1854.	0.	853.	1214.	574.	8496.	533.	8668.	6851.	5849.	11529.	1036.	2304.	170663.
FARM	0.	0.	0.	0.	0.	0.	440.	0.	0.	0.	0.	0.	0.	0.	440.
Totals	51700.	358098.	58100.	123399.	188199.	95099.	13700.	155099.	185188.	51856.	103712.	51856.	200015.	333359.	

BIBLIOGRAPHY

Armstrong, Regina B., "The Enterprise Zone Concept: Fiscal and Urban Policy Issues," *City Almanac,* Vol. 16, No. 1, June, 1981.

Bearse, Peter J., "Government as Innovator: A New Paradigm for State Economic Development Policy," *The New England Journal of Business and Economics,* Vol. 2, No. 2, Spring, 1976.

Birch, David and Peter Allaman, "Components of Employment Change for States by Industry Group 1970–72," *Working Paper No. 5,* Cambridge, Mass.: Joint Center for Urban Studies, Harvard and MIT, September, 1975.

Business Week, "An End Run Around U.S. Ports," March 16, 1970.

City of New York, Office of the Comptroller, *Comprehensive Annual Report of the Comptroller, Fiscal Years 1968, 1981, and 1983.*

City of New York, Office of Management and Budget, *City of New York, Financial Plan,* January, 1984.

City of New York, Office of Management and Budget, *Message of the Mayor,* April, 1983.

Council of Economic Advisors, *Economic Report of the President,* 1979, 1980, and 1984.

Crow, R.T., "An Econometric Model of the Buffalo SMSA: A Progress Report," Working Paper No. 161, School of Management, State University of New York at Buffalo, 1973.

Drennan, Matthew, "The Local Economy and Local Revenues," *Setting Municipal Priorities, 1984,* C. Brecher and R. Horton, editors, New York: New York University Press, 1983.

——, "Economy," *Setting Municipal Priorities, 1982,* C. Brecher and R. Horton, editors, New York: Russell Sage Foundation, 1981.

Engle, R. *et al.,* "An Economic Simulation Model of Intra-Metropolitan Housing Location: Housing, Business, Transportation, and Local Government," *American Economic Review,* Papers and Proceedings, Vol. 62, 1972.

Forbes Magazine, "The Great Port War," October 16, 1978, pp. 168–70.

Ginzberg, Eli and George J. Vojta, "The Service Sector of the U.S. Economy," *Scientific American,* Vol. 244, No. 3, March, 1981.

Glickman, Norman, *Econometric Analysis of Regional Systems,* New York: Academic Press Inc., 1977.

Glickman, Norman, "Son of 'The Specification of Regional Econometric Models,' " *The Regional Science Association Papers,* Vol. 32, Philadelphia: The Regional Science Association, 1974.

Goldman, R., "The Structure of the Santa Clara County Model," County of Santa Clara, California, Planning Department, 1965.

Grossman, David, "What Kemp-Garcia Would Do for New York City," *City Almanac,* Vol. 16, No. 1, June 1981.

Hall, O.P. and J.A. Licari, "Building Small Region Econometric Models: Extension of Glickman's Structure to Los Angeles," *Journal of Regional Science,* Vol. 14, 1974.

Hansen, E. and S. Touhsaent, "Comparative Analysis of Tax Burden on Families at Four Income Levels," Center for Governmental Research, Rochester, New York, 1980.

Kelejian, Harry and Wallace E. Oates, *Introduction to Econometrics,* New York: Harper and Row, 1974.

Knight, Richard V., *Employment Expansion and Metropolitan Trade,* New York: Praeger, 1973.

Kolesar, Peter and Kenneth L. Rider, "Fire," *Setting Municipal Priorities, 1982,* C. Brecher and R. Horton editors, New York: Russell Sage Foundation, 1981.

Mattila, J.M., "A Metropolitan Income Determination Model and the Estimation of Metropolitan Income Multipliers," *Journal of Regional Science,* Vol. 13, 1973.

Middleton, William D., "True-Train Tip-Off," *Trains,* March, 1971.

Mieszkowski, Peter, "Recent Trends in Urban and Regional Development," *Current Issues in Urban Economics,* Peter Mieszkowski and Mahlon Straszheim, editors, Baltimore: The Johns Hopkins University Press, 1979.

Moody, H.S. and F.W. Puffer, "A Gross Regional Product Approach to Regional Model Building," *Western Economic Journal,* Vol. 7, 1969.

Netzer, Dick, "Public Sector Investment Strategies in the Mature Metropolis," *The Mature Metropolis,* Charles L. Leven (ed.), Lexington, Mass.: Lexington Books, 1978.

President's Commission for a National Agenda for the Eighties, *A National Agenda for the Eighties,* Washington: U.S. Government Printing Office, 1980.

Schwartz, Gail, *Bridges to the Future: Forces Impacting Urban Economies,* Economic Development Administration, U.S. Department of Commerce, 1978.

Smith, Dennis C., "Police," *Setting Municipal Priorities, 1982,* C. Brecher and R. Horton, editors, New York: Russell Sage Foundation, 1981.

U.S. Department of Commerce, Bureau of the Census, "Money Income of Families and Individuals," 1972 and 1977.

U.S. Department of Commerce, Bureau of the Census, *Statistical Abstract of the United States: 1972,* 93rd edition, Washington: 1972.

U.S. Department of Commerce, Bureau of Economic Analysis, *Business Statistics,* 1977.

U.S. Department of Commerce, Bureau of Economic Analysis, *Local Area Personal Income 1970–1975,* Vol. III, Middle Atlantic Region, 1977.

U.S. Department of Commerce, Bureau of Economic Analysis, *The National Income and Product Accounts of the United States, 1929–1976,* A Supplement to the *Survey of Current Business,* 1981.

U.S. Department of Commerce, Bureau of Economic Analysis, "National Income and Product Accounts," *Survey of Current Business,* July issues.

U.S. Department of Labor, Bureau of Labor Statistics, *Employment and Earnings, 1909–75,* Bulletin 1312–10.

U.S. Department of Labor, Bureau of Labor Statistics, *Employment and Earnings, States and Areas, 1939–78,* 1980.

U.S. Department of Labor, Bureau of Labor Statistics, *Employment, Hours and Earnings, States and Areas, 1939–82,* 1984.

U.S. Department of Labor, Bureau of Labor Statistics, *Employment and Earnings* (monthly), April, 1984.

U.S. Department of Labor, Bureau of Labor Statistics, *Handbook of Labor Statistics,* 1976.

U.S. Department of Labor, Bureau of Labor Statistics, *The National Industry-Occupation Employment Matrix, 1970, 1978, and Projected 1990,* Bulletin 2086, Vols. I and II, 1981.

U.S. Department of Labor, Bureau of Labor Statistics, "Occupational Employment Survey," unpublished data, New York-Northeastern New Jersey Regional Office of Bureau of Labor Statistics.

Vaughn, Roger and Mark Willis, "Economic Development," *Setting Municipal Priorities 1982,* eds. C. Brecher and R. Horton, New York: Russell Sage Foundation, 1981.

INDEX